China Joins
Global Governance

China Joins Global Governance

Cooperation and Contentions

Edited by Mingjiang Li

LEXINGTON BOOKS
Lanham • Boulder • New York • Toronto • Plymouth, UK

Published by Lexington Books
A wholly owned subsidiary of The Rowman & Littlefield Publishing Group, Inc.
4501 Forbes Boulevard, Suite 200, Lanham, Maryland 20706
www.rowman.com

10 Thornbury Road, Plymouth PL6 7PP, United Kingdom

British Library Cataloguing in Publication Information Available

Library of Congress Cataloging-in-Publication Data
China joins global governance : cooperation and contentions / edited by Mingjiang Li.
    p. cm.
  Includes bibliographical references and index.
  ISBN 978-0-7391-7677-1 (alk. paper) — ISBN 978-0-7391-7678-8 (electronic) 1.
China—Foreign economic relations. 2. China—Foreign relations. 3. China—Economic
policy—2000- I. Li, Mingjiang.
  HF1604.C4534 2012
  337.51—dc23
                                                                    2012027951

♾™ The paper used in this publication meets the minimum requirements of
American National Standard for Information Sciences—Permanence of Paper
for Printed Library Materials, ANSI/NISO Z39.48-1992.

Printed in the United States of America

Contents

Acknowledgments

This volume is the output of a conference on China's role in global and regional governance that the China Program at the S. Rajaratnam School of International Studies (RSIS), Nanyang Technological University, organized in March 2011. RSIS, my home institute, provided funding for the conference. I thank many colleagues at RSIS who have provided intellectual and logistical assistance for this project in one way or another. A few other colleagues, including Alan M. Wachman, Peng Dajin, Katherine Morton, Bryony Lau, David Fouquet, Alessio Patalano, James Manicom, Zhang Jiadong, Ramon Pacheco Pardo, Liu Yawei, Lee Dongmin, and Wang Jianwei also participated in the conference. The contributors to this volume benefited from their comments that were raised at the conference. I would like to express my deep gratitude to Ms. Chan Boh Yee who has provided invaluable editing assistance for this volume.

Introduction

Mingjiang Li

China's international relations have been undergoing tremendous changes in the past decade or so. One area where China faces both an enormous challenge and a good opportunity is global governance, a concept and international policy issue area that has already been much debated on.[1] The growing trend of globalization, coupled with China's increasing integration into the existing international system amid the rising salience of various global issues such as financial instability, trade imbalance, climate change, and nuclear proliferation—have pushed China to the forefront of global governance.

Global governance is a serious challenge for China simply because it is a relatively new foreign policy area for China's decision makers. Many analysts would probably agree that many elements in China's erstwhile and current international policy do not support the further enhancement of global governance. Yet, the international community is increasingly calling on China to take on more responsibility in almost every arena of international affairs, including international security, non-proliferation, global economic and financial stability, climate change, and international development. Any decision to be more actively involved in these issues would necessitate a dramatic change of mindset among the Chinese leadership and consequently notable transformations in China's foreign policy. It remains to be seen whether China is fully prepared to pay the price for adopting a proactive posture toward global governance or to seek some sort of leadership role in this regard.

At the same time, active participation in global governance could be a good opportunity for the acceleration of China's rise in the international system. It could be an inevitable step toward the realization of China's national aspiration of restoring its past glory in the world, an objective that generations of Chinese elite have sought after since the mid-nineteenth century. A larger Chinese role in tackling various major global challenges would elevate China's international status and expand its soft

1

power, a longstanding goal among Chinese leaders. Enhanced engagement in global governance could also be a good opportunity for China to help create or reform international institutions and regimes that would at least partially reflect China's preferences and interests. A larger Chinese contribution to global governance would also very likely enable China to obtain more decision-making power in various international organizations and institutions.

CHINA'S GROWING INTEREST IN GLOBAL GOVERNANCE

It is worth noting that global governance is not a totally alien concept for the Chinese elite today. In fact, over the past two decades, the domestic intellectual debate on global governance and China's role in global governance has been intense. Chinese research institutions have organized many conferences and workshops on these issues. Chinese analysts have closely followed the discourse and debate on global governance in the West. Numerous research papers have been published in various Chinese media outlets and journals in the past twenty years or so.[2] The Chinese scholarly community has attempted to relate almost any international issue to global governance. To give a few examples, Chinese scholars have discussed the relationship between China's energy security and global governance,[3] food security and global governance,[4] and China's "harmonious world" thesis and its theoretical implications for global governance.[5]

Over the years, the Chinese scholarly community has urged the government to pay more attention to global governance. They argue that the rapid rate of globalization has left individual states incapable of handling internal problems caused by globalization or countering the effects of globalization. It is thus inevitable for China to participate in the discussion and resolution of these global problems. Chinese analysts also argue that China's own development necessitates more active participation in global governance, particularly in the economic arena. At the same time, Chinese policy advisors believe that with the rise of China's economic power, external expectation for China's larger role in international economic issues has risen and it would be too costly for China to simply gloss over the international demand.[6]

It is fair to say that the recent financial and economic crisis has served as a catalyst for China's growing interest in global governance. Li Zuojun, a senior analyst at the State Council Center for Development Studies, argues that the root cause of the recent global financial and economic crisis, which has generated quite significant costs to China, is the lack of sufficient global governance.[7] A group of scholars at the Central Party School believe that China's policy measures and actions since the outbreak of the global financial crisis in 2008 indicate that China's participation in global governance has entered a new phase.[8]

In spite of scholarly enthusiasm in global governance, it seems that the official acceptance of and serious interest in the notion is a fairly recent phenomenon. Top Chinese decision makers only started to genuinely regard global governance as part of China's foreign policy agenda in recent years. Chinese State Councilor Dai Bing-guo proclaimed, for the first time, China's official positions on global governance at the Dialogue Meeting between the Leaders of G8 and Developing Nations in L'Aquila, Italy, in July 2009, albeit in a broad-brush manner.

Dai outlined China's stances on the goal of governance, the subject of governance, the methods of governance, and the mechanisms of governance.[9] He noted that the ultimate goal of the global economic governance is to advance economic globalization toward balanced development, shared benefits and win-win progress. Dai proposed that all countries, big or small, strong or weak, rich or poor, should first, get involved in global economic governance, and second, participate equally in decision making. He emphasized that good global economic governance involves negotiations and cooperation between countries to solve problems so opinions from all sides and the interests of each country, especially those of the developing countries, should be taken into consideration. Dai argues that due to the rapid development of the global economy, some of the current mechanisms cannot fully reflect the requirements of the international society; in order to meet the global challenge the governance mechanisms must be more inclusive. A multifaceted strategy for global governance is required.

Dai gave the speech at the L'Aquila dialogue on behalf of Chinese president Hu Jintao, who decided to return to China earlier than planned due to the outbreak of social unrest in Xinjiang. But at the 11th Conference of Chinese Diplomatic Envoys Stationed Abroad in July 2009, Hu urged senior Chinese diplomats to work hard to further enhance China's political influence, economic competitiveness, amicable image, and moral appeal in the world.[10] This slight amendment to China's erstwhile "low profile" international strategy has arguably laid the foundation for more active Chinese engagement in global governance. The fifth plenary session of the 17th Central Committee of the Chinese Communist Party held in Winter 2010 emphasized that China should actively participate in global economic governance and regional cooperation.[11] At the central meeting on economic work in December 2010, the Chinese leadership again stressed that China should strive to enhance its capacity to participate in world economic governance in the wake of the financial crisis.[12]

From the discussion above, it is clear that there are a few notable themes in China's growing interest in global governance. First of all, it is worth noting that China tends to emphasize the economic aspect of global governance. Zhang Yansheng, a senior policy analyst at the Institute of External Economic Studies of the State Development and Reform Commission, argues that the reform of global governance structure should always focus on the theme of economic development.[13] This policy emphasis is ostensibly illustrated in the leadership's statements and Dai's remarks. Also, China's actual behavior and actions in various multilateral institutions in the past few years indicate that Beijing is primarily interested in global economic affairs.

China's preference for economic global governance is no surprise since Chinese growing official enthusiasm in global governance takes place at a very peculiar context, that is, the financial/economic crisis that started in 2008. The mainstream view within China is that the crisis marks the relative rise of the emerging powers and the slight decline of the Western developed world. Many Chinese analysts seem to be convinced that the trends of faster economic growth rate in the developing economies and sluggish growth in the developed countries is likely to persist in the near future. Because of this context and perception, China seems to believe that more active participation in global economic governance serves to advance its national interests of meeting the government's priority needs of sustaining rapid economic growth, achieving better coordinated global governance in the financial and economic sectors, and managing external economic uncertainties and instability.

In contrast, there seems to be no notable change in China's policy toward major political and security issues in the world in recent years. This is because China still feels uncomfortable in further engaging with the international society on political and security issues. China's official policy toward many challenging political and security issues are still at much variance with many other countries in the world, particularly the West, for instance on issues such as human rights, non-proliferation, and international intervention. In the foreseeable future, it is difficult to imagine that China would have a strong interest in joining global governance on political and security issues.

Second, it seems that China is keen to take the opportunity to increase its presence in global governance and at the same time attempt to grab more political power in the international system. China seems to be happy to see the foundation of some of the major global institutions shaken due to the financial crisis because it believes that the recent crisis symbolizes the defects of the existing patterns and institutions of global governance. China has demonstrated confidence that its enlarged presence would help overcome some of the shortcomings in global governance. Many Chinese analysts have a fairly sanguine view of the prospect of the G20, believing that the G20 would gradually replace the G8 as the main architecture for global governance. They believe that the emergence of the G20 and the expansion of its functions would most likely allow China to play a larger role in global governance.

But China is primarily interested in competing for more decision-making power in the international arena. China has enjoyed some degree of success so far. Chinese observers often cite the increase of China's share and voting power at the IMF as a good example. Despite the limits set by the dominance of the United States and European Union and China's own capabilities, there is strong indications of China's growing role in global governance. To overcome these limits, China has found it effective to unite with emerging powers. This is clearly demonstrated in China's strong support for the BRICS institution. In April 2011, China hosted the BRICS summit in which the leaders of the five countries discussed various global issues including international monetary and financial system reform, economic and trade cooperation, global climate change, food security, and nuclear safety. Chinese president Hu Jintao emphasized that increasing the decision-making power and representation of the emerging markets and developing world is part of the reform of global economic governance.[14] Zhang Yuyan, a scholar at the Chinese Academy of Social Sciences, even suggested that eleven emerging economies, including Argentina, Brazil, China, India,

Indonesia, South Korea, Mexico, Russia, Saudi Arabia, South Africa, and Turkey, form a grouping to provide a new platform for world governance. He further proposes that the E11 group should strengthen their internal unity and insist on the principle of "common but differentiated responsibilities" to deal with the developed countries.[15]

Third, it seems plausible to argue that China will not strive for a prominent leading role in global governance in the near future. Song Hong, an expert on China and WTO affairs, notes that with the growth of Chinese power, China's international positions and objectives are also likely to change. He further argues that even though China has actively participated in global governance, it is still in the process of learning to pursue a more active role.[16] Furthermore, growing interest in global governance notwithstanding, China seems to have various reservations regarding involvement as well. The views by Pang Zhongying, a leading expert in China on global governance, perhaps represent some of the major concerns in China about China's role in global governance.

Pang argues that the Western powers that still dominate the creation and implementation of international rules and norms, are very vigilant against any potential Chinese challenge to the existing international regimes. The Western world wants China to take on more responsibilities in various international organizations but at the same time the Western powers "strictly restrict" China's possible influence on the creation and implementation of the rules in order to maintain Western dominance. Pang believes that the Western countries continue to persuade China to join those international organizations in which China is not a member yet and their real purpose is to "govern China" through various international regimes. Pang further argues that China should no longer unilaterally make concessions to the Western world. He gives the example of China's aid to Africa, saying that if China observes the norms of the "Paris Club" on international assistance, African countries will no longer look to China and China's attraction to Africa will be significantly reduced.

Therefore, Pang argues that China should no longer agree to be simply integrated into the international regimes without being given more substantive decision making power. He makes three proposals for China to deal with the challenge. First, China should unite with like-minded countries, for instance the BRICS countries, to put pressure on the West to reform some of the international rules. Second, instead of providing more resources to the World Bank and the IMF, China could pursue an active "unilateralism" by working with individual countries in other parts of the world on international development programs through China's State Development Bank and the Bank for Import and Export. Third, China should attempt to work with various parties to strengthen multilateral governance at the regional level in other parts of the world.[17]

INTENDED CONTRIBUTIONS OF THE BOOK

This book joins the growing literature on the impact of China's rise in the international society. Numerous scholarly writings have concluded that China's rise is real and phenomenal. With its rapid rise, China's presence and influence are felt at very corner of the world and in almost every multilateral institution in the world. The existing literature focuses much on China's foreign policy in general and Beijing's bilateral relations with other major powers and regions. Unfortunately, for a long time, the scholarly community has neglected these very important questions: How has China dealt with major global institutions and regimes? How has China helped address various global challenges? How has China's rise changed the international approach to global governance? Finding some answers to these questions is the purpose of this book.

This book attempts to contribute to our understanding of China's rise and the impact of its rise on the rest of the world through a specific angle, that is, China's influence on global governance. This book is a comprehensive study of the subject matter. It covers Beijing's vision and grand strategy in global multilateralism and governance. Five chapters describe and analyze China's role in global economic/ financial/trade governance. Two chapters explore China's policy toward global energy issues and climate change. The last chapter examines China's policy and approach to global security such as nuclear disarmament and non-proliferation.

For many years, policy–makers and analysts have debated on the impact of China's rise on the stability of the international system that was set up post-World War II. International observers have also debated on whether China would be a status quo power or a revisionist power and whether China would observe the rules and regulations of international institutions and regimes. This volume would also make a significant contribution to our understanding of these issues. Some of the conclusions that are reached in this book would certainly be very significant in helping us understand the future trajectory of China's behavior in its international policy.

CONTENTS OF THE BOOK

Chapter 1 examines China's aspiration to play a greater role in global governance as evidenced by its proactive participation in global institutions and its endeavours to make its voice heard by the existing powers in the West. The authors analyze the different political discourses that Chinese leaders have articulated concerning the country's foreign policy as well as preferences for global governance positions ranging from a responsible state to peaceful rise or peaceful development, including a harmonious world. They also examine some of the new concepts or conceptual frameworks such as the all-inclusive *tianxia* (all-under-Heaven) system that Chinese scholars have put forward as alternatives to the West-centric paradigms of international relations. However, the authors try to scrutinize whether or not China has such a vision for global governance. And they also attempt to provide some answers to the question of whether China wants to reimpose the *tianxia* system onto the world and whether it can be a legitimate ruler of "all-under-Heaven" in the twenty-first century.

Chapter 2 addresses a much-debated question: what impact will the rise of China have on the existing international system? The chapter attempts to provide some clues for a better understanding of this issue by examining China's views on and policy toward international multilateralism in general and some of the newly emerging multilateral mechanisms in particular, including the G20 and the BRICS. Mingjiang Li contends that while China will become more proactive in its multilateral diplomacy in selective cases, and increase its influence in global multilateral settings, various concerns and constraints will make it unlikely for China to completely overhaul or even dramatically reshape the multilateral architecture at the global level. China is stuck in defining its identity, and caught up between posturing as a leader of the developing world on some issues and siding with the developed countries on other policy issues. Given all these constraints, Li believes that China's involvement in global multilateralism is likely to be guided by pragmatism rather than grand visions. He argues that China is likely to repeat what it has done in the East Asian regional multilateralism in the past decade: participation, engagement, pushing for cooperation in areas that would serve Chinese interests, avoiding taking excessive responsibilities, blocking initiatives that would harm its interests, and refraining from making grand proposals. He concludes that China will most likely strive to rise from within the existing international order.

In November 2001, China finally acceded to the World Trade Organization after a marathon accession negotiation that lasted fifteen years. As China's accession coincided with the launch of the Doha Round, many commentators predicted that China's participation in the trade negotiations will have significant impact on the Round. However, this has not proven to be the case. What are the approaches taken by China in global trade negotiations? Why did China adopt such approaches? How do China's different negotiating approaches affect the dynamics of trade negotiations? Henry Gao in chapter 3 addresses these questions. The chapter starts with a brief discussion on how trade negotiations on nonagricultural market access, rules on non-tariff barriers, and services are conducted in the WTO, followed by a summary of China's participation in the Doha Round so far. Gao notes that China started as a reluctant player in the negotiations, and only gradually made its way into the core decision-making group of the WTO rather late during the Round. He further argues that even though China has now been accepted as a member of the G-7, the most powerful group in the WTO, it has been playing only supportive rather than leading roles. Gao explains the reasons for such low profile approaches, and also examines the value of the Chinese proposals so far from both quantitative and qualitative perspectives. The chapter concludes with some thoughts on how China will act in future negotiations.

Xiaojun Li in chapter 4 explores China's approach to trade dispute settlement. He notes that since its accession into the World Trade Organization (WTO) in 2001, China has gradually transformed from a cautious observer to an active participant in the WTO's Dispute Settlement Body (DSB). In this chapter, the author reviews China's experience in managing frictions associated with its growing role in world trade through formal WTO dispute settlement proceedings over the past decade, using both case studies and quantitative data. He argues that in addition to the lack of legal and administrative capacity, normative constraints and the concern for reputation and status in particular were crucial in explaining Beijing's absence from WTO litigation in the initial period. These obstacles were later overcome through a learning and socialization process leading to an attitudinal shift in China's normative orientation regarding the use of the WTO dispute settlement procedure to both defend its domestic industry and push for market access abroad. He concludes with a suggestion that China's expanded role and involvement in the DSB could strengthen the multilateral trade regime and generate positive externalities in other areas of regional and global governance.

Chapter 5 examines the much-debated exchange rate of the Chinese currency renminbi. Yale H. Ferguson discusses the need to correct serious "imbalances," a prominent feature of present-day discourse regarding the world economy in such international institutions as the G8, G20, and IMF. He notes that "imbalance" has not always been a watchword. Prior to the recent global financial crisis, for example, Niall Ferguson and Moritz Schulaerick coined the term "Chimerica" to describe what they argued was a beneficial "combination" of the Chinese and American economies. However, the "marriage made in heaven" began to "fail" in the wake of the financial crisis, with a lot of attention focused on China's neo-mercantilist policies, including a significantly undervalued renminbi. Soon the renminbi/dollar exchange rate became a major issue in the increasingly fractious U.S.-China relations. Indeed, there was widespread concern about the looming possibility of "currency wars" throughout the global economy. Ferguson traces the evolution of this key issue through its latest peak in early 2011 when China finally agreed to allow a gradual appreciation of its currency. The author notes that attention has now shifted to other matters, such as combating dangerous inflation in China and emerging economies, the effect of "dampening" measures on growth rates, and China's evolving strategies for diversifying its huge foreign exchange reserves and investing them abroad.

Chapter 6 addresses China's role in monetary and financial affairs in East Asia. Wei Li notes that with its rapid rise as an economic and political power, China is burdened with growing costs for its over-reliance on the US dollar due to its relatively disadvantaged position in the international monetary structure, even when compared with some smaller economies. China's "dollar trap" and its vulnerability were exposed in the U.S.-triggered global financial crisis of 2008, arousing domestic concern and fear. He observes that hot debate on China's new international monetary strategy has fueled a set of instrumental adjustments to monetary diplomacy and policies in the past three years to cope with the dollar-based global monetary system and enhance the international use of RMB. The author argues, however, that in terms of long-term orientation of its monetary strategy, China is still vacillating between the choices of a multilateral union like Germany and unilateral expansion like Japan, because of the regional security dilemmas and its ambiguous national grand strategy. He further suggests that whichever path it takes, China's new international monetary strategy will inevitably exert great influence on the future regional monetary order building.

Chapter 7 seeks to analyze China's trade initiatives in East Asia by examining free trade and economic partnership agreements. Park notes that while trade negotiations are lagging at the multilateral level in the Doha Round, countries have found a better way to tackle trade issues via an alternative—bilateral free trade agreements and economic partnership agreements that offer states bargains and options to protect certain industries and agricultural markets. In particular, China has become more active in its pursuit for regional trade via FTAs. Yet China's aggressive positions in WTO trade disputes and unfair trade policies remain a grave concern for its trading partners, dimming China's prospective role in global and regional governance. In analyzing China's trade motives through FTAs, Park first accounts for the background and driving force behind China's active engagement in trade deals, and compares case studies of China's FTAs and those of South Korea and Japan. She then proceeds to review the dilemmas of China's trading activities by examining China's intent for market protection and adamant trade policies at the multilateral level. Park concludes with the implications of China's bargaining strategies in trade for the future.

China's status is rising not only geopolitically but also geoecomically as it has turned out to be a formidable geoeconomic power venturing actively into the world market, most visibly into the energy market over the past decade. In chapter 8, Jieli Li applies the geopolitical theory of "Marchland Position" to the case of China in historical-comparative context. The theoretical framework points out that a state in a "marchland" geoposition with fewer rivals on its path is likely to grow stronger and enjoy more geoeconomic opportunities. As a result, the state's geoeconomic fortunes are likely to be gained through its geopolitical prowess within a regional or global system as the state's power-prestige tends to facilitate its business deals. And conversely, geoeconomic space is likely to diminish in direct proportion to the contraction of the state's geopolitical influence. The author points out that China seems to follow the historical pattern of any rising power in world history—along with growing geopolitical power-prestige comes a global extension for geoeconomic space. He argues that by taking advantage of the declining influence of Western powers, China has acted quickly in its thrust into the world energy market and made a great effort to establish strongholds in Africa, Latin America, and Central Asia. China's global search for natural resources reflects its urgent need to diversify its energy suppliers to meet the demand of its fast-growing economy. And this mega-scale geoeconomic move is made possible largely due to China's enhanced geopolitical rise in the world over the past decade. To be more specific, China's quick market expansion has benefited directly from its favorable geopolitical environment resulting from the 9/11 incident in the United States (2001) and widespread financial crisis that started in 2008. This chapter employs some empirical cases to buttress the above theoretical assumption.

Chapter 9 addresses China's policy toward global climate change negotiations. Zhong Xiang Zhang notes that China's unilateral pledge to cut its carbon intensity by 40–45 percent by 2020 relative to its 2005 levels raises both the stringency issue and the reliability issue. Given that China's pledge is in the form of carbon intensity, reliability issues are related to concerns about China's statistics on energy and GDP. He further argues that as long as China's commitments differ in form from that of other major greenhouse gas emitters, China is constantly confronted with the threats of trade measures and criticized for inadequate commitment to the reduction of carbon intensity. To respond to these concerns and to put China in a positive position, this chapter maps out a realistic roadmap for China's specific climate commitments toward 2050. Some of its distinctive features include China taking on absolute emission caps around 2030 and the three transitional periods of increasing climate obligations before that. Given the fact that the current international climate negotiations are flawed with a focus on commitments on the targeted date of 2020 (that does not accommodate well the world's two largest greenhouse gas emitters), the chapter suggests a new direction to break the current impasse in international climate negotiations.

Chapter 10 explores China's role in influencing and shaping nuclear disarmament and non-proliferation institutions. Tong Zhao notes that as the New START Treaty enters into force and nuclear weapon stockpiles in the United States and Russia continue to drop, China becomes a critical player in determining the future direction of the global nuclear disarmament process. Tong Zhao argues that the existing nuclear arms control framework between the United States and Russia has to be revised to include China's concerns regarding the potential impact of advanced conventional weapons, missile defense, and space military assets in order to engage China in serious nuclear disarmament discussions. China's emphasis on regulating nuclear operation policies and reinforcing nuclear taboo is reflective of its relatively unique nuclear philosophy and its interest in confidence-building measures with other nuclear weapons states. On the non-proliferation side of the equation, China's historically complex relationship with the nuclear non-proliferation regime needs to be taken into account. China's upholding of the non-discrimination principle is very much related to its own experience of undergoing serious economic sanctions in previous decades, and should not be entirely dismissed as a political excuse and bargaining chip.

NOTES

1. See for instance, John Fonte, "Sovereignty or Submission: Liberal Democracy or Global Governance?" Foreign Policy Research Institute, http://www.fpri.org/enotes/2011/201110 .fonte.sovereignty.html; John Fonte, *Sovereignty or Submission: Will Americans Rule Themselves or Be Ruled by Others?*" (New York: Encounter Books Inc., 2011); Robert Cooper, *The Breaking of Nations: Order and Chaos in the Twenty-First Century* (New York: Atlantic Monthly Press, 2003).

2. A quick search in the China National Knowledge Infrastructure database would display a few hundred Chinese articles that focus on global governance.

3. Wang Li, "nengyuan ziyuan canyu quanqiu zhili: zhongguo nengyuan zhanlue de biran xuanze" [Participation in global governance in energy and resources: the inevitable choice for China's energy strategy], *jingji cankao bao* [economic reference newspaper], Nov. 13, 2007.

4. Yu Hongyuan, "liangshi weiji riyi yanjun, quanqiu zhili youdai gaishan" [food crisis intensifies and global governance needs to be improved], *jiefang ribao* [liberation daily], Dec. 31, 2008

5. Lu Xiaohong, "Hexie shijie: zhongguo de quanqiu zhili lilun" [harmonious world: China's theory on global governance], *Waijiao pinglun* [Foreign Affairs Review], Dec. 2006, No. 92.

6. Zhou Zixun, "zhongguo canyu quanqiu zhili ying liang li er xing" [China should participate in global governance in accordance with its capability], *zhengquan shibao* [securities times], Oct. 25, 2010; Zhang Yanbing, "jueqi de zhongguo yu quanqiu zhili" [a rising China and global governance], *zhongguo shehui kexue bao* [Chinese social sciences bulletin], Feb. 4, 2010.

7. Li Zuojun, "guoji jingji weiji de zhenzheng genyuan shi quanqiu zhili queshi" [the real source of global economic crisis is the lack of global governance], *zhongguo jingji shibao* [China economics daily], Aug. 11, 2009.

8. Zhang Boli, "bawo quanqiu zhili taishi, zengqiang quanqiu zhili guannian" [understand the trend in global governance, strengthening awareness of global governance], *People's Daily*, Aug. 11, 2010.

9. http://www.gov.cn/ldhd/2009–07/09/content_1361635.htm, accessed Jan. 4, 2012.

10. http://politics.people.com.cn/GB/1024/9687405.html, accessed Jan. 5, 2012.

11. Xinhua News Agency, *Communiqué of the fifth plenary session of the 17th central committee of the Chinese Communist Party*, Oct. 18, 2010.

12. http://www.gov.cn/ldhd/2010–12/12/content_1764046.htm, accessed Jan 10, 2012.

13. Zhang Yansheng, "zhoumi guancha quanqiu zhili jiegou gaige buneng hushi fazhan zhuti" [closely examine the reform of global governance structures, the theme of development not to be ignored], *zhongguo jingji daobao* [China economics herald], May 21, 2011.

14. Zhang Youwen, "canyu quanqiu zhili: zhongguo guoji diwei tisheng de xin zhuti" [participation in global governance: a new issue for upgrading China's international status], wenhui bao [wenhui newspaper], April 25, 2011.

15. *Zhongguo jingying bao* [China management newspaper], "xin xing jingjiti jixu 'shangwei' shijie zhili xin pingtai" [emerging economies should urgently create a new platform for world economic governance], December 20, 2010.

16. Jiang Wei, "canyu lingdao quanqiu zhili, women hai chuzai xuexi jieduan" [China learns to be part of leading global governance], *ershiyi shiji jingji baodao* [21st century economic reporting], Oct. 24, 2011.

17. Pang Zhongying, "tupo xifang 'quanqiu zhili' kunjing" [breaking the dilemma posed by Western global governance], *zhongguo shehui kexue bao* [China social sciences bulletin], Oct. 27, 2011.

I

CHINA'S VISION
AND STRATEGY

1

China's Vision of Global Governance: A Resurrection of the "Central Kingdom"?

Lai-Ha Chan, Pak K. Lee, and Gerald Chan

China's rapid ascendancy in the past decades has sparked off lively debates in the mass media as well as in academic and policymaking circles as to what China will do with its newfound power. Previous studies about China's rise and its gradual integration in the world can be broadly divided into three different groups. Scholars in the first group examine if China would comply with the norms and rules made and proffered by the West.[1] They query whether China can adjust itself to the norms and rules that have been set and preferred by the dominant powers since World War II. The second group of scholars has pondered whether China will attempt to challenge the position of the United States as a hegemon in the world. Similar to those in the first group, they tend to gauge China's commitment to the liberal international order and ask whether China is a status quo power,[2] a (dis)satisfied power,[3] a regional threat,[4] or a responsible state.[5] The third group of scholars argues that China seeks great power status, clamoring for "a seat at the table" of the elite club of major powers.[6]

Informative and persuasive notwithstanding, the studies of these three groups focus on the strategy of attaining equal status with Western powers but do not address the more crucial issue as to whether China has a vision of global governance in its increasing engagement with the world and whether this vision is at odds with Western preferences. Without examining this key issue, one cannot say whether or not China will be respected and treated by the established powers as an equal partner. Inspired by Jeffrey Legro, who contends that the impact of China's relative power and its growing interdependence with the rest of the world should be "mediated through the doctrines [Chinese] leaders use to justify action and establish authority,"[7] this chapter explores China's underlying intentions of engaging global governance.

Global governance is understood here as a dynamic process about the making and implementation of global norms and rules by the joint effort of various actors in an anarchical world to provide global public goods (or regulate global public ills). It is aimed at tackling a host of transsovereign problems and creating a stable and responsive political order.[8] A study of China's vision of global governance will lead us to examine in depth what constitutes "a stable and responsive political order" in the minds of Chinese leaders. Orville Schell, director of the Centre on US-China Relations in Asia Society, holds the view that China "will increasingly seek to reinvent the old tributary system."[9] The traditional tributary system was based on the notion that the Chinese emperor was the Son of Heaven who held the Mandate of Heaven and was therefore the legitimate ruler of "all-under-Heaven" (*tianxia*). All states beyond China were, in theory, subordinate to this Central Kingdom (*Zhongguo*). Those close to China, especially Korea, Ryukyu, and Annam/Vietnam, had to pay tribute to the Chinese emperor periodically and to ask for investitures from the Chinese emperor. In contrast with the Westphalian international order in which formal equality forms the foundation of interstate relations in Europe, the tributary system was a non-egalitarian, hierarchical and hegemonic world order.

What is the Chinese vision of global governance? Does China want to re-impose this world order on the world? Can China be the legitimate ruler of "all-under-Heaven" in the twenty-first century? Will China take an aggressive foreign policy to achieve its goal, and will there be a pernicious effect on the world order? This chapter will first examine the notion of *tianxia* and how the Chinese scholarship has recently revisited this notion as well as its contemporary implications. Second, it will illustrate China's preferences for world order, including its values and approaches to global governance. Third, it will examine if China possesses the legitimacy to rule the world, if it is willing to lead, and if other states are inclined to defer to it.

TRIBUTARY SYSTEM AS THE WORLD ORDER?

David Kang studied the role of the tribute system in maintaining stability in the early modern East Asia from the founding of the Ming dynasty in 1368 to the Opium War of 1839–1842. He has demonstrated that a tributary system was basically conducive to providing a stable regional order.[10] During the 471 years between 1368 and 1839, there were only two major wars involving China and its neighbouring Sinicized states (Korea, Japan, and Vietnam). They were the Chinese invasion of Vietnam in 1402–1428 and the Japanese invasion of Korea in the Imjin War (1592–1598). Although the tributary system was a hierarchical and asymmetrical order, it was more defensive than imperialist. The Ming came to Korea's rescue in the latter war. Japan partook in the system for only 145 years between 1404 and 1549, but China did not force Japan to rejoin it afterwards.[11] At the heart of the hierarchical tributary system was an implicit "social contract" between China and the Sinicized states (especially Korea and Vietnam) whereby China provided them with security and aid in times of need and with credible commitments not to abuse its power in return for their acceptance of China's civilizational supremacy.[12] As a status-quo legitimizing hegemon,

China respected the sovereignty, independence, and autonomy of its vassal states, so they felt no need to employ balancing strategies against China.

The initial reason for China to conquer Vietnam in the early fifteenth century was due to an appeal from the deposed Tran dynasty to restore it to power from the illegitimate ruler, Ho Quy-ly, originally named Le Quy-ly. Probably because of the defeat at the hands of the Ho forces at the border, the Ming made a "disastrous decision" to invade and occupy Vietnam. However, Vietnam remained as a tributary state of China even after the end of the unsuccessful conquest in 1427. Le Loi, the leader of the Vietnamese resistance force, was invested by China as the ruler.

Later, the Qing did not aspire to reannex Vietnam even though it intervened as a "legitimizing patriarch" in 1788 in the domestic politics of Vietnam. It helped restore the Le dynasty in the wake of the Tay Son rebellion, but was defeated in the following year by Nguyen Hue of the Tay Son. In spite of the victory, Nguyen Hue did not cease the annual tribute missions to China and accepted a place of honor at the eightieth birthday celebrations of Emperor Qianlong in 1789. Having defeated the Tay Son, Nguyen Ahn (no relation to Nguyen Hue) completed the overthrow of the Le dynasty in 1802. He changed his name to Gia Long and proposed to the Qing that his country be renamed "Nam Viet" ("Nan Yue" in Chinese) when he sought investiture from the Chinese imperial court. The latter disapproved of the name "Nan Yue" because it referred to an old Chinese state located in parts of modern Guangdong and Guangxi. The Qing suggested reversing the two words and bestowing the name "Viet Nam" to Gia Long's territory in 1803. Chiang Kai-shek declined an offer from Franklin Roosevelt to return both Indochina and Hong Kong to China.[13] China did not pose any threat to Korea either. Ming China joined the Imjin war after Hideyoshi's troops invaded Korea in 1592 with an ultimate target at China.[14]

Outlines and key points of the Korea-China and Vietnam-China borders were demarcated through negotiations and remained largely intact.[15] China also provided regional public goods (to use modern-day terminology), namely, regional peace and security based on a functional Confucian bureaucratic system of selecting scholar-officials through competitive examinations for the secondary Sinicized states to emulate.[16] So the tributary system is argued to be a socially recognized legitimate order, a major contributing factor to the highly stable and nonviolent East Asian order in the 470 years or so between the fourteenth and mid-nineteenth centuries.[17] In other words, one may posit that even if China of the early twenty-first century wishes to reimpose the tributary world order on the world, one cannot immediately jump to the conclusion that China will become increasingly assertive and aggressive. And it is not necessarily pernicious for present-day China to look back to the past for its future role in contemporary global governance.

Interestingly, in the past few years, China scholars inside and outside the country have shown growing interest in the notion of *tianxia* and the associated tributary system.[18] Are Chinese elites looking for a return to the ancient tributary system in organizing China's international relations of the early twenty-first century? How do they understand and interpret *tianxia* and the associated tributary system? Zhao

Tingyang, a philosopher and a proponent of reconceptualizing Chinese traditional conception of world governance, published his seminal work titled *Tianxia System: A Philosophy for the World Institution* in 2005.[19] According to him, the theory of *tianxia* (all-under-Heaven) is the most ideal solution to world problems and the system could form a world government. The book has captured the attention of both scholars and the masses and has swiftly become one of the best-selling books in China. It has also become a new reference point for some international relations scholars both inside and outside China, to discuss China's conception of world order.

According to Zhao, *tianxia* as a model of world order has three different notions defined by a trinity of the geographical, psychological, and political worlds.[20] Geographically, *tianxia* looks at world problems and world order from a global perspective. Its "all-inclusive" nature includes everything in the world; it is regarded as "almost equivalent to the universe" within the embrace of the Sinic civilization. This "oneness" of the world is also reflected in the political principle of "inclusion of all."

From a social and psychological perspective, *tianxia* means "hearts of all people." By referring to Xun Zi's (313BC–238BC) essay "On Kingship and Supremacy," Zhao underlines the importance of normative power. He claims that the autonomy of people to follow or not to follow is regarded as a fundamental question in Chinese political philosophy as the matter of "people's heart" or the "general will of the people." He concludes that an emperor cannot maintain his empire of all-under-Heaven "unless he receives the sincere and true support from the people on the land."[21] In other words, *tianxia* (here meaning heaven or the world) could only be obtained through people's willingness to follow, rather than by force.

From a political point of view, *tianxia* could be understood as a world institution and because of the "oneness," it would be a more effective channel to solve global problems. Zhao explains that "our supposed world is now still a non-world, for the world has not yet been completed in its full sense."[22] While claiming that he is not criticizing the United Nations (UN) as an international organization, but given the "limitations in the potentiality of the UN pattern," he argues that we are now facing the prospect of a "*failed world*," not "failed states." The reason is that the UN is a political platform that only satisfies developed countries' interests, or more specifically the United States' interests. It cannot stop "a superpower from universalizing itself alone in the name of globalization."[23] In order to solve this problem, Zhao proposes that the all-under-Heaven system be the ideal form of the world institution.

Although Zhao is not a political scientist, his work has generated a continuing debate about the possibility of a non-Western world order. His discourse on the normative structure of international relations, particularly in regard to its ability to address global problems, has been picked up by other China scholars. In formulating his strategy of China's rise, Yan Xuetong, dean of the Institute of International Studies at Tsinghua University and one of the influential IR scholars in China, also uses Xun Zi's thoughts on international politics to discuss Zhao's idea about normative power. In Yan's words, true kingship is a higher form of world leadership than 'hegemony' because *tianxia* is attained through voluntary submission, not by force.[24] Here it is worth noting that the Chinese concept of 'hegemony' is interpreted differently from the Western one.[25] The term 'hegemony' is understood and used pejoratively by the Chinese as *baquan* or *badao* (coercive dominance); in the Western social-science literature, it refers to "the way in which the dominant social groups achieve rulership or leadership on the basis of attaining social cohesion and consensus."[26] So, in the Chinese literature, a closer term to the Western social-science interpretation of hegemony is "kingship" (*wangtao*) or "benevolent governance." *Wang* means the leader of the state or the world; and *tao* is the path to the rulership.

Yan continues his explanation on China's strategy by stating,

> If China becomes a true kingship country—a super state grounded in high morals and ethics—it should bring about a world order more peaceful and secure than that today. True kingship may not be the perfect international system but, compared with the current hegemonic system, would be one imbued with greater cooperation and security . . . Certain countries worry that a rising China might revive the old East-Asian tributary system. But any such renewal would inevitably lessen China international political mobilization. Objectively, however, big and small states are not equal as regards power. Establishing a hierarchical norm, therefore, could help maintain a balance of power and responsibility, thereby reducing international conflict and strengthening cooperative relationships.[27]

Here Yan makes three propositions. First, true kingship is a higher form of world leadership than 'hegemony' (*baquan*) because *tianxia* is attained through voluntary submission, not by force. Second, to attain true kingship, China should place greater attention to Xun Zi's notion of "*yi*" (moral and ethical principles) in projecting its power by foreign policy and securing its legitimacy to rule the world. Third, while the country's economic wealth has strengthened its material power in the past three decades, China has not gained much respect from the world. To remedy this situation, China should make its moral responsibility to the world commensurate with its growing national power.

Shang Huipeng of Peking University says that the tributary system was an extension of the Confucian notion of family. In this family of nations (*guoji jiating*), China was the patriarch, enjoying the highest status while shouldering the greatest responsibility toward subordinate states. For Shang, the three relationships discussed by Alexander Wendt in his *Social Theory of International Politics*—enemies, rivals, or friends—are not applicable to the tributary system. Although it is true that the mutual relations were not equal, they were not exploitative or coercive. There were exchanges of benevolence (from above) and reverence (from below). China's leadership was not simply built on material prowess but also on moral authority.[28]

Zhang Feng asserts that the tributary system can be understood at two levels: discourse and institution. At the discourse level, the Sinocentrism was used to demonstrate China's centrality and supremacy in East Asia even when China was weak in military terms, for example, in the Song dynasty (960–1279); at the institutional level, the tributary system and the identification of Chinese emperors as the sons of Heaven served to affirm and maintain China's legitimate status and security.[29]

In summary, instead of imposing its values on the surrounding subordinate states, China's leadership under the tributary system was built on moral authority. The "Central Kingdom" possessed legitimacy to rule as well as ability to attract other states to follow. At the heart of this system was an implicit "social contract" between China and East Asian states: an exchange of the provision of security and aid for the acceptance of China's supremacy. As a legitimizing hegemon (or *wangtao* in Chinese), China respected their sovereignty, independence and autonomy, so they felt no need to employ balancing strategies against China. An interesting, contemporary implication is whether Chinese leaders are looking for a return to the ancient tributary system in organizing China's international relations with its previous subordinate states, and more importantly with the world at large while participating in global governance.

CHINA'S VALUES AND ITS APPROACHES TO GLOBAL GOVERNANCE

How does the study of the pre-modern tributary system impact on our understanding of the Chinese present vision of global governance? Until the late Qing dynasty, the Chinese had perceived China as the Central Kingdom, the center of the universe.[30] However, this world view underwent a fundamental change in the nineteenth century, particularly in the wake of its defeat in the Opium War (1839–1842).Between 1840 and 1860, China was forced to sign numerous unequal treaties with Western powers, which brought an end to the notion of *tianxia* as well as the institution of tributary system.[31] In the twentieth century, China suffered from humiliating defeats at the hands of foreign powers until the end of World War II.

The impact of this treaty system on Chinese contemporary history and its foreign policy is momentous. China was forced to experience and embrace the Westphalian world order, which is based on sovereign equality, absolute sovereignty and nonintervention into other states' domestic politics. It was forced to recognize the state-centric, *realpolitik* notion of international order during the Opium War. After 1949, China has employed this doctrine to defend its territorial integrity, stave off external intervention, and ask for equal treatment by the West.

As a result of the Western encroachment on Chinese sovereignty and territory for about a century, China has given national sovereignty and autonomy much prominence in its foreign policy, particularly in the area of international peace and security, human rights protection and the associated humanitarian intervention. For the Chinese, the ideal order is a pluralist and harmonious world order, which lays emphasis on the principles of national sovereignty and non-intervention and the right to choose one's path to development.

In line with its understanding of national sovereignty, China formulates the mantra of a "harmonious world" (*hexie shijie*), which both upholds the principle of nonintervention and stresses the predominant role of the state in governance as a way to defend itself on the global stage. "Harmonious society" is Hu Jintao's new vision for both his nation and the world. In the Fourth Plenum of the 16th Chinese Communist Party (CCP) Central Committee, held in Beijing in September 2004, Chinese leaders proposed to build a "harmonious socialist society" in China. In the United Nations 60th Anniversary Summit in New York in September 2005, Hu further elaborated that a "harmonious world" is to be built on a world composed of sovereign nation-states that respect a plurality and diversity of cultures, ideologies, and politico-economic systems, and handle their relations on the basis of "respect for sovereignty and territorial integrity, as well as respect for countries' right to independently choose their own social systems and paths of development."[32] Since then, Chinese scholars have expounded their views on the concept of a "harmonious world" at great length. It is said that the notion represents China's overall goal and theory of global governance.[33] Based on the official doctrine, Lu Xiaohong of China Foreign Affairs University and Yu Keping of the CCP Central Compilation and Translation Bureau have pointed out that the principal actors in global governance are nation-states and the United Nations.[34]

A decoding of the Chinese explanatory notes of a harmonious world and its theory of global governance reveals that the idea of a harmonious world shares the same logic as the Westphalian international system. China's advocacy for strengthening the United Nations-based multilateralism and constructing a harmonious world is obviously targeted at the hegemonic role of the United States and its mission to transform the prevailing Westphalian international system into a self-proclaimed "more peaceful" world based on the solidarist values of liberty, human rights, and democracy. In other words, China would like to maintain the Westphalian international system rather than follow in the footsteps of democratic countries to transform the international order into a post-Westphalian one. The Chinese notion of the international order bears a striking resemblance to the English School's pluralist conception of international society where sovereign states, acting as the principal actors in the international society, aim to achieve a minimal degree of order despite holding varying conceptions of human rights and global justice.[35] For Chinese leaders, the primary goal of building a harmonious world is to safeguard the principles of sovereignty and nonintervention in domestic politics as well as protect China's endowed right to choose its own path to development. China does not, however, harmonize very well with the evolving liberal international order, which emphasizes sovereignty's entailment of responsibility and the notion of responsibilities to protect.

With reference to the earlier question, "Does China want to reimpose the *tianxia* system on to the world?", China's preference for the world order in the twenty-first century is somewhat different from that of the tributary system. Since the establishment of the People's Republic of China, the doctrine of sovereignty and the principle of nonintervention have been the cornerstone of its vision for the world order. While participating in global governance, China emphasizes that cooperation should be based on equal footing among all states. Unlike the tributary system, which was a non-egalitarian and hierarchical world order, China is now at pains to maintain the

Westphalian international order in which formal equality forms the foundation of interstate relations. Although the study of the tributary system may not bear any apparent impact on China's present diplomatic practice, it may pave the way for Beijing to play a more intrusive role in world affairs in the future, as the country continues to grow in power and status.

THE QUESTION OF LEGITIMACY

As mentioned earlier, Yan argues that to attain true kingship, China should "maintain a balance of power and responsibility." This means that China should project its foreign policy with moral and ethical principles and match its moral responsibility for the world with its growing national power. To address the issue of whether China can be a legitimate ruler of "all-under-Heaven" in the twenty-first century, two important questions need to be tackled: (1) Is China willing to play the leadership role in managing a variety of global issues in order to maintain a stable and responsive political order? (2) Does China possess the legitimacy to rule or ability to attract other states to follow or defer to it? The following sections will provide both an inside-out and an outside-in perspective—China's willingness and preparedness to lead; and the legitimacy of its claim to leadership—as evidence to prove that China lacks the legitimacy to re-impose the tributary system in the twenty-first century.

China's Contribution toward Global Pubic Goods for Health

One way to gauge if China can lead others in a hierarchy of states is to examine if it is willing to contribute to the provision of global public goods. Is China willing to play the leadership or hegemonic role in addressing a variety of global issues so as to maintain a stable and responsive political order? More specifically, is it willing to take the lead to help the world's poor in times of need? China's ascendancy and its accumulated wealth over the past three decades have raised international concern about its share of responsibility for resolving various global problems. This section explores China's contribution in the field of global health and how China can address the global challenge in health, in particular in relation to the achievement of the Millennium Development Goals (MDGs). Global health is chosen as a specific test case here, partly because this issue has assumed increasing importance as a nontraditional security issue in global affairs and partly because China has been a source of some serious outbreaks of contagious diseases such as severe acute respiratory syndrome (SARS), bird flu, and swine flu in recent times.

Historically, developed countries, especially the G7 and the European Union (EU) countries, have been the largest donors to international health programs. Their tremendous financial power allows them to extend their leverage over agenda setting in global health governance, particularly on the priority in dealing with different kinds of health issues. For example, during the G8 summit in Okinawa, Japan, in 2000, the group was committed to advancing the fight against HIV/AIDS, tuberculosis, and malaria. Their commitment subsequently set the stage for the formation of the Global Fund in 2002, which led to an allocation of considerable resources to the prevention and treatment of these diseases globally. In 2005, the group further pledged in Gleneagles, Scotland, an extra US$50 billion aid for development. Together with its previous US$80 billion commitment, the group made a pledge of nearly US$130 billion on international development assistance by 2010.[36] Although there was US$10 billion shortfall in the group's delivery of their commitment as of June 2010, there is no doubt that the G8 or the Global Fund is the dominant financier in the fight against HIV/AIDS, tuberculosis, and malaria. For example, of the US$8.7 billion–worth total international assistance on HIV/AIDS in 2008–2009, more than 82 percent (US$7.6 billion) comes from the G8 countries.[37]

However, with the onset of global recession in 2008, international donors, particularly the more developed countries, are cutting back on AIDS support, directly hurting the fight against the epidemic across Africa. In 2008–2009, the G8, EU, and other donor governments only provided US$7.6 billion for AIDS relief to developing nations. Compared with US$7.7 billion disbursed in 2007–2008, funding remained essentially flat.[38] Concomitant with the global economic downturn is a power shift from the more developed industrialized countries in the North to the emerging economies in the South. The focus of global health governance has correspondingly shifted from G8 to a larger group, G20, created in 1999. In addition to the members of G8 and the EU, G20 consists of Argentina, Australia, Brazil, China, India, Indonesia, Mexico, Saudi Arabia, South Africa, South Korea, and Turkey. The original concern of G20 was primarily financial stability and sustainable economic growth with scant attention to global health or social development.[39] However, in October 2010, initiated by South Korean president Lee Myung-bak, a G20 working group on development was established.[40] It is the first working group that emphasizes development assistance and strives for achieving the MDGs, in particular Goal 2 on improving education quality. Considering that there are deep political divisions among the member states, it is still uncertain whether the pro-development approach can be sustained within the group.[41] Nevertheless, it is an important step forward, contributing to the provision of global public goods in line with the growing influence of this group. While international donors are reducing their pledge to AIDS support, will the emerging economies of the G20 grouping, especially China, become new significant players in global health governance? Is China willing to shoulder more responsibilities in the area of global health?

Paradoxically, although most of the major emerging market economies have gone through the global economic downturn relatively unscathed, they remain as major recipients of aid for their domestic health programs. According to the Institute of Health Metrics and Evaluation, India and China were among the top ten recipients in health assistance between 2002 and 2007.[42] While China has overtaken Japan as the world's second largest economy, and accumulated US$3.18 trillion in foreign exchange reserves by the end of 2011,[43] it is the fourth-largest recipient of the Global

Fund, after Ethiopia, India, and Tanzania. Between 2002 (when the Global Fund was launched) and 2010, China received US$964 million, of which 40 percent went to combat HIV/AIDS in the country.[44] Considering that China could afford to spend US$46 billion on organizing and staging the 2008 Olympic games and the 2010 Shanghai Expo and another US$586 billion on a national economic stimulus package, global health experts debate whether China should remain as a recipient of Global Fund. Critics also question the wisdom of financing anti-malaria programs in China.[45] It is argued that "China's Health Ministry seeks aid only because the Chinese government chooses instead to lavish funds on "hard power" agencies or to invest it in other sectors."[46]

It is little wonder that Michel Kazatchkine, then the executive director of the Global Fund, asked China (and India) to increase their contributions to fight against the HIV/AIDS pandemic. Based on a country's national income and the amount that donor is expected to contribute, the Global Fund suggested in 2010 that the Chinese government should contribute US$96 million to the fund over the next three years, amounting to 16 times its current annual donation.[47] However, during the Global Fund donors' meeting in October 2010 in New York, China only pledged US$14 million to the fund for the 2011–2013 funding cycle, slightly larger than that of Nigeria (US$10 million), a new donor to the fund, but far less than Kazatchkine's expectation.[48] Overall, the Global Fund will need US$13 billion to US$20 billion in 2011–2013 to fulfill Goal 6 of the MDGs on time.[49] At the fund's meeting in October, donors committed US$11.7 billion in total for the three years. While it is claimed to be the largest ever financial pledge for a collective international effort to fight the three pandemics, the Global Fund noted that it fell short of the expected minimum demand. This shortfall "could slow down the effort to beat the three diseases."[50] The proponents of the Global Fund were disappointed that "hopes for contributions from several emerging nations from the G20 group have not materialized," even though some African countries such as Nigeria, Namibia, and Tunisia made their commitments for the first time.[51] Finally, under donor pressure to reduce aid to the fast-growing China, the Global Fund and China agreed in October 2011 to cut US$95 million from the fund's grants to the country.[52]

While China is now the world's second largest economy, its donations to the WHO, the principal major intergovernmental organization on health, are not generous either. Between 2008 and 2009, its voluntary contributions were a mere US$4.23 million, accounting for less than 0.3 percent of the total contributions from member states, far less than the United States or many members of the G8. For the year 2010, while it might be understandable why the contributions from G8 members went down, owing to the global economic downturn, China's economic growth remained resilient. However, its voluntary contribution to the WHO declined to 1.22 million, accounting for only 0.16 percent of the total contributions from member states (see Table 1.1). China also lagged far behind some medium

Table 1.1. China and G8 contributions to the World Health Organization, 2008–2009, and 2010

Countries	Voluntary Contributions in US$ (% of Total Contributions of Member States), 2008–2009	Voluntary Contributions in US$ (% of Total Contributions of Members States), 2010
United States	$424,540,852 (29.56%)	279,949,098 (36.18%)
United Kingdom	$205,510,011 (14.31%)	115,182,487 (14.89%)
Canada	$96,356,532 (6.71%)	60,803,103 (7.86%)
Japan	$24,520,679 (1.71%)	32,711,415 (4.23%)
Germany	$48,150,583 (3.35%)	17,557,058 (2.27%)
France	$19,401,505 (1.35%)	11,740,264 (1.52%)
Russia	$20,050,000 (1.40%)	10,341,651 (1.37%)
Italy	$37,157,862 (2.59%)	7,284,065 (0.94%)
China	$4,232,333 (0.29%)	1,220,000 (0.16%)

Sources: World Health Organization, "Voluntary contributions by fund and by donor for the financial period 2008-2009," Sixty-Third World Health Assembly, A63/INF.COC./4, 29 April 2010; http://apps.who.int/gb/eb wha/pdf_files/WHA63/A63_ID4-en.pdf (accessed January 11, 2011); and *World Health Organization*, "Voluntary contributions by fund and by donor for the year ended 31 December 2010," Sixty-Four World Health Assembly, A64/29Add.1, 7 April 2011; http://apps.who.int/gb/ebwha/pdf_files/WHA64/A64_29Add1-en.pdf (accessed 22 January 2012).

or even small powers such as Norway (US$55.88 million), the Netherlands (US$ 27.14 million), Spain (US$24.04 million), Australia (US$31.92 million), Sweden (US$18.81 million), and Luxembourg (US$10.76 million).[53] A comparison with the contribution during 1992–1993, when the Chinese economy began to take off, reveals surprisingly that China's contribution has been decreasing over time. During 1992–1993, it paid US$5.80 million to the WHO, accounting for 0.77 percent of the total contributions from member states.[54]

While China has utilized multilateral cooperation to mobilize international health aid to tackle its mounting internal AIDS crisis,[55] its contributions to global health do not seem to be commensurate with its growing economic wealth and status. On the one hand, this may be another incidence of China's maxi/mini principle, described by Samuel Kim in the 1990s, whereby China wants to maximize its rights while minimizing its responsibilities and commitments. Thus, one has valid grounds for asking whether China is a system-exploiting power, tending to take a free ride on multilateral effort to manage global diseases. On the other hand, Chinese officials have often referred to China's developmental status and its low per capita GDP. The country faces a lot of well-known domestic problems. They also claim that "the biggest contribution China can make to global health is to provide adequate healthcare to its 1.3 billion people."[56] The small contributions to the Global Fund may also reflect China's reservations about engaging non-state actors in global governance.

The Legitimacy to Rule

From an outside-in perspective, does China's foreign policy or its approach toward global governance project any set of moral values and norms? If so, are they the same as those embodied in the imperial tributary *tianxia* system? Are they attractive to the rest of the world in the current age of globalization and growing interdependence? This section addresses the crucial issue of whether or not the rest of the world will perceive the Chinese worldview as legitimate. Will the previously subordinate states and the United States, which was not involved in the pre–Opium War East Asian order, defer to China's leadership?

We would argue that it is less likely. Respect for and protection of national sovereignty might be conducive to preventing or at least reducing interstate wars in early East Asia (the fourteenth to nineteenth centuries) and the Cold War period, but they are no longer helpful in resolving the host of transnational issues of global concerns in the present era of globalization and increasing integration. The *tianxia* system and the state-centric concept of international politics embodied in it would be inimical to the interests of international society of the early twenty-first century, for failing to address the proliferation of weapons of mass destruction (e.g. the North Korean nuclear weapons program), global financial instability, human rights violations leading to brutal internecine wars, global warming, spread of contagious diseases, energy shortages, and transnational organized crime. The Westphalian notion is at odds with the growing demand for global governance and global collective action.

China's soft power is also spread unevenly across the globe with negative views toward it being higher in East Asia and the United States. Results from a Chicago Council on Global Affairs survey on soft power in Asia reveals that large majorities of the people in the United States, Japan, South Korea, Indonesia, and Vietnam are not aware of the China's notion of a "harmonious world" and that for the people in the United States, Japan, and South Korea, China is unable to portray its ideas of the best global order.[57] According to an international polling conducted for BBC World Service between December 2010 and February 2011, opinions of China's influence are in general positive in Africa and Latin America but are less favorable in the Anglo-Saxon countries of Canada, the United Kingdom, and the United States (the views are divided in Australia) and in Europe (except Russia). More essential to our study is the finding that a majority of South Korean (53 percent), Japanese (52 percent), and Indian (52 percent), hold negative views of China.[58]

Also, the legacy of the unequal tributary relationship may not be helpful for China to assume the leadership role in East Asia. Since 1949, both North Korea and Vietnam have been highly sensitive about being seen as subordinate to or dependent on China. In various occasions they did not defer to China. China does not have any followers in East Asia. The nationalist Kim Il-sung had repeatedly sought help from Stalin since March 1949 to invade South Korea. He did not have any face-to-face discussion with Mao until May 1950 after obtaining Stalin's approval of his plan in his visit to Moscow in March-April 1950. He did so simply because Stalin attached a condition that if he met any troubles in the war, he had to ask Mao to bail him out.[59] When Mao asked Kim if North Korea needed any military assistance from China,

Kim reportedly answered "arrogantly" that the North Korean forces (including those Koreans who assisted the CCP in the Chinese civil war) and the Communist guerrillas in the South could handle the war themselves.[60] The preferences of China and North Korea also differ in the latter's development of a nuclear weapons program in the early years of the twenty-first century.[61]

China had heated disputes with South Korea in 2004 over the history of Koguryo (37 BC–AD 668). Koguryo, an ancient Korean kingdom, was defeated by the alliance between Silla and Tang dynasty in 668.[62] It was partly located in today's Chinese northeast, so Chinese historians under the "Northeast Project" undertaken by the Chinese Academy of Social Sciences argue that the ancient kingdom was part of the Chinese nation and history. The kingdom's relations with China were central-local relations. Some in South Korea interpreted this "revisionist" historiography as part of China's grand intention to reassert influence over its tributary states.[63]

After this conflict, results from several international opinion surveys in recent years have indicated that the majority of South Korean respondents do not view China positively. One shows that 60 percent of South Koreans see that China's economic growth is a bad thing for their country, 89 percent think that China's growing military power is a bad thing, and 56 percent believe that China hurts the environment the most.[64] Another survey indicates that from 2002 to 2010, the percentage of South Koreans who have a favorable opinion of China has decreased from 66 percent in 2002 to 38 percent in 2010 and more South Koreans have perceived China as an enemy (28–37 percent) than as a partner (23–25 percent) in 2008–2010.[65] In yet another survey, only 21 percent of the South Korean respondents are comfortable with the prediction that China will become a leader of Asia.[66]

In the Vietnam War, North Vietnam did not share China's hostility toward the Soviet Union. As China warned North Vietnam against receiving aid from the Soviet Union, Hanoi argued that the Sino-Soviet conflict sabotaged united action among the three Communist parties and countries to promote Vietnamese unification. The worsening relations between the CCP and the Vietnam Workers Party eventually led to a war between the two countries in 1979. The two countries did not normalize their mutual relations until 1991.[67]

In addition, despite the fact that China's overland borderline with Vietnam was set and mutually recognized in the eleventh century, the two countries have had disputes over their maritime boundary in the South China Sea since the 1970s.[68] Territorial disputes have also taken place between China and Japan in the East China Sea. China's neighboring countries now have grounds for worrying that a rising China is no longer the benevolent status quo power under the old tributary system.

CONCLUSION

This chapter addresses three interrelated issues. First, in light of the tendency that China looks back to its glorious past for possible guidance on how to reclaim its rightful position in the world in the future, we asked what the *tianxia* notion and the tributary system meant. Second, considering China's involvement in global governance, we discussed the core values as well as the social order China projects to the world with the aim of exploring whether there are similarities between the *tianxia* concept and China's current preferences for world order. Third, we examined the contributions of present-day China to the provision of global public goods, using the case study of public health, to gauge if China is willing to assume global leadership, and whether other states would admirably perceive the Chinese way as a model for them to emulate.

Some analysts have argued that China's tributary system did not threaten the security of its neighboring states, as the Central Kingdom was not imperialist and aggressive. It instead provided regional peace and security and a viable governance model for them to follow, which may be regarded as regional public goods. Its legitimacy was not wholly based on material power. In comparison with the European states in the same period of time, Ming and Qing China were peace-loving as long as the other states or semi-state entities accepted and recognized China's supremacy.

Two long-standing consistencies in China's preferences for world order are noted. First, it has attached great importance to the role of the state, focusing on interstate relations and thus not regarding non-state actors as significant players. Second, the Chinese have had a strong belief that China is East Asia's center of gravity. Wars broke out after 1839 when external powers posed direct challenges to its centrality and supremacy in East Asia.

While it may be premature to claim that China has any intent to resurrect the *tianxia* system in the region in the future, it is quite obvious that today's China does not possess any similar discernible soft power for others to emulate. Still an inward-looking country, China is loath to supply global public goods to address the transnational problems many of us are facing today. China's preferred world order indeed offers little meaningful and practical solutions to them either. Unlike the situations in the fourteenth to nineteenth centuries, East Asian countries are concerned that China will use its newfound power to exploit or coerce them and that they should be treated as equal sovereign states by China. In short, without followers, China can less likely reclaim its previous position of the Central Kingdom. The real challenge we are going to face in the foreseeable future is rather a global leadership deficit or vacuum in which both the United States and China cannot lead on their own while they do not want the other to lead.

NOTES

1. Examples are Gerald Chan, *China's Compliance in Global Affairs: Trade, Arms Control, Environmental Protection, Human Rights* (Singapore: World Scientific, 2006); Alastair Iain Johnston, *Social States: China in International Institutions, 1980–2000* (Princeton, NJ: Princeton University Press, 2008); Ann Kent, *Beyond Compliance: China, International Organizations, and Global Security* (Stanford, CA: Stanford University Press, 2007).

2. Alastair Iain Johnston, "Is China a Status Quo Power?" *International Security*, 27(4), Spring 2003: 5–56.

3. Alastair Iain Johnston, "Beijing's Security Behavior in the Asia-Pacific: Is China a Dissatisfied Power?" in J. J. Suh, Peter J. Katzenstein, and Allen Carlson (eds.), *Rethinking Security in East Asia: Identity, Power and Efficiency* (Stanford, CA: Stanford University Press, 2004), 34–96; Shaun Breslin, "China's Emerging Global Role: Dissatisfied Responsible Great Power," *Politics*, 20 (S1) (2010): 52–62.

4. Richard Bernstein and Ross H. Munro, *The Coming Conflict with China* (New York: A. A. Knopf, 1997).

5. Xia Liping, "China: A Responsible Great Power," *Journal of Contemporary China*, 10(26), 2001: 17–25.

6. Yong Deng, *China's Struggle for Status: The Realignment of International Relations* (Cambridge: Cambridge University Press, 2008); Deborah Welch Larson and Alexei Shevchenko, "Status Seekers: Chinese and Russian Responses to U.S. Primacy," *International Security*, 34 (4), Spring 2010: 63–95; idem, "Status Concern and Multilateral Cooperation," in I. William Zartman and Saadia Touval (eds.), *International Cooperation: The Extents and Limits of Multilateralism* (Cambridge: Cambridge University Press, 2010): 182–207.

7. Jeffrey W. Legro, "What China Will Want: The Future Intentions of a Rising Power," *Perspectives on Politics*, 5 (3), September 2007: 515–34, at 515.

8. Gerald Chan, Pak K. Lee and Lai-Ha Chan, *China Engages Global Governance: A New World Order in the Making?* (Abingdon: Routledge, 2012), chapter 1.

9. David Pilling, "Beijing's foreign policy," *Financial Times*, 19 January 2011, http://www.ft.com/cms/s/0/56a99fdc-2405–11e0–bef0–00144feab49a.html (accessed 29 January 2011).

10. David C. Kang, *East Asia before the West: Five Centuries of Trade and Tribute* (New York: Columbia University Press, 2010). The classic study of the tributary system is John King Fairbank (ed.), *The Chinese World Order: Traditional China's Foreign Relations* (Cambridge, MA: Harvard University Press, 1968).

11. Samuel S. Kim, *China, the United Nations, and World Order* (Princeton, NJ: Princeton University Press, 1979): 45.

12. This kind of "social contract," however, did not exist between China and the nomadic people at China's western and northern frontiers for the latter refused to accept China's cultural superiority. Endemic wars happened between China and them. Kang, *East Asia before the West*, chapter 7.

13. Kang, *East Asia before the West*, 58, 98–103; Brantly Womack, *China and Vietnam: The Politics of Asymmetry* (Cambridge: Cambridge University Press, 2006): 119, 125–29, 134, 136.

14. Marius B. Jansen, *The Making of Modern Japan* (Cambridge, MA: Belknap Press, 2000): 20.

15. Womack, *China and Vietnam*, 129, 133

16. Kang, *East Asia before the West*, chapter 3. Womack argues that Le Thanh Tong, the ruler of Vietnam from 1460 to 1497, "managed for the first time in the history of independent Vietnam to establish the scholar-bureaucracy as the core of central administration." Womack, *China and Vietnam*, 132.

17. Kang, *East Asia before the West*. See also Shang Huipeng, "'Lun ren' yu 'tianxia'—jiedu yi chaogong tixi wei hexin de gudai Dong Ya guoji zhixu" ('Human relations' and 'all under Heaven': an interpretation of the tribute-centred ancient East Asian international order), *Guoji zhengzhi yanjiu* (*International Politics Studies*), No. 2 (2009): 38.

18. See, e.g., Zhao Tingyang, *Tianxia tixi: Shijie zhidu zhexue daolun (The Tianxia System: A Philosophy for the World Institution)* (Nanjing: Jiangsu jiaoyu chubanshe, 2005); William A. Callahan, "Chinese Visions of World Order: Post-Hegemonic or a New Hegemony?" *International Studies Review*, 10 (4), December 2008: 749–61; Zhang Feng, "Rethinking the 'Tribute System': Broadening the Conceptual Horizon of Historical East Asian Politics," *Chinese Journal of International Politics*, 2 (4), Winter 2009: 545–74; Allen Carlson, "Moving beyond Sovereignty? A Brief Consideration of Recent Changes in China's Approach to International Order and the Emergence of the *Tianxia* Concept," *Journal of Contemporary China*, 20 (68), January 2011: 89–102.

19. Zhao Tingyang, *Tianxia tixi (The Tianxia System)*.

20. A brief but more concise explanation of this proposition can be found in Tingyang Zhao, "Rethinking empire from a Chinese concept 'All-under-Heaven' (Tian-xia)," *Social Identities*, 12 (1), January 2006: 29–41; and idem, "Tianxia tixi de yige jianyao biaoshu" (An introduction to all-under-Heaven system), *Shijie jingji yu zhengzhi (World Economics and Politics)*, No. 10 (2008): 57–65.

21. Zhao,"Rethinking empire from a Chinese Concept 'All-under-Heaven'" (Tian-xia)': 30.

22. Ibid.

23. Ibid., 37. Emphasis is from the original.

24. Yan Xuetong, "Xun Zi's Thoughts on International Politics and Their Implications," *The Chinese Journal of International Politics*, 2 (1), Summer 2008: 159.

25. Throughout this chapter, 'hegemony,' in inverted commas, refers to the Chinese understanding of the notion. Otherwise, it refers to the meaning in the Western social-science literature.

26. Jonathan Joseph, *Hegemony: A Realist Analysis* (London: Routledge, 2002): 1.

27. Yan Xuetong, "Xun Zi's Thoughts on International Politics and Their Implications": 159, 163 (emphasis added).

28. Shang Huipeng, "'Lun ren' yu 'tianxia' ('Human relations' and 'all under Heaven'): 29–43.

29. Zhang Feng, "Rethinking the 'tribute system'".

30. This section draws on Lai-Ha Chan, *China Engages Global Heath Governance: Responsible Stakeholder or System-Transformer* (New York: Palgrave Macmillan, 2011): 33–36 and 137–42.

31. For more details of these unequal treaties, see Jonathan D. Spence, *The Search for Modern China,* 2nd edition (New York: W. W. Norton, 1999):160–166.

32. Hu Jintao, "Building towards a Harmonious World of Lasting Peace and Common Prosperity" (speech delivered at the High-Level Plenary Meeting of the United Nations 60th Session, New York, 15 September 2005); available at http://lb2.mofcom.gov.cn/aarticle/chinanews/200511/20051100766746.html (accessed 2 June 2008).

33. Lu Xiaohong. "'Hexie shijie': zhongguo de quanqiu zhili lilun (A 'harmonious world': China's global governance theory)", *Waijiao Pinglun (Foreign Affairs Review)*, December 2006: 63–68; Pang Zhongying, 'Guanyu Zhongguo de quanqiu zhili yanjiu (On the research on global governance in China)', in Pang Zhongying, ed. *Zhongguo xuezhe kan shijie 8: quanqiu zhili juan (World Politics—Views from China, Vol. 8, Global Governance)* (Hong Kong: Heping tushu youxian gongsi, 2006): xvii-xxx; and Yu Keping, 'hexie shijie yu quanqiu zhili (A harmonious world and global governance)', *Zhonggong tianjin shiwei dangxiao xuebao (Journal of the CCP Tianjin Municipal Party School)*, No. 2, 2007: 5–10.

34. Lu Xiaohong, "'Hexie shijie': Zhongguo de quanqiu zhili lilun ('Harmonious world': China's global governance theory)." *Waijiao Pinglun* (Foreign Affairs Review), December

2006: 63–68; and Yu Keping, 'Hexie shijie yu quanqiu zhili (A harmonious world and global governance)', *Zhonggong Tianjin Shiwei dangxiao xuebao (Journal of the CCP Tianjin Municipal Party School)*, No. 2, 2007: 5–10.

35. Hedley Bull, *The Anarchical Society: A Study of Order in World Politics*, 3rd edition (Houndmills, Basingstoke: Palgrave Macmillan, 2002); and Andrew Linklater, "The English School," in Scott Burchill et al., *Theories of International Relations*, 3rd edition (Basingstoke: Palgrave Macmillan, 2005): 84–109; Andrew Linklater and Hidemi Suganami, *The English School of International Relations* (Cambridge: Cambridge University Press, 2006): 59–68.

36. Laurie Garret and El'Haum Alavian, "Global Health Governance in a G-20 World," *Global Health Governance*, 4 (1), Fall 2010: 6–7.

37. Jennifer Kates, Kim Boortz, Eric Lief, Carlos Avila, and Benjamin Gobet, *Financing the Response to AIDS in Low- and Middle-Income Countries: International Assistance from the G8, European Commission and Other Donor Governments in 2009* (Kaiser Family Foundation and UNAIDS, July 2010): 12.

38. Kates et al., *Financing the Response to AIDS in Low- and Middle-Income Countries.*

39. Garrett and Alavian, "Global Health Governance in a G-20 World": 5.

40. "The G20 and development: A new era (Updated)," October 2010; http://www.relief-web.int/rw/RWFiles2010.nsf/FilesByRWDocUnidFilename/MMAH-8A846A-full_report.pdf/$File/full_report.pdf (accessed 10 January 2011).

41. Garrett and Alavian, "Global Health Governance in a G-20 world": 5.

42. Institute for Health Metrics and Evaluation, *Financing Global Health 2009: Tracking Development Assistance for Health* (Seattle: Institute for Health Metrics and Evaluation, 2009): 50, Figure 32, http://www.healthmetricsandevaluation.org/print/reports/2009/financing/financing_global_health_report_full_IHME_0709.pdf (accessed 9 January 2011).

43. "China's Foreign Currency Reserves Decline," *BBC News*, 13 January 2012, http://www.bbc.co.uk/news/business-16541661 (accessed 26 January 2012). See also Chan, Lee, and Chan, *China Engages Global Governance*, chapter 4, for the growth of China's economic clout.

44. Ingham, "China, India Should Open Wallets for AIDS War." However, owing to the disputes about China's capability and willingness to meet the Global Fund's standards in allocating an appropriate share of the funds to grass-roots organizations inside the country, the Global Fund has frozen the disbursement of a US$283 million AIDS grant to the country since November 2010. Beijing had pledged to give 35 percent of the US$283 million to community-based organizations; however, a report by Global Fund Watch, an NGO, indicates that China only allocated less than 11 percent of it to non-governmental groups. The freeze was lifted in August 2011. See Gillian Wong, "Health Fund Freezes Payments to China Amid Dispute," msnbc.com, 24 May 2011; http://www.msnbc.msn.com/id/43148520/ns/world_news-asia_pacific/t/health-fund-freezes-payments-china-amid-dispute/# (accessed 26 May 2011); Sharon LaFraniere, "AIDS funds frozen for China in grant dispute," *New York Times*, 20 May 2011, http://www.nytimes.com/2011/05/21/world/asia/21china.html (accessed 25 May 2011); Gillian Wong, "Global Fund lifts China grant freeze," CNSNews.com, 23 August 2011, http://cnsnews.com/news/article/apnewsbreak-global-fund-lifts-china-grant-freeze (accessed 26 January 2012).

45. Andrew Jack, "Global Diseases Agency Forces Chief to Quit," *Financial Times*, 24 January 2012, http://www.ft.com/cms/s/0/5978206c-46af-11e1–bc5f-00144feabdc0.html (accessed 25 January 2012).

46. LaFraniere, "AIDS Funds Frozen for China in Grant Dispute."

47. China's pledges and contributions are US$30 million for 2003–2013. The annual pledges and contributions in 2008, 2009, and 2010 were US$2 million. The Global Fund to Fight HIV/AIDS, Tuberculosis and Malaria, "Pledges and Contributions," http://www .theglobalfund.org/en/pledges/?lang=en (accessed 9 January 2011). See also Ingham, "China, India Should Open Wallets for AIDS war"; Jack C. Chow, "China's Billion-Dollar Aid Appetite," *Foreign Policy*, 21 July 2010.

48. The Global Fund to Fight AIDS, Tuberculosis and Malaria, "Global Fund Third Voluntary Replenishment 2011–2013 Pledges for 2011–2013 at 5 October 2010," available at http://www.theglobalfund.org/documents/replenishment/newyork/Replenishment_New YorkMeeting_Pledges_en.pdf (accessed 13 January 2011); and "The Global Fund's Voluntary Replenishment Round Brings Hope, but Not Plenty," available at http://www.africa-health. com/articles/november_2010/Global%20Fund.pdf (accessed 13 January 2011).

49. The Global Fund to Fight AIDS, Tuberculosis and Malaria, *Resource Scenarios 2011–2013: Funding the Global Fight against HIV/AIDS, Tuberculosis and Malaria* (Geneva: The Global Fund to Fight AIDS, Tuberculosis and Malaria, March 2010), p. 5; available at http://www.theglobalfund.org/documents/replenishment/2010/Resource_Scenarios_en.pdf (accessed 10 January 2011).

50. The Global Fund to Fight HIV, Tuberculosis and Malaria, "Press Releases: Donors Commit US$11.7 Billion to the Global Fund for Three Years," 5 October 2010, http://www .theglobalfund.org/en/pressreleases/?pr=pr_101005c (accessed 10 January 2011).

51. Communications Department, Global Fund to Fight AIDS, Tuberculosis and Malaria, "The Global Fund's Voluntary Replenishment Round Brings Hope, but Not Plenty," *Africa Health*, November 2010, pp. 26–27, http://www.africa-health.com/articles/november_2010/ Global%20Fund.pdf (accessed 12 January 2011).

52. "Global Health Fund, China Agree to Cut $95 Million from Grants Amid Donor pressure," Global Health Council, 31 October 2011, http://www.globalhealth.org/news/ article/13878 (accessed 26 January 2012).

53. World Health Organization, "Voluntary Contributions by Fund and by Donor for the Year Ended 31 December 2010," Sixty-Four World Health Assembly, A64/29Add.1, 7 April 2011; http://apps.who.int/gb/ebwha/pdf_files/WHA64/A64_29Add1–en.pdf (accessed 22 January 2012).

54. Javed Siddiqi, *World Health and World Politics: The World Health Organization and the UN System* (London: Hurst & Co., 1995): 216.

55. For an analysis on how China's rational utilitarian calculations have helped the country to receive external resources to halt its HIV/AIDS disease, see Chan, *China Engages Global Health Governance*: 125–127.

56. Samuel S. Kim, "International organizations in Chinese Foreign Policy," *Annals of the American Academy of Political and Social Science*, Vol. 519 (1992): 140–57; idem, "China's International Organization Behaviour," in Thomas W. Robinson and David Shambaugh (eds.), *Chinese Foreign Policy: Theory and Practice* (Oxford: Clarendon Press, 1994), pp. 401–34. The saying is quoted from an official from the Ministry of Health of the PRC during the Workshop on South-South Health Cooperation, organized by the Institute of Global Health at Peking University, Beijing, China on 12–23 July 2010.

57. The Chicago Council on Global Affairs, *Soft Power in Asia: Results of 2008 Multilateral Survey of Public Opinion* (Chicago, IL: The Chicago Council on Global Affairs, 2009): 17, http://www.thechicagocouncil.org/UserFiles/File/POS_Topline%20Reports/Asia%20

Soft%20Power%202008/Soft%20Power%202008_full%20report.pdf (accessed 11 March 2011).

58. "Brazil and South Africa More Popular," *BBC News*, 7 March 2011, http://www .bbc.co.uk/news/world-latin-america-12654446. Details of the poll results are available at http://www.bbc.co.uk/pressoffice/pressreleases/stories/2011/03_march/07/poll.pdf (accessed 26 January 2012).

59. William Stueck, *Rethinking the Korean War: A New Diplomatic and Strategic History* (Princeton, NJ: Princeton University Press, 2002): 69–74. That Kim did not inform Mao of the date of his attack was also due to the fact that there was a "Yan'an faction" in Kim's communist party that was believed by him to be intimately close to China. Ibid.: 103. The Yan'an faction was purged in 1957–1959. Andrei Lankov, *From Stalin to Kim Il Sung: The Formation of North Korea, 1945–1960* (London: Hurst & Company, 2002), chapter 3.

60. Chen Jian, *China's Road to the Korean War: The Making of the Sino-American Confrontation* (New York: Columbia University Press, 1994): 85–90, 111–12.

61. Chan, Lee, and Chan, *China Engages Global Governance*, chapter 3.

62. Like Koguryo, Silla (57 BC–AD 935) was one of the Three Kingdoms of Korea.

63. Bruce Klingner, "China Shock for South Korea," *Asia Times Online*, 11 September 2004, http://www.atimes.com/atimes/Korea/FI11Dg03.html (accessed 10 March 2011); Jae Ho Chung, "China and Northeast Asia: A Complex Equation for 'Peaceful Rise,'" *Politics*, 27 (3), October 2007, 159–61; idem, "China's 'Soft' Clash with South Korea: The History War and Beyond," *Asian Survey*, 49 (3), May/June 2009: 468–83.

64. Only 27 percent of Japanese and 48 percent of Indians think that China's growing economy is a bad thing for their countries, 80 percent of Japanese and 59 percent of Indians see that China's growing military power is a bad thing, and 34 percent of Japanese and 10 percent of Indians believe that China hurts the environment the most. The Pew Global Attitudes Project, Spring 2007 Survey, http://pewglobal.org/files/pdf/256topline.pdf (accessed 11 March 2011).

65. The Pew Global Attitudes Project, Spring 2010 Survey, http://pewglobal.org/files/pdf/ Pew-Global-Attitudes-Spring-2010–Report.pdf (accessed 11 March 2011).

66. The Chicago Council on Global Affairs, *Soft Power in Asia.*

67. Nicholas Khoo, "Breaking the Ring of Encirclement: the Sino-Soviet Rift and Chinese Policy toward Vietnam, 1964–1968," *Journal of Cold War Studies*, 12 (1), Winter 2010: 3–42; Womack, *China and Vietnam*, 174–83, esp. 177, 200–02; Xiaoming Zhang, "Deng Xiaoping and China's Decision to Go to War with Vietnam," *Journal of Cold War Studies*, 12 (3), Summer 2010: 3–29.

68. For the background, see Womack, *China and Vietnam*, 181–83.

2

Rising from Within: China's Search for a Multilateral World and Its Implications for Sino-US Relations

Mingjiang Li[1]

China's phenomenal rise in recent decades has sparked an intense international debate on the impact which the reemergence of the "Middle Kingdom" will have on the existing international system. An important dimension in addressing this issue is China's policy toward multilateralism, particularly major global multilateral institutions. Scrutinizing China's perception and policy toward multilateral institutions and regimes may provide some useful clues for observers to ascertain whether it is rising as a status quo or as a revisionist power.[2] Understandably, most studies thus far have focused on the implications of China's approach to multilateralism for Sino-US relations and US global leadership, heating up the debate on China's rise with a wide range of views. Generally speaking, there are three camps of thought in the debate, including those who believe that China will successfully integrate into the existing order; those who argue that China has been selectively participating in and using multilateralism for other purposes; and those observers who believe that China will ultimately overhaul the system.

Some scholars are unequivocally sanguine about the prospect of China becoming an integral part of the existing international order. This profuse optimism, to a large extent, is built on a positive assessment of China's involvement in various international institutions.[3] Kent, for instance, concludes that, as compared to its behaviors prior to the early 1980s, China's "acceptance of, and integration into, the international system have been nothing short of extraordinary."[4] Johnston observes that China has demonstrated a cooperative attitude toward international security regimes from 1980 to 2000 largely as a result of social learning.[5] Steinfeld argues that China has continued to integrate itself into the Western economic order and adheres to the rules set and dominated by the West.[6] Foot posits that China has chosen accommodation to cope with a US-hegemonic global order, while simultaneously attempting to hedge and dilute US supremacy by seeking to establish solid relations with other partners and attempting to push for a more egalitarian world system.[7] Ikenberry has put forth a strong argument that while the rise of China will inevitably weaken US power and dislodge the unipolar structure, the US-led liberal international order will persist and ultimately integrate a more powerful China into that order.[8]

The second school of thought maintains that China has pragmatically regarded multilateral institutions as political tools for the furtherance of its national interests. Among the observers in this category, some are cautiously optimistic and others are more concerned about the uncertainties that China's involvement in global multilateralism might engender. Those who are cautiously optimistic highlight China's willingness to accept and participate in the existing international system, while noting that it mostly uses the system in a pragmatic fashion to maximize its own interests. They believe that China prioritizes participation in multilateral institutions where it can exercise more decision making or bargaining power; facilitate its domestic economic development; restrain the hegemony of the United States for the purpose of pushing for "multipolarity" in the international system; and improve China's international image.[9]

On the other hand, pessimistic pragmatists believe that China has been taking a "supermarket" approach in its participation in the international institutions. They allege that China is merely "buying what it must, picking up what it wants, and ignoring what it doesn't" largely because the Chinese leaders "see the international scene as fundamentally one of competition, not condominium."[10] Many scholars believe that China's sheer size and rapid increase of power and current display of growing assertiveness "represent a challenge to the established global order" and the future global multilateral architecture is "far from clear and not at all determined."[11] There is always the possibility that China might "use its influence in international institutions as a spoiler instead of a partner."[12] Others are concerned that some Chinese values or normative preferences might lead to a clash with the West over how to jointly address global issues, especially with regard to humanitarian intervention.[13]

The third and final school of thought is firm in its pessimistic view regarding China's participation in international multilateral institutions. Mearsheimer strongly believes that there is almost no possibility of China successfully becoming part of the existing international order and "China and the United States are destined to be adversaries as China's power grows."[14] Believing that the widespread positive view of China embracing the existing international order is deeply mistaken, Jacques argues that "an increasingly powerful China will seek to shape the world in its own image." He cautions that "in coming decades, the West will be confronted with the fact that its systems, institutions and values are no longer the only ones on offer."[15]

The debate has gained new momentum in the wake of the financial crisis when Beijing displayed unprecedented confidence in engaging with various international institutions and started to make new proposals to reform various global economic and financial regimes.[16] The 2008/09 financial crisis was widely perceived in China as marking the decline of the Western powers, particularly the United States, and the weakening of their dominance in the global system.[17] Related to this percep-tion, many Chinese believe that it is opportune for China to play a more active role in shaping the future multilateral world. Certainly, designing a proper strategy in China's multilateral diplomacy is a herculean undertaking and, in recent years, there has been a heated debate in China as to what kind of multilateral world that best serves China's national interests and what China should do to pursue its goals in its multilateral diplomacy.[18]

This chapter seeks to examine China's recent changing posture and policy toward the major emerging multilateral institutions and attempts to read into the debate among Chinese policy analysts to gain a better understanding of the trends in China's search for global multilateralism in the foreseeable future. The focus is on the motivations of China's growing activism in multilateralism and China's percep-tions and attitudes toward some of the newly emerging multilateral regimes and processes. This chapter concludes that various concerns and constrains will render it impossible for China to completely overhaul or even dramatically reshape the multilateral architecture at the global level, even as it becomes more proactive in its multilateral diplomacy, albeit selectively in many cases, and seeks to increase its influence in global multilateral settings. China is likely to repeat what it has done in East Asian regional multilateralism in the past decade: increasing participation and engagement, pushing for cooperation in areas that would serve Chinese interests, avoidance of taking on excessive responsibilities, blocking initiatives that would harm its interests, and refraining from making grand proposals. Another notable constrain is the fact that China is faced with a difficult task of identity definition as it is caught up between posturing as a leader of the developing world on some issues and siding with the developed countries on other policy issues. Given all these constraints, China's involvement in global multilateralism is likely to be guided by pragmatism rather than grand visions. It is hard to imagine, at least in the foreseeable future, that much of China's morality-ridden rhetoric with regard to multilateralism will be easily translated into concrete policy proposals to be embedded in the future multilateral world. Based on the findings which support the views of the pragmatist school of thought, this chapter argues that China will most likely strive to rise from within the existing international order and recommends that Washington should be prepared to plan its China policy on this basis. On this note, this chapter posits that Sino-US relations will largely be shaped by the dynamics of contentions for power and interest, as well as cooperation and coordination between China and the United States in various multilateral institutions.

CHINA VIEWS EMERGING MULTILATERAL INSTITUTIONS: EXPECTATIONS AND CONSTRAINTS

The origins of China's interest in global multilateralism can be traced to the reform and opening up program launched by Deng Xiaoping in the late 1970s. China began the continuous process of integration into the international system with its accession to numerous international institutions and regimes in the 1980s. However, the pace of China's activism in multilateralism and participation in the international system increased ostensibly after its accession to the World Trade Organization (WTO) in 2001. As seen from its actual behaviours and various policy pronouncements by top Chinese decision makers, China has indeed entered a historical new phase in its participation in global multilateralism.[19]

China's interest and confidence in global multilateral processes further surged in the wake of the 2008/2009 financial crisis. As mentioned earlier, the policy community in China believes that the recent financial crisis has marked a notable decline of the West and a significant reduction of Western influence in global multilateralism. While acknowledging that there are many constraints preventing China from assuming significant leadership in global multilateralism, many Chinese policy analysts believe that the time has come for China to rise up as a more important player in international institutions. This combination of euphoria and concerns is well reflected in the mainstream views in China regarding BRICS and G20, two of the newly emerging multilateral institutions.

Multilateralism for Multipolarity

Among the Chinese policy community, there is a strong conviction that multilateral diplomacy is a powerful instrument for the building and acceleration of a multipolar world. It is their firm belief that multilateralism is an effective tool for checking the unilateral impulses of the United States. From the Chinese perspective, a more institutionalized international order would be more stable than the current one which is dominated by one single superpower. China regards participation in multilateralism as a useful means to push for a more equitable and fairer international political and economic order and ultimately strive for a larger share of decision-making power in various international institutions, especially in the economic and financial institutions (the World Bank and IMF), and boost its international influence.[20] Beijing feels that it will be too difficult for China alone to wrestle power from the Western developed countries, but it would be more possible if China collaborates with other like-minded emerging powers as a joint venture.

Such considerations have led China to be very supportive of the BRICS grouping. Beijing's positive attitude in the BRICS is rooted in three major considerations. First of all, the BRICS countries boast strong economic power. Even before the addition of South Africa to the grouping, Chinese analysts frequently make the point that the BRIC countries boast 42 percent of the global population, 14.6 percent of the global GDP, and 12.8 percent of the global trade. In recent years, the economic growth rates of the original four countries have also been impressive, contributing to almost half of global economic growth. And the four countries together hold a huge amount of international foreign reserves.[21] Second, China believes that this joint venture among BRICS countries is possible because they have many common positions and interests in international relations, in particular in the economic arena.[22] Third, for China, the BRICS, as a new institution, is not only significant in and for itself, but more importantly, it could serve as a powerful proxy to push for the reforms of other major existing international institutions. As such, Chinese analysts believe that the BRICS countries should get united to negotiate with the developed world to promote their common interests in world politics. They believe that the BRICS mechanism will have "major significance for the whole world" because this new multilateral institution is likely to accelerate the development of the multi-polarization of the international structure and to reform the unfair and unreasonable international political and economic system.[23]

China's expectations of the BRICS mechanism have been translated into concrete policy behaviors in recent years, for instance in the IMF. Before the G20 summits, the finance ministers and governors of their central banks have met to discuss issues of their common concern and coordinate their positions. For instance, during the April 2009 London G20 Summit, the BRICS countries publicized a joint statement requesting for more voting power and representation in the IMF.[24] These emerging powers have had several ministerial meetings to synchronize their positions on climate change and have also worked together to pressurize the developed countries to take more responsibilities for the reduction of carbon emissions. More recently, China hosted the first summit of the BRICS after South Africa was admitted into the group at the Bo'ao Forum in April 2011. The primary goal of the summit was to coordinate the positions of the member countries on major international issues before the French summit of the G20.[25]

Compared to the BRICS grouping, the G20 is perhaps far more important for China. Besides its importance in tackling many challenging global economic and financial issues, the G20 is also viewed by Beijing as a tangible and crucial step toward multi-polarization of the global power structure. China believes that the G20, to some extent, represents the current balance of power in the world. Many Chinese analysts subscribe to the belief that the G20, with a membership encompassing the developed G8, the BRICS countries and other developing countries, and the European Union, signifies the growing importance of emerging economic powers and reflects the changing economic power balance between the developed nations and newly emerging powers. They maintain that the growing importance of the G20 also means that American hegemony is being challenged and confirms that the indispensability of emerging powers in solving global problems.[26] China believes that the G20 is a forum in which emerging powers, especially China itself, can make their voices heard and attempt to obtain a larger share of representation and voting power in major international economic and financial institutions.[27]

Furthermore, China believes that the institutionalization of the G20 and the greater voting power given to the emerging economies will have profound implications for the shaping of the future international order. Chinese policy analysts argue that the gradual displacement of the G8 by the G20 suggests that the global governance system is readjusting in accordance with the international economic power structure, which is moving from the complete dominance of the developed countries toward "North-South co-governance." Also, the emergence of the G20 signifies the recognition by the rest of the world, especially the Western world, of China's rise.[28] The G20, although presently an economic forum in nature, is likely to have a ca-talysing effect on the emergence of new orders in the global political and security sectors as well.[29] They thus conclude that the G20 is "a great positive historical move" and "a major breakthrough" in the evolution of a new world order. By and large, Beijing is satisfied with its achievements through the G20 meetings in the past few years. China believes that because of its growing economic clout, its participation in the G20 has contributed to the shift of power and a structural change within G20 to-ward emerging economies.[30] Moreover, the functioning of the G20 has significantly upgraded China's global status.[31]

Multilateralism for Cooperation

It would be misleading to suggest that China regards global multilateralism as a completely zero-sum game. As a major power and with its economy becoming increasingly interdependent with the rest of the world, China does believe that mul-tilateral diplomacy can provide new platforms for international cooperation, primar-ily for the realization of Chinese interests, but at the same time for the provision of international public goods. In some respects, China now understands that many of the newly emerged transnational externalities such as climate change, global financial instability, resource depletion, international terrorism, environmental degradation, and pandemics cannot be tackled effectively by any single country but have to be addressed through multilateral cooperation with other states. Over the past decades, participating in multilateral cooperation in dealing with various regional and global challenges has been a good learning experience for China as well. The evolution of China's behaviours in multilateral cooperation in dealing with the SARS epidemic, international peace-keeping operations, and nuclear non-proliferation demonstrates the positive impact of social learning on China becoming more supportive of rel-evant international norms.

For the BRICS mechanism, since it is still in its emerging stage, China has not developed clear ideas of how the five countries could forge effective cooperation, except its avid interest in using it as a proxy to contend with the developed West as noted above. However, Chinese analysts have mentioned that in general the BRICS countries could further explore bilateral and multilateral cooperation in their eco-nomic relations, for instance, currency swaps, more liberal trading arrangements, investment facilitation measures, climate change, and the development of new energy resources. These countries could also work together to resist protectionist trade measures by some developed countries. They believe that such cooperation has become even more necessary in the wake of the financial crisis.[32]

The G20, since its inception in 1999, has always focused on some of the most challenging economic problems facing the world, especially problems in the international financial system. China maintains that the G20 is a good mechanism for the common economic good of many countries.[33] It views the G20 as a good platform for coordinating the macroeconomic policies of the world's major economies in order to stabilize the global economy so that China's own economy is not negatively affected by dramatic fluctuations.[34] China also believes that the G20 will create many opportunities for China to participate in international affairs and cooperate with other countries for tangible economic benefits. According to Chinese policy analysts, the main tasks for China in the G20 include collaboration with other members to oppose trade protectionism, to push for a low-carbon economy in dealing with global climate change, and to establish a new global financial order. In the global financial sector, China could work to push for further international financial monitoring cooperation and further reform of the international monitoring system and the international credit rating system. They recommend that China should also strive to bring about further reform of various international financial institutions, primarily involving the decision-making and higher representation for developing countries in the IMF, and push steadily for the diversification of the international currency system and support the stability of the system.[35] In some respects, China has been successful. For instance, it has been able to increase its own IMF quotas from 3.72 percent to 6.39 percent and its voting power from 3.65 percent to 6.07 percent to become the third most powerful member at the IMF.[36]

Multilateralism for China's "Peaceful Rise"?

Chinese officials and scholars have frequently argued that China's active participation of global and regional multilateralism epitomizes its intention of "peaceful rise." They also argue that further engaging with multilateralism is one path that China could realize its "peaceful rise." The fact that the Chinese elite harbor this perception is noteworthy, regardless whether China's participation in multilateralism will eventually help its peaceful rise. Beijing believes that its participation in multilateralism could help diminish the "China threat" theory and build a "responsible power" image for China.[37] Contrary to its earlier perception that many of the international institutions were simply policy tools controlled by the most powerful countries, Beijing has realized that active participation in various multilateral regimes can help reduce the apprehensions of other countries toward China's rise. In addition, China has attempted to sugarcoat its preference for global multilateralism in highly moral terms, with repeated statements that one of its purposes of building global multilateralism is to achieve the goal of *hexie shijie* (a harmonious world). In recent years, the Chinese leadership has laboriously preached the Confucian vision of a new world order centered on the concept *he* (peace, harmony, union). Official statements constantly advocate *he er bu tong* (harmonious but different) and *he wei gui* (peace as the ultimate objective). Beijing believes that this rhetoric can help build and project a pacifist cultural image for China.[38] It also helps demonstrate Beijing's cautious approach to putting itself in the limelight by working within the current international framework through its membership in the UN and regional cooperative initiatives.[39]

In the security realm, China has advocated new ideas in multilateral security arrangements. To cope with the new international situation and challenges in the 1990s, the Chinese government proposed a New Security Concept in a series of Defense White Papers and advocated this concept numerous times in various multilateral forums. According to this New Security Concept, the post–Cold War order requires all states to pursue a security policy that features "mutual trust, mutual benefit, equality and coordination."[40] China's advocacy of a new security concept, in the eyes of some external observers, is an update and expansion of the Five Principles of Peaceful Coexistence formulated during the Cold War.[41] China has offered very little thought as to how the New Security Concept can be put into practice to ensure international peace in an anarchic world. This has led to the suspicion that China has certain pragmatic objectives in promoting this concept, for instance, trying to expand China's influence in ways seen as nonthreatening to its neighbors and trying to balance US global power in a manner that serves China's interests.[42]

As China holds the G20 in high regard, some Chinese analysts have argued that the G20 could potentially contribute to China's "peaceful rise." Although the G20 may not be the best platform and while there are still many uncertainties about its future (more discussion on this in the next section), they prescribe the G20 as a preferred choice during the transitional period for China's "peaceful rise" and the upgrading of its status to a major world power. In their opinion, the next three decades will be a crucial period for China's rise and more frictions with the United States are to be expected. At the same time, China needs a fairly predictable, flexible, and non-confrontational external environment to ensure the smooth progression of its grand plan for national rejuvenation. As such, these analysts believe that the G20 possesses certain characteristics, such as elasticity, representation, flexibility, and maneuverability to help create that external environment. They think that the G20 can serve as a useful mechanism for mitigating conflicts between China and the United States and advert the potential clashing of the two titans, given that many bilateral thorny issues could be discussed and possibly solved through multilateral mechanisms. On the other hand, it would be easier for China to deal with the sole superpower with the support of like-minded states within the grouping and at the same time divert or reduce pressures on it. In this sense, China believes that the G20 is a fairly ideal institution for China, at least at this stage.[43]

Constraints of the BRICS and G20

Beijing also realizes that there are significant limitations for cooperation in these emerging multilateral institutions. China understands that there are also quite a number of constraints for multilateral cooperation among the BRICS countries. In addition to the different economic structures and levels of development among the five countries, a number of other differences have surfaced—India and Brazil have different preferences regarding the liberalization of agricultural products; China and India have engaged in competition over oil and gas resources in Russia and Central Asia; and the other BRICS countries are not happy to see an acceleration of the internationalization of the Chinese currency, the renminbi or yuan (RMB).[44] Some Chinese analysts note that the cooperation among BRICS countries could also be limited at the global level because the West still enjoys predominant economic and technological prowess. In the foreseeable future, the BRICS countries will have to give priority to their respective cooperation with the Western developed countries instead of cooperation among themselves.[45] Beijing understands that the other members of the BRICS grouping may be attracted by other multilateral regimes. Russia is a member of the G8. Ideologically, India as "the largest democracy" in the world is strongly interested in forging cooperation with the "most powerful democracy"—the United States. Brazil is a member of the Organization of American States (OAS), in which the United States serves as the leader. India, Brazil, and South Africa have a separate loose gathering in the name of "dynamic democracies."

Therefore, even if China is keen to further strengthen BRICS cooperation, other parties may not reciprocate China's enthusiasm.[46] China has also realized that the BRICS mechanism is likely to generate some impact on global economic issues, but will have little impact on global security matters. Ultimately, China is likely to regard the BRICS grouping as a useful multilateral platform for other larger political goals, for instance, contending with the Western powers for a larger share of decision-making power at the global level, as noted above.

As for the G20, many Chinese analysts have noted a number of challenging constraints, despite acknowledging it as is a good opportunity for China. First of all, the G20 is generally an expedient, ad hoc, and under-institutionalized forum. As a result, its policy proposals and prescriptions are of a non-binding nature for its members. It will take more time and effort to upgrade the G20 into an institution for dealing with global governance, including broad international consensus on the definition of its functions, the establishment of a long-term and effective mechanism, the balance between representation and efficiency, and the differentiation of roles between the G20, the UN, and other international organizations.[47] Some Chinese analysts believe that it may be unrealistic to expect significant institutionalization of the G20 at all because the 2008/2009 financial crisis that gave birth to the G20 has not generated as deep a global recession as the one in the 1930s and consequently, the dominant position of the West has not been fundamentally weakened. In this sense, the G20 may have to contend with the G8 for leadership if the former is to become the leading institution in global governance.[48]

In addition, the G20 was initiated by the developed countries. Analysts in China have a fairly consensual view that the developed countries only intended to use the G20 as a policy tool to encourage the major developing countries to contribute to the solution of various global economic and financial problems. The creation of the G20 was intended neither to fundamentally reform the existing global economic and financial system, nor to genuinely allow the developing countries to enjoy a greater role in the global economic system.[49] Many Chinese analysts note that the United States' willingness to engage in the G20 mechanism stems from its primary interest to integrate other powers, including China, into the existing rules and regimes and to persuade the developing countries to share international responsibilities.[50]

Moreover, China believes that given the diversity of its members in terms of economic development and concerns, rivalry and competition are inevitable in the G20. Ultimately, the developing countries in the G20 may be disappointed by the mechanism because they may not be able to contend with the developed countries on an equal footing. At the global level, there is still a wide gap in wealth and knowledge between the developed and developing economies. And the Western developed countries still dominate the agenda-setting and discourse in global governance. The status quo of "global governance equals Western governance" has not been fundamentally changed.[51] Many Chinese scholars note that within the G20, there is relatively little divergence among the developed countries, whereas there is much divergence among the developing countries. Furthermore, the internal political and economic structures of the emerging powers are still very much flawed. There are still many concerns about long-term political stability and the prospect of economic restructuring in many emerging powers.[52] As a result, the G20 may not be able to coordinate the positions and policies of its members effectively.[53]

Many Chinese observers note that the G20 is unlikely to become the key multilateral institution and there are still many uncertainties with regard to the future of the G20.[54] It may gradually become more institutionalized and play a more important role in world economy as globalization deepens and economic interdependence among major economies further develop. It is also possible that the regime could eventually become irrelevant as the world financial and economic situation improves and member states of the G20 may find it more convenient to turn back to various regional groupings or smaller groupings, such as the G8, EU, NAFTA, and BRICS.[55]

Regarding the future relations between the G8 and the G20, Chinese analysts are divided in their views. Broadly speaking, there are three proposals. One view is that with the mitigation or possibly the end of the financial crisis, the ministerial meeting of the G20 will resume its function to serve as a dialogue mechanism between the developed and developing countries under the Bretton Woods system and the G8 will continue to tackle problems such as climate change, African development issues, and global trade under the G8+5 mechanism. The second view is that the G20 will become more institutionalized and is likely to expand to include security, social, and environmental issues in its discussions and replace the G8 as the center for global governance. The third view is that the G20 will become more institutionalized but it will confine itself to economic and financial issues and the G8 will continue to play its role in other areas under the G8+5 mechanism.[56]

Many analysts in China believe that the second scenario would be preferable for China. They argue that replacing the G8 with G20 would mean a significant move toward the realization of a multipolar world. They support this argument further by justifying the displacement of the G8 by the G20 with the fact that it is far more representative and influential economically and, in the coming decades, the growth rate of the G20, especially the emerging economies, will continue to be faster than that of the G8 and the emerging economies will account for a much larger share of the total global economy.[57]

DILEMMAS IN CHINA'S SEARCH FOR A MULTILATERAL WORLD

In addition to the pragmatic approach to various multilateral institutions and regimes, China has a few notable dilemmas to overcome if it attempts to come up with grand designs for global and regional multilateralism and seeks to play a leading role in regional and global multilateralism.

Multipolarization versus "China First"

For many years, China has advocated for a multi-polar world. The Chinese vision for multi-polarity was largely aimed at checking the global influence of the United States. However, this vision has an inherent dilemma for China. To build a multi-polar world, China would have to allow and encourage other emerging powers to become stronger and play a larger role in international politics. These powers would include some of China's neighboring countries such as Russia, India, and Japan, with which China has had unpleasant historical relations. Such unpleasant historical issues with these regional powers include Tsarist Russia's territorial expansion into the Far East at the expense of the Chinese empire and the Sino-Soviet hostilities during much of the Cold War, the Sino-Indian border war in 1962, and the militaristic Japan's bullying of China from the late nineteenth century to the end of World War II. Today, in the Asian continent, the relationships between China and these neighboring powers are rife with competition and rivalry in Central Asia, South Asia, and East Asia. Encouraging these powers to be independent poles in international politics would entail a larger role for these neighboring giants in sub-regional and global affairs, which may contradict with China's own aspiration of becoming a dominant power in East Asia and eventually a global power.

Although Chinese analysts believe that China could obtain a better position in the global multilateral order by joining hands with other emerging powers, such as Russia, India, Brazil, and South Africa, it also poses a serious challenge for China. It is essentially the same logic as noted above. To encourage other emerging powers to work with China to build a multi-polar world, Beijing will need to support a larger political role of those countries in various international multilateral institutions. Chinese analysts tend to believe, perhaps rightly so, that augmented profiles of other emerging powers in world politics would weaken China's international influence. This is exactly the reason why China has straightforwardly resisted any effort for the admission of certain emerging powers to the United Nations Security Council as new permanent and veto-wielding members. This dilemma is clearly evident in the case of the BRICS grouping. While Beijing regards the BRICS mechanism as a useful vehicle for China to promote multi-polarity in world politics and to push for major reforms of international multilateral institutions, it is also concerned that other members of this loose coalition, particularly India and Brazil, might attempt to utilize this platform to aggrandize their own international influence in order to support their admission into the UN Security Council as permanent members. In fact, at the end of the first summit of the BRICS countries in June 2009, India and Brazil did attempt to bring up this issue. China resisted the attempt by saying that the BRICS forum was mainly tasked to discuss the impact of the financial crisis only and was not supposed to discuss the reform of the UN Security Council membership.[58]

Leadership, Identity, and Responsibility

At the current stage, China is worried that a Chinese leadership role in major multilateral institutions and regimes would incur unbearable responsibilities for China. China's apprehension of taking on too much international responsibility is evident in China's refusal of the G2 proposal. China believes that the G2 concept was an American conspiracy to nominally upgrade China's international status but in reality to get China to accept international responsibilities that would be beyond China's capability.[59] Many Chinese analysts believe that China should continue its "low profile" strategy in global multilateral diplomacy due to several considerations. First, China has been the main beneficiary of the existing international regimes. At this stage, China should continue to integrate itself into the existing regimes instead of creating new ones. Also, China's economic and military power is still limited and it has a huge population with mounting domestic problems. Therefore, China does not have the power to change or challenge the existing global regimes, which are still dominated by Western powers. Even if China should attempt to do so, it would only invite suspicion and even hostility from the West and as a result, China's ascent in the international system may be hampered. Second, China should focus on its contiguous neighborhood and play an even more active role in East Asian multilateral institutions. As China is currently one of the leading powers in the region, it should bide its time and move on to assuming world power only when regional states have recognized China's dominance.[60]

The leadership versus responsibility debate in China is also largely about China's questions of its own identity: How should China define its identity? Is China a developing country or a developed power? This quandary is clearly evident in its consideration of joining the G8. Many Chinese analysts are against the idea of China becoming an official member of the G8 on the basis of several considerations. In addition to various economic reasons, Beijing is not sure how it should present itself in the G8. Some Chinese observers argue that if China joins the G8, it would lose much freedom in its actions and would find it hard to convince other developing countries that China represents their interests. This will be contradictory to China's international strategy of positioning itself as the protector of and pioneer for the interests of the vast developing world.[61]

In light of these considerations, some Chinese policy analysts argue that the best option for China is to engage with the G8 as a dialogue partner. In this way, China can avoid taking responsibilities that are beyond its capabilities and at the same time, China can be free to position itself as a bridge between the developing world and the developed countries to push for global multilateralism and solutions of global problems in a fashion that best serves China's national interests.

There are many other issues that make it difficult for China to clearly define its international identity. On many economic issues, China shares the same or similar views with the developed countries. But on many other issues regarding global governance, China tends to side with the vast developing world. The mainstream thinking in China, both in the official policy-making circle and the scholarly community, seems to stress that China should still treat "South-South solidarity" as a cornerstone in China's foreign policy. This means that in multilateral diplomacy, China will more or less side with the developing world and at the same time pay attention to coordination with the developed countries. China is aware that, in order to transforming itself into a major global power, it should also consider taking on certain international responsibilities and international obligations that are commensurate with its national strength and capabilities.[62]

No matter how the situations in China and the rest of the world evolve, it will inevitably be a significant challenge for China to balance its views and positions in the G20. To overcome this dilemma, some analysts suggest that because the future international structure is likely to be multipolar, China may have to opt for multilayer international multilateral institutions in different functional areas. They propose that China should promote an implicit G2 (China and the United States) and an explicit G20, and use these two institutions to promote and participate in other institutions. They also suggest that China should pay attention to three key issues: first, regarding the Sino-US strategic dialogue as the key to China's peaceful rise; second, treating the G20 as the most important platform for China's international economic cooperation; third, using the ASEAN Plus Three platform as the most important one for China's regional cooperation. They conclude that China should regard the G20 highly, but should not overestimate its role. While China seeks to maintain its low profile, it should simultaneously attempt to play an important role in the G20 and finally it should continue to define its role as a major power advocating and representing the common interests of the developing world.[63]

Tianxia versus Westphalia

If there has been any Chinese thought for a grand design of a new multilateral world at all, it would have to be the Chinese discourse on the concept of *Tianxia* (all under heaven). Chinese scholars argue that historically the Chinese view of the world order was heavily influenced by the *Tianxia* concept. In the twenty-first century,

China's quick rise in the international system has made its foreign policy community rethink whether and how China should have its own vision of world order that may lead to a post-hegemonic world. To fulfill the goal of developing the Chinese school of international relations studies and applying China's perspective on the new international order, some Chinese scholars and philosophers like Zhao Tingyang suggested that rather than borrowing concepts developed out of western experiences in international relations, China should create its own concepts about the world order and world institutions by reviving the idea of *Tianxia* as the key concept in restructuring the world order.[64] Zhao argues that the traditional China has always favored peace, stability, order, and generosity toward other nations as traditionally, its relations with neighboring countries have been very different from the Western experience, which has been rife with violence, wars, power politics, and hegemony. Zhao suggests that the *Tianxia* conceptualization could lead to "a form of selfless global unity" supported by "a global hierarchy where order is valued over freedom, ethics over law and elite governance over democracy and human rights."[65] From the imperial China's perspective, *Tianxia* blurs the conceptual boundaries between empire and the world, domestic politics and international politics, and nationalism and cosmopolitanism. These scholars advocate an all-inclusive cosmopolitan system that would help solve global problems through building multi-layer multilateral institutions that promote cooperation and embrace divergences in a magnanimous way.

Despite the lofty objective in the Tianxia notion, many factors are likely to render the vision of building a future world order on the ground of China's traditional *Tianxia* worldview a utopian endeavor. First of all, since the beginning of its modernization and open-door process more than a century ago, China started to accept the norm of sovereignty established by the Westphalia system and looked at the world politics using a similar lens as the westerners. In fact, China has become a staunch defender of the Westphalia system by maintaining a rigid stance on the inviolability of sovereignty and noninterference in domestic affairs. Second, "the *Tianxia* system's main problem is that it doesn't explain how to get from an unstable and often violent present to the harmonious future."[66] Third, the *Tianxia* has yet to receive Beijing's official endorsement. The Chinese leadership worries that official support to the *Tianxia* discourse would feed into the "China Threat" thesis and thus be harmful for China's rise.

CONCLUSIONS

The analyses of this chapter provide abundant evidence to support the second school of thought on China's role in the international order. The analyses in this article suggest that China harbors no grand revisionist ambition to overthrow the existing international system. China would be happy if it could play a bigger role in the existing system and is prepared to attempt to achieve this goal by gradually reforming the decision-making structure of various existing multilateral institutions and regimes.

The findings of this article also confirm the mainstream Chinese argument that China has no incentive to create a new international system because it has been the biggest beneficiary of the existing system over the past three decades. China seems to be confident that it can continue to use these existing multilateral institutions to achieve its pragmatic objectives, for instance, balancing the predominant power of the United States, having a voice on major international issues, striving for more influence in world politics, improving its own international image, and pushing for cooperation in areas and on issues that would serve Chinese interests.

Despite the fact that China has attempted to use various multilateral forums to advocate ideas, some of which are derived from its traditional Confucian philosophy, such as "a harmonious world," a *Tianxia* worldview, and its New Security Concept, it remains generally weak in shaping discourse in international forums.[67] China is still undergoing an intense domestic debate on whether it should abandon and how it should modify the late Deng Xiaoping's *tao guang yang hui* (hide brightness and nourish obscurity) or "low profile" international strategy. Until the debate produces some sort of consensus, China's multilateral policy is likely to be at least partially affected by the path dependence of the low profile policy prescription. Pragmatism, however, does not mean that China will not seek to be more active in international multilateralism. On the contrary, various signs in recent years unmistakably indicate that China will attempt to be more broadly and deeply involved in multilateral diplomacy at the regional and global levels. However, China's involvement in international multilateralism is likely to be highly selective, as the cautiously pessimism school of thought has argued. China is very likely to treat the United Nations as the most important multilateral institution to deal with international political and security issues and regard the G20 as the most important multilateral arrangement to cope with international financial and economic problems. At the same time, Beijing will meticulously utilize other *ad hoc* multi-party regimes and platforms such as the BRICS grouping to protect its national interests and aggrandize its international influence.

China's "rising from within" option will be a tough challenge for Washington and very likely will also, to a large extent, help shape the patterns of Sino-US relations in the near future. On the one hand, this approach will help soothe American anxiety toward China's rapidly rising power. It will contribute to the mitigation of negative perceptions and attitudes associated with power transition. American policymakers and analysts who prefer an engagement policy with China will be able to find positive evidence in China's accommodation of the global order to make their case. More importantly, if China is keen to rise from within the existing international institutions, it would help create potential opportunities for China and the United States to cooperate and collaborate on many international issues of common concerns. Such cooperation would in return further bind the bilateral relations between the two countries.

On the other hand, the ultimate goal for China, as discussed in this chapter, is to secure Chinese interests and compete for more decision-making power in the international system. China has demonstrated three pathways to realize these goals. First, it has attempted to use its own power and influence to balance American hegemonic power on issues that do not serve Chinese interests. This was usually done in coalition with other developing countries, for instance in areas of human rights and humanitarian interventions. Secondly, it has sought to leverage on the collective influence of other emerging powers to bargain and wrestle power from the incumbent Western leading powers. And thirdly, it has attempted to trade "burden sharing" for "power sharing." In the Chinese understanding, the United States and other Western powers are eager to bring China and other emerging powers on board to share responsibilities in tackling various global issues, but they are not willing to give up their much larger share of decision-making power. China, together with other emerging powers, is likely to continue to press hard to have a larger say in international affairs when it is urged to take more responsibilities. This has evidently been the case during the recent financial crisis, particularly with regard to the restructuring of the IMF. It appears that China and other emerging powers will continue to be successful in gradually grabbing more decision-making power from the United States and other Western powers. A reasonable option for the United States is perhaps to "support reconfiguration of the global architecture to incorporate China into the discussion both of the development of international rules and of what it means to be a "responsible stakeholder."[68] Barring any dramatic change of the United States' China policy, China's "rising from within" behavior is likely to allow the current state of "frenemies" or "neither friends nor foes" in Sino-US relations to be sustained in the foreseeable future.

NOTES

1. This chapter has appeared in *Global Governance*, Vol. 17, No. 3, July–Sept. 2011, pp. 331–352. The author thanks the journal for allowing it to be reprinted in this volume.

2. Iain Johnston, "Is China a Status Quo Power?" *International Security* 27:4 (Spring 2003).

3. For instance, Harold K. Jacobson and Michel Oksenberg, *China's Participation in the IMF, the World Bank, and GATT* (Ann Arbor: University of Michigan Press, 1990); Hongying Wang and James N. Rosenau, "China and Global Governance," *Asian Perspective*, Vol. 33, No. 3, 2009, pp. 5–39; Ann Kent, "China, International Organizations and Regimes: The ILO as a Case Study in Organizational Learning," *Pacific Affairs*, Vol. 70, No. 4 (Winter, 1997–1998), pp. 517–532; Pieter Bottelier, "China and the World Bank: How a Partnership Was Built," *Journal of Contemporary China* (2007), 16(51), May, 239–258; Hui Feng, *The Politics of China's Accession to the World Trade Organization: The Dragon Goes Global* (London: Routledge, 2006).

4. Ann Kent, *Beyond Compliance: China, International Organizations, and Global Security* (Palo Alto: Stanford University Press, 2007), pp. 222–23.

5. Alastair Iain Johnston, *Social States: China in International Institutions, 1980–2000* (Princeton; Oxford: Princeton University Press, 2008).

6. Edward S. Steinfeld, *Playing Our Game: Why China's Rise Doesn't Threaten the West*, (New York: Oxford University Press, 2010).

7. Rosemary Foot, "Chinese Strategies in a US-Hegemonic Global Order: Accommodating and Hedging," *International Affairs*, 82, 1 (2006) 77–94.

8. G. John Ikenberry, "The Rise of China and the Future of the West: Can the Liberal System Survive?" *Foreign Affairs*, January/February 2008.

9. Guoguang Wu and Helen Lansdowne, "International Multilateralism with Chinese Characteristics: Attitude Changes, Policy Imperatives, and Regional Impacts," in Guoguang Wu and Helen Lansdowne, eds., *China Turns to Multilateralism: Foreign Policy and Regional Security* (Oxon: Routledge, 2008).

10. Gary J. Schmitt, "Introduction," in Gary J. Schitt, ed., *The Rise of China: Essays on the Future Competition* (New York: Encounter Books, 2009); David Shambaugh, "Beijing: A Global Leader With 'China First' Policy," *YaleGlobal*, June 29, 2010.

11. Jing Gu, John Humphrey, and Dirk Messner, "Global Governance and Developing Countries: The Implications of the Rise of China," *World Development* Vol. 36, No. 2, , 2008, pp. 274–292.

12. David Shorr; Thomas Wright, "Forum: The G20 and Global Governance: An Exchange," *Survival*, 52: 2, 181—198, 2010.

13. Lai-Ha Chan, Pak K. Lee, and Gerald Chan, "Rethinking Global Governance: a China Model in the Making?" *Contemporary Politics*, Vol. 14, No. 1, March 2008, 3–19; Gregory Chin and Ramesh Thakur, "Will China Change the Rules of Global Order?" *Washington Quarterly*, 33:4, 2010, pp. 119–138.

14. John J. Mearsheimer, *The Tragedy of Great Power Politics* (New York and London: W. W. Norton & Company, 2001), p. 4.

15. Martin Jacques, *When China Rules the World: The End of the Western World and the Birth of a New Global Order* (New York: the Penguin Press, 2009).

16. See for instance, David Shambaugh, "Beijing: A Global Leader with 'China First' Policy," *YaleGlobal*, June 29, 2010; William A Callahan, "China's Grand Strategy in a Post-Western World," http://www.opendemocracy.net, 1 July 2010.

17. There are, of course, different views in China regarding the resilience of the United States. But it seems to be the mainstream Chinese view that China's national strength has gained ground vis-à-vis the United States.

18. Zhao Tingyang, "*Tianxia gainian yu shijie zhidu*" [The concept of *Tianxia* and world system], in Qin Yaqing, ed., *World Politics—Views from China: International Order* (Hong Kong: Peace Book, 2006), pp. 3–46; Liu Mingfu, *Zhongguo meng: hou meiguo shidai de daguo siwei yu zhanlue dingwei* [*The China Dream: Great Power Thinking and Strategic Positioning of China in the Post-American Era*] (Beijing: China Friendship Press, 2010).

19. For a brief introduction of China's participation in multilateralism, see Li Mingjiang, "Rising from Within: China's Search for a Multilateral World and Its Implications for Sino-US Relations," *RSIS Working Paper*, No. 225, March 25, 2011.

20. Guo Xiangang, "zhongguo waijiao xin liangdian: yu xinxing guojia hezuo de tansuo yu shijian" [new spotlight in China's diplomacy: exploring and practicing cooperation with emerging powers], *guoji wenti yanjiu* [international studies], issue 1, 2010, pp. 5–9, 31.

21. Zhang Maorong, "jin zhuan si guo: heli you duo qiang?" [BRICS countries: how strong is their unity?], *shijie zhishi* [world knowledge], issue 14, 2009, pp. 52–54; Wang Yusheng, "jinzhuan si guo de meili he fazhan qushi" [the charm of the BRICS and the trend of its development], *ya fei zongheng* [Asia-Africa studies], issue 5, 2009, pp. 27–29.

22. Wang Yusheng, [the charm of the BRICS and the trend of its development].

23. Ibid.

24. Zhang Maorong, [BRICS countries: how strong is their unity?].

25. http://www.zaobao.com.sg/zg/zg110414_001.shtml, accessed April 15, 2011.

26. Zhao Zongbo, "*Guanyu ershi guo jituan huodong chengguo de ruogan sikao*" [Thoughts on the achievements of the G20], *Dangdai jingji* [Contemporary Economy], February 2010, pp. 60–63.

27. *Ibid.*

28. Liu Rui and Xu Yiming, "jinrong weiji zhi hou zhongguo dui G20 yingdang chiyou de jiben lichang" [some basic positions that China should take towards the G20 in the wake of the financial crisis], *shehui kexue yanjiu* [study on social sciences], issue 2, 2010, pp. 67–72.

29. Zhao Xiaochun, "G20 fenghui yu shijie xin zhixu de yanjin" ["G20 summit and the evolution of the new world order"]. *Xiandai guoji guanxi* [*Contemporary international relations*] 11 (2009).

30. Mark Beeson and Stephen Bell, "The G-20 and International Economic Governance: Hegemony, Collectivism, or Both?" *Global Governance*, Vol.15 No. 1 (January-March 2009), pp. 67–86.

31. Geoffrey Garrett, "G2 in G20: China, the United States and the World after the Global Financial Crisis," *Global Policy*, Issue 1, Vol. 1 (January 2010), pp. 29–39.

32. Zhang Maorong, [BRICS countries: how strong is their unity?].

33. Zhao Zongbo, [thoughts on the achievements of the G20].

34. Ibid.

35. Liu and Xu, ["Basic positions China should take "], 67–72.

36. http://www.caijing.com.cn/2010–11–06/110561191.html, accessed January 15, 2011.

37. Lu Chenyang, "Zhongguo dui duobian waijiao de canyu ji duice sikao" [China's participation in multilateral diplomacy and policy suggestions], *xuexi yu tansuo* [study and exploration], No. 2, 2008, Serial No. 175, pp. 90–92.

38. Qing Cao, "Confucian Vision of a New World Order? Culturalist Discourse, Foreign Policy and the Press in Contemporary China," *International Communication Gazette,* 2007, Vol. 69(5), p. 435.

39. Yongnian ZHENG & Sow Keat TOK, "Harmonious Society and Harmonious World: China's Policy Discourse under Hu Jintao," Briefing Series, Issue 26, The University of Nottingham, China Policy Institute, p. 10.

40. Information Office of the State Council: *China's National Defence in 2008,* http://www.bjreview.com.cn/document/txt/2009–02/06/content_177309.htm.

41. See, for example, Dennis J. Blasko, "China's Views on NATO Expansion: A Secondary National Interest." *China Brief* 9, no. 5 (March 2009), 3; Bates Gill, *Contrasting Visions: United States, China and World Order*. Remarks presented before the US-China Security Review Commission Session on the US-China Relationship and Strategic Perceptions, Washington DC, 3 August 2001; http://www.brookings.edu/views/testimony/gill/20010803.pdf.

42. Kerry Dumbaugh: *China's Foreign Policy: What Does It Mean for U.S. Global Interests?* CRS (Congressional Research Service) Report for U.S. Congress, July 18, 2008, p. 2.

43. Chen, Fengying. "G20 yu guoji zhixu da bianju" ["G20 and the dramatic transformation of the international order"]. *Xiandai guoji guanxi* [*Contemporary international relations*] 11 (2009).

44. Ibid.

45. Liu Jianfei, "jin zhuan si guo he zuo bing fei tantu" [BRIC cooperation not always a smooth way], *dang zheng luntan* [forum of party and government officials], issue 9, 2009, p.39.

46. Ibid.

47. Cui Liru. "G20 kaiqi le tansuo 'quanqiu zhili' xin lujin de jihui zhi chuang" ["G20 opens a window of opportunity for exploring a new approach to 'global governance'"], *Xiandai guoji guanxi* [*Contemporary international relations*] 11 (2009).

48. Liu Zongyi, "G20 jizhihua yu zhongguo canyu quanqiu jingji zhili xueshu huiyi zongshu" [a summary of the conference on G20 institutionalization and China's participation in global economic governance], *guoji zhanwang* [international trend], issue 2, 2010, pp. 98–103.

49. Xiao Shu and Gong Yuping, "san ci fenghui hou kan ershi guo jituan de fazhan qianjing" [an analysis on the G20's prospect after three summits], *dangdai shijie* [contemporary world], issue 11, 2010, pp. 51–53.

50. Liu Zongyi, ["A summary of the conference"].

51. Xiao and Gong, ["An analysis of the G20's prospect "].

52. Huang Renwei, "Xinxing daguo canyu quanqiu zhili de libi" ["Benefits and drawbacks of new emerging powers' participation in global governance"]. *Xiandai guoji guanxi* [*Contemporary international relations*] 11 (2009), 21–2.

53. Zhao Zongbo, [thoughts on the achievements of the G20].

54. Xiao and Gong, [an analysis on the G20's prospect]; Huang Renwei, ["Benefits and drawbacks of new emerging powers' participation in global governance"].

55. Zhao Zongbo, [thoughts on the achievements of the G20].

56. Chen Suquan, "ba guo jituan, ershi guo jituan yu zhongguo" [G8, G20 and China], *dongnanya Zongheng* [Around Southeast Asia], 2009, pp. 77–80.

57. Ibid.

58. Interview with Chinese diplomats, August, 2009.

59. Liu Feitao, "G2 yu dangqian zhongmei guanxi de bozhe" [G2 and the fluctuations in Sino-US relations], *shijie jingji yu zhengzhi* [world economics and politics], vol. 449, no.3, 2010, pp. 45–46.

60. Lu Chenyang, ["China's participation in multilateral diplomacy and policy suggestions"].

61. Liu and Xu, ["Basic positions China should take"].

62. Lu Chenyang, ["China's participation in multilateral diplomacy and policy suggestions"]; Wu Hongying, "quanqiu hua yu G20" [globalization and G20], *xiandai guoji guanxi* [contemporary international relations], no.11, 2009, pp. 5–6.

63. Liu Zongyi, ["A summary of the conference"].

64. Zhao Tingyang, [The concept of *Tianxia* and world system].

65. William A Callahan, "China's Grand Strategy in a Post-Western World," http://www.opendemocracy.net, July 1, 2010.

66. Ibid.

67. Chen Kaihe, "lun wo guo zai duobian waijiao huodong zhong de guoji gonggong guanxi celue" [China's international public relations strategies in multilateral diplomacy], *waijiao pinglun* [foreign affairs review], no. 100, December 2007, pp. 68–74.

68. C. Fred Bergsten, Charles Freeman, Nicholas R. Lardy, and Derek J. Mitchell, *China's Rise: Challenges and Opportunities* (Washington, DC: Peterson Institute for International Economics, 2008).

II

CHINA AND GLOBAL
ECONOMIC GOVERNANCE

3

China's Participation in Global Trade Negotiations

Henry Gao

On November 11, 2011, China acceded to the WTO in Doha, Qatar, at the 4th Ministerial Conference, which also launched the first negotiating Round of the new trade body since its establishment. As China is the largest country which has ever acceded to the WTO after the formation of the new trade organization, many commentators predicted that its accession will change the dynamics of the negotiations, but they differ in their interpretations on how such change will affect the multilateral trading system. Some viewed this in a more positive light by pointing out that the addition of China will strengthen the developing country bloc and make the WTO a more balanced institution. Others, however, were not so optimistic. Instead, they argued that the Chinese accession will upset the existing power structure of the WTO and make it more difficult to conduct negotiations and reach decisions.

Now in its tenth year of WTO membership, how has China changed the dynamics in the global trade negotiations? In this paper, I will try to answer this question by reviewing China's record in WTO negotiations. The paper will start with a brief discussion on how trade negotiations are conducted in the WTO, followed by a summary of China's participation in the Doha Round so far. I will also offer several reasons for China's adoption of particular negotiation approaches, and conclude with some thoughts on China's behavior in future negotiations.

TRADE NEGOTIATIONS IN THE WTO: A PRIMER

Like all international negotiations, trade negotiations are never easy to begin with. Moreover, trade negotiations demand a lot more resources and skills than most other international negotiations due to the following unique features:

First, while most other international negotiations are concerned with only the national interests of the countries involved, trade negotiations affect both the national interests of the countries as well as the commercial interests of the private firms that conduct trade across the border. Thus, private firms play an important role in trade negotiations and many countries find it necessary to consult private firms through various means. Moreover, as private firms have different objectives from the governments, their interests are not necessarily aligned with their own governments' interests. This not only makes it difficult for any government to negotiate trade matters, but it also makes the formulation of negotiating positions and the enforcement of negotiating results very difficult.

Second, even if the government manages to align its position with that of private firms, it still has to carry out another difficult and unpleasant task: coordinating among different ministries. Unlike other foreign policy issues, which are usually taken care of by the Foreign Ministry, trade issues often involve several different Ministries. Even in the relatively simple dates of the General Agreement on Tariffs and Trade (GATT), when the multilateral trading system covers only manufactured goods and agricultural products, trade negotiations command the attention of at least four ministries: the Foreign Ministry, the Ministry of Trade (which in large countries is often separate from the Foreign Ministry), the Ministry of Agriculture and the Ministry of Industry. In some countries, this list is supplemented by the ministries of fisheries, forestry, mining, and even textile products. When the World Trade Organization (WTO) came into being, new subjects such as services and intellectual property rights were brought into its scope and the ministerial matrix is further expanded to include ministries of telecommunication, transportation, finance, health, culture, and numerous other government agencies. As trade ministries usually do not have a domestic constituency, they often find themselves in a weak bargaining position in the turf war with the other Ministries, and this makes their job as trade negotiators even more difficult.

Third, even if the Trade Ministry manages to muster the support of the entire government, it will find negotiating at the WTO a task more daunting than at any other international institutions. The WTO has two negotiating rules which can hardly be found at any other international institutions. The first rule is Most Favored Nation (MFN) principle, which states that a country cannot cut sweetheart deals with another country alone: the same treatment has to be offered to any other WTO member. While this might be unthinkable in other areas of international relations, it makes perfect sense in the WTO. Otherwise the WTO could be quickly undermined by the cross-cutting bilateral deals between various Members. The second rule is "reciprocity," which basically means that in order to get something in trade negotiations, a country is expected to give something in return. If the MFN rule is designed to deal with external pressures, the reciprocity rule deals with internal pressures so that exporting interests in support of liberalization in foreign markets can be mobilized to check against the import-competing interests which are against trade liberalization in the home markets. Again this principle is rarely followed in other areas of international relations. For example, when the United States bombed Iraq, it certainly did not envisage the possibility of being bombed back by the Iraqis one day. Under these two rules, the countries have to weigh and balance their different policy objectives to arrive at the proper negotiating positions. According to the MFN rule, they have to make sure that when they offer some concessions to one country, there will not be unexpected free-riders who will reap more benefits. According to the reciprocity rule, they have to calculate the value of the potential gains they can get from accessing other countries markets versus the potential losses they have to suffer when they open their own markets to foreign firms. Even with highly sophisticated econometrics tools, the trade negotiators often find the process of arriving at the best negotiating positions an art rather than a science because there are so many variables that defy accurate predictions.

Nonetheless, over the years, the GATT and WTO have designed various negotiating devices which made the lives of trade negotiators a little less unpleasant. These include the following:

First, with regards to trade in goods, the most common instrument of trade policy is tariff. Here, the negotiations were initially conducted according to the bilateral request-offer approach. Each country would pick the products it is interested in exporting to other countries, and present its request for tariff reduction on those products to the foreign countries it wishes to gain access to. At the same time, the same country shall also provide the products that it wishes to grant foreign exporters access, and make the offer available to all countries. While this approach provides the most accurate way of trade negotiation as it focuses on individual products, it is also highly complicated and time-consuming as each country has to make requests and offers on potentially thousands of products. Thus, with the gradual expansion of the GATT membership, the countries started to look for other alternative negotiating approaches.

Such approach shall not be based on individual tariff lines; instead, the new approach shall enable massive reduction of tariffs in broad strokes. The obvious choice for the new approach is a formula-based approach, that is, where each country is required to cut its tariff by a certain percentage. There are two variations of the formula approach. The first is called linear-cut formula, whereby each country is required to cut its tariff by a certain percentage. This is the approach taken from the Kennedy Round. The most straight-forward liner-cut formula would require the same percentage of tariff cut from every country. However, developing countries opposed this idea and argued that they should not be required to provide the same level of tariff reductions as they are located at lower levels of economic development. Thus, in the Tokyo Round, tariff reductions were conducted according to the following formula: developed countries would cut their tariffs by 60 percent, while developing countries would cut theirs by 30 percent.

While this approach takes into account the different development levels of different countries, it does not address the differences in the preexisting tariff levels between different countries before the negotiation. For example, suppose we have two countries: Country A with an average initial tariff of 100 percent, while Country B has an average tariff of 10 percent. If we apply a 30 percent tariff reduction to both countries, the final tariffs will be 70 percent and 7 percent respectively, which means that the average tariff of Country A is still ten times that of Country B. The tariff difference is not a simple developed-versus-developing country question, as different tariff levels exist even among developing countries as well, with some countries (e.g., Singapore) applying very low tariffs while some countries (e.g., India) apply an average tariff level of 30 percent or even more.

To address this problem, the Swiss Formula was introduced during the XX Round. The Swiss Formula can be expressed as follows: $Z=AX/(A+X)$ where X is the initial tariff rate, A is a maximum tariff rate that also serves as a co-efficient, and Z is the final tariff rate after tariff reduction. As the initial tariff X rises to infinity, $X/(A+X)$ approaches 1, resulting in $Z=A*1=A$. To understand the effect of the Swiss formula, let's look at how a formula with a coefficient of twenty-five works over six years for countries with different initial tariff rates.

As we can see in table 3.1, the higher the initial tariffs of a country, the more it has to reduce its tariffs. Thus, the Swiss Formula has the effect of harmonizing the tariffs among different countries.

Second, as tariffs are gradually lowered in successive rounds of negotiations, countries increasingly resort to various non-tariff instruments, such as subsidies, antidumping, safeguard measures, technical regulations, and various licensing regimes to regulate their imports and exports. The existing negotiating approaches that have been used for tariff reductions are ill-equipped to deal with these non-tariff barriers (NTBs) as the latter tend to be qualitative rather than quantitative in nature. Instead, the negotiations here take a text-based approach. Draft texts on each subject are prepared by different countries with the help of the secretariat. On issues they disagree,

Table 3.1. Effect of the Swiss Formula on Countries with Different Initial Tariff Rates

Starting Tariff Year	150%	125%	100%	75%	50%	25%	10%
Year 0	150	125	100	75	50	25	10
Year 1	128.57	107.64	86.67	65.63	44.44	22.92	9.52
Year 2	107.14	90.28	73.33	56.25	38.89	20.83	9.05
Year 3	85.71	72.92	60	46.88	33.33	18.75	8.57
Year 4	64.29	55.56	46.67	37.5	27.78	16.67	8.1
Year 5	42.86	38.19	33.33	28.13	22.22	14.58	7.62
Year 6	21.43	20.83	20	18.75	16.67	12.5	7.14
Annual steps (%)	21.43	17.36	13.33	9.38	5.56	2.08	0.48
% cut over 6 years	85.71	83.33	80	75	66.67	50	28.57

Source: WTO, Tariff Reduction Methods, available at http://www.wto.org/english/tratop_e/agric_e/agnegs_ swissformula_e.htm#formula.

the countries might propose several different languages and put them in brackets, meaning "yet to be agreed." Then the countries will work together to try to reach agreement, and when they do agree they will formulate a language that is acceptable to everyone to replace the bracketed texts. In a way, this process is very similar to the legislative drafting process in domestic parliaments.

Third, for services trade negotiations, the formula approach is not suitable as the services regulations are mainly qualitative in nature. On the other hand, the text-based approach is not feasible as there are too many different services sectors. Thus, the bilateral request-offer approach is taken, where each country makes its request to other countries to open specific services sectors, and also table offers on service sectors which it is willing to offer to other countries.

CHINA'S EXPERIENCE IN THE DOHA NEGOTIATIONS

Joining the WTO at the Ministerial Conference that also launched the new Round is both a blessing and curse for China: on the one hand, China was able to participate in the new Round as a full member since the very beginning; on the other hand, as a new member, China did not have time to prepare for a more effective participation in the Round, which turned out to be not only the biggest, but also the longest and most difficult in the history of the multilateral trading system.

The Elephant in the Room

In the beginning phase of the Doha Development Agenda (DDA), China took a rather cautious approach. While it submitted its first negotiating proposal as early as six months after its accession, most of its earlier years in the WTO were spent on observing the negotiations rather than making active interventions. Most of the time, the Chinese delegates would sit quietly in the negotiating room and take notes. On the rare occasion that they took the floor, they usually just recited word by word from pre-prepared notes and refrained from interacting with other delegations.

There are several reasons for China's reticence. First, it has to do with the Recently-Acceded Member Argument. Having been under the spotlight for fifteen years in one of the longest accession negotiations[1] in the history of the GATT/WTO, the first explanation for China's low profile in public in the DDA is that the Chinese government wanted some quiet breathing space to digest and implement its heavy accession commitments. Indeed, China's concessions on both trade in goods and services greatly exceeded those of other WTO Members, most of which have not changed since the conclusion of the Uruguay Round. As argued by Shi Miaomiao, deputy director-general of the Department of WTO Affairs of MOFCOM:[2]

> In terms of industrial products, if applying the Uruguay Round modality for tariff-reduction, China would only be required to reduce its tariff from a base point of 42.7%

to the final bound tariff of 32.4% in year 2004, with an average reduction by 24.1%. According to its accession commitments, however, China's tariff reduction level is much greater. In 2004, China's average tariff rate on industrial products was reduced to 9.5%. After China's fulfillment of its commitment on accession into WTO, it has reduced its tariff rate by as much as 78.9%, which is much bigger than the 33% tariff reduction commitment made by other countries during the Uruguay Round. Moreover, even if the new round of Doha negotiation concludes with a reduction rate of as much as 68.5%, the total tariff cut of China would still exceed the total tariff cut of other countries during the Uruguay Round and Doha Round combined.

Independent experts affirm this view. For example, Mattoo notes that China's services commitments are generally higher than other WTO members in terms of both the width of coverage and the depth of market-opening. Indeed, he praises China's commitments under the General Agreement on Trade in Services (GATS) as "the most radical services reform program negotiated in the WTO."[3] This observation is shared by Lardy, who noted in his study of China accession package that China's commitments "far surpass those made by founding members of the WTO and, in some cases, go beyond those made by countries that have joined the organization since its founding in 1995."[4]

Because of its substantial accession commitments, China has been arguing that it, along with other "Recently Acceded Members (RAMs)," should not be required to make the same level of concessions as the founding WTO members.[5] As the flip side of this strategy, China also tries to refrain from making aggressive demands in the negotiation and keeps a low profile in general to avoid unwanted attention from the other players.

To be fair, many WTO members were initially sympathetic to the call for special treatments for RAMs. For this reason, the Hong Kong Ministerial Declaration explicitly states that "[w]e recognize the special situation of recently-acceded Members who have undertaken extensive market access commitments at the time of accession. This situation will be taken into account in the negotiations."[6] Indeed, had the DDA been concluded according to the original schedule, it is not unlikely that China could have avoided making substantial concessions on agriculture or Non-Agricultural Market Access (NAMA) by hiding under the RAM label.

Unfortunately, however, as the Doha Round drags on, fewer members are willing to give a "free ride" to members such as China that acceded a decade ago. Moreover, the United States and European Union face increasing pressures: on the one hand, their negotiating partners ask them to make more concessions; on the other hand, vocal domestic constituencies (such as labor and farmer groups) have been calling for the government to seek more inroads into foreign markets without giving access to their own domestic markets. Thus, they need to find another scapegoat to divert part of the attention. What could be a better target than China—the economic superpower on rapid rise? Thus, starting from 2006, the United States and European Union have been pushing China from both sides. For example, the United States has repeatedly urged China, as the biggest beneficiary of the multilateral trading system, to take more responsibilities at the WTO.[7]

Similarly, the EU has argued that China should be required to make contributions just like other WTO members.[8] While the United States and European Union use ambiguous terms such as "leadership" to describe such "responsibilities" and "contributions," a careful reading between the lines of their messages reveals that what the United States and European Union have in mind is really asking China to provide more concessions in key areas such as agriculture, NAMA, and services so that they can have a better report card to show to their domestic stakeholders.

While China fought hard to avoid making new concessions by being recognized as a RAM, it seems that China has lost the battle. According to the latest negotiating drafts, the prevailing consensus seems to be that flexibility will be extended mostly to small, low-income RAMs and "very recently acceded Members," that is, those that acceded to the WTO after the Doha Round was launched.

Second, it has to do with a lack of expertise. As a new member, China was not familiar with the rules of game. This is the case for both the substantive rules as well as the procedural rules. Regarding the substantive rules, while the most important rule has been compiled in the Secretariat publication entitled *The Legal Texts: The Results of the Uruguay Round of Multilateral Trade Negotiations*,[9] there are also numerous GATT protocols, decisions, and other legal instruments that are not available in a readily-accessible format.[10] On top of those, as noted by the Appellate Body in *Japan—Alcoholic Beverages II*,[11] there are many panel reports adopted during the GATT era, which, as "an important part of the GATT *acquis* . . . create legitimate expectations among WTO Members, and, therefore, should be taken into account where they are relevant to any dispute."[12] In addition, in line with the tradition of "constructive ambiguity," many WTO rules are drafted in such a way that they are difficult to interpret for any member, let alone newer ones. For new members, it is a major challenge to understand these legal rules.

Compared with the substantive rules, the procedural rules of the WTO are even more difficult for new members to decipher. While Articles IX and X of the Marrakesh Agreement Establishing the WTO (WTO Agreement) provide a set of elaborate rules for the voting requirements for various decisions, formal voting has been rare in the history of the GATT and WTO.[13] In practice, most if not all decisions are made by "consensus." But what is "consensus"? According to the footnote to Article IX(1) of the WTO Agreement, consensus is defined as the situation where "no Member, present at the meeting when the decision is taken, formally objects to the proposed decision." However, such cryptic explanation offers little help to the uninitiated. Ironically, that is probably the reason why the consensus rule is preferred over the clearly defined and easily understood rules, such as two-thirds or three-fourths majority. To make it even more hopeless, even the consensus rule itself is of little use in reality as it applies to decision-making in formal meetings, which unfortunately is not where most decisions are made at the WTO. As acknowledged by the WTO Secretariat,

[i]mportant breakthroughs are rarely made in formal meetings of [WTO] bodies, least of all in the higher level councils. Since decisions are made by consensus, without voting, informal consultations within the WTO play a vital role in bringing a vastly diverse membership round to an agreement.[14]

Thus, the only way to acquire essential negotiating skills such as agenda-setting and coalition-building is through actual participation in the real work of the WTO.

Unfortunately, as China did not join the WTO as a formal member until six years after the WTO was formed, it faced a rather steep learning curve. In this regard, the thirty years of experience China had already acquired as a member of the UN at the time it joined the WTO were not of much help for two reasons. First, the nature of trade negotiations is very different from the political grand-standing at the UN. As one WTO official observed, "The UN is a talk-shop; the WTO is for getting real business done."[15] Second, at the UN, China has been a member of its key decision-making body—the Security Council—from the very beginning. In contrast, there is no such formal institutional arrangement at the WTO. Also, the key players in the global trade arena have been rather reluctant to grant China a seat at the table of the informal negotiating groupings for fear of diluting their own power.[16] While China has substantial trade volume, this alone has not guaranteed China a position as a key player in WTO negotiations.

Similarly, the fifteen-year accession negotiation did not teach China much about negotiating as a full member as the nature of accession negotiation is very different from that of normal negotiations in the WTO. The accession negotiation is a one-way process: while every existing WTO Member can make any request against the acceding member, the acceding member does not have any say on the existing rules of the WTO and have to accept them on a "take it or leave it" basis. In a way, the accession negotiation is easier to handle as the acceding country only has to worry about its defensive interests. In the normal WTO negotiations, however, each member not only has to look after its defensive interests, but also has to launch offensive requests against other countries. This requires considerable skills in assessing a country's own interests, coordinating positions among various domestic interests groups and different ministries, and formulating and executing its negotiating strategy, all of which China lacked during its early years as a new WTO member.

Enter the Dragon

Since its beginning, the GATT has been largely a trans-Atlantic scheme, where the most important initiatives and decisions were first brokered between the United States and European Union and then presented to the rest of the membership for acceptance. Later, this arrangement was expanded to include two more countries, that is, Canada and Japan. Known as "the Quad" among the GATT observers, they controlled the GATT during most of its history.

In the 1980s, things started to change. An early example of this is the strong resistance of the developing countries to the launch of the Uruguay Round.[17] After the conclusion of the Uruguay Round and the establishment of the WTO, the developing countries became even more assertive. Led by India and Brazil, the developing countries fought hard against the launch of a new round as they believed that they received a bad bargain in the Uruguay Round. The Round was only launched in 2001 after the developed countries agreed to make important concessions to developing countries. These include, among others, the official recognition of the "utmost importance"[18] of implementation issues—the central demand of developing countries—in the Doha Declarations, and the adoption of a separate Ministerial Declaration explicitly allowing developing countries the right to grant compulsory licenses to deal with public health crises.

As the negotiations went under way, the power gradually shifted from the Quad to the new G-4, that is, United States, European Union, Brazil and India, and then to the "Five Interested Parties" (FIPS), that is, the G-4 plus Australia. This later expanded into the G-6 with Japan. However, China, the biggest developing country, has been conspicuously absent in the inner circle. In a way, China behaved liked the proverbial elephant in the room. Notwithstanding its enormous size, it chose to sit quietly in a dark corner, while the other members also largely pretended not to notice its presence.

How could this happen? The reasons are two-fold:

First, during the early stages of the Doha Round, the negotiations focused mostly on agriculture. This why the FIPS countries were selected as they each had a strong interest in agriculture: the United States was eager to open markets abroad while shielding its subsidy programs to its farmers; the European Union wished to keep its subsidy program while maintaining the preferential deal it had with its former colonies; Brazil and Australia were highly competitive producers of many agricultural products in the world with strong interests in pushing open foreign markets as leaders of the Cairns Group; while India was most interested in protecting its own vulnerable agriculture sector, the sole livelihood of many of its millions of subsistence farmers. In contrast, China is a net importer of agricultural products and most of its agriculture products were sold in its huge domestic market. Thus, China did not have a strong interest in the agricultural negotiations.

Second, at least for the first few years after its accession, China was preoccupied with the discriminatory clauses that are tailored-made for China, which China reluctantly accepted as the price for its accession. They can be further divided into two categories: (1) WTO-plus obligations, that is, obligations that are beyond those normally required of WTO members; and (2) WTO-minus rights, that is, rights that are below those generally enjoyed by WTO members. WTO-plus obligations include the obligation to translate all foreign trade laws into one of the official languages of the WTO, a special transitional review mechanism for the first ten years after China's accession, and national treatment to both foreign products and persons. The WTO-minus rights include non-market economy status in antidumping investigations, alternative benchmarks in subsidy and countervailing measures (SCM) investigations, a special textile safeguard mechanism, and a transitional product-specific safeguard mechanism.

As these provisions were specifically designed to soften the impact of China's WTO accession on other members, they have a much more direct impact on Chinese exports than general WTO rules applicable to other members, at least during the transitional period. While the exact relationship between China's special provisions and the normal WTO rules is still subject to debate,[19] most commentators would agree that the

China-specific provisions would take precedence in accordance to the principle of *lex specialis derogat legi generali* (a special rule prevails over a general rule). Thus, at least until 2017 (before the expiration of these China-specific provisions), China would regard the revision of these special provisions rather than the revision of the general WTO rules as a more urgent task. Unfortunately, revising the China-specific accession provisions through the WTO negotiations will be extremely hard, if not impossible. To start with, the WTO is ill-equipped for this task. Among the WTO Agreements, none contain explicit rules on how to revise the accession protocol. In practice, other than a few isolated cases of minor revisions of accession commitments,[20] there has been no precedent of comprehensive revisions of accession terms for particular countries. Thus, if China were to insist on revising its accession provisions, the default consensus rule would probably apply. As we have seen from the history of the WTO, consensus among all WTO members is extremely hard to come by—indeed, it is one of the reasons why the Doha Round is taking so long. More importantly, most other WTO members are not interested in the idea of revising China's terms of accessions. Furthermore, even if assuming, that China could somehow persuade other members to accept its request to revise its accession commitments, it probably will have to provide compensation to other members according to the current rules on the renegotiation and modification of schedules.[21] Such compensation will have to take the form of additional concessions to other members beyond the commitments China made upon accession. However, as I explained earlier, it is very unlikely that China will be willing to provide such additional concessions.

Against this context, the recent calls by the United States and European Community for China to shoulder more responsibility and make more concessions in the Doha Round are a bit ironic: on the one hand, the United States and European Community imposed these harsh conditions in the accession negotiation and effectively denied China the normal membership status;[22] on the other hand, the United States and European Community now want China to behave like a normal WTO Member, or better still, go beyond what normal WTO members would offer by taking up the leadership responsibility. Before the United States and European Community abandon such a double-standard and start to treat China on a non-discriminatory basis, why should China be expected to contribute to the Round above and beyond what is expected of a normal member?

While its interests differ from many developing countries, China has decided, for political reasons, to align itself with the developing country camp. Thus, in August 2003, when the major developing country camp, the G-20,[23] was formed, China quickly jumped on board. While many observers welcomed this as the beginning of China's leadership role among developing countries, they were soon disappointed to find a silent China at the Ministerial Conference in Cancun hiding behind Brazil and India rather than leading other developing countries. One obvious reason is the lack of experience of Chinese diplomats. The less obvious reason, however, is probably more relevant: as with most other groupings in the WTO, the G20 is an issue-specific group. Its main mandate is to pressure developed countries to remove their domestic support and export subsidies on agriculture. However, as one of the largest importers of many agricultural commodities such as wheat, soybean, and cotton, China actually stood to lose out if the developing countries were granted their wish: the removal of subsidies would certainly raise international market prices of these products, and China would have to pay more for its agricultural imports. Thus, China remained silent from the Cancun Ministerial in 2003 through the Hong Kong Ministerial in 2005.

In 2006, things started to change. After resisting the demands of developing countries for a long time, the United States and European Union started to show more flexibility and moved closer to the targets of developing countries on agricultural issues. For example, the European Union finally agreed, during the Hong Kong Ministerial, to eliminate its agricultural subsidies in 2013. At the same time, the United States also agreed to cut its trade-distorting farm subsidies from US$22.5 billion to US$17 billion per year.[24] Partly encouraged by the progress on agriculture negotiations, partly to shift the blame from themselves to the developing countries, the United States and European Union started to push for movement in another key area: industrial tariffs (referred as NAMA). This completely turned the table in the negotiations: In agricultural market access negotiations, the developing countries tend to play the offensive role of demandeurs, while the developed countries largely assume the defensive position as demandees. In contrast, in nonagricultural market access negotiations, the developed countries are the demandeurs against developing countries. The reason for this is that developed countries have, due to the five decades of trade negotiations under the GATT, lowered their industrial tariffs to below 5 percent on average; while developing countries have much higher levels of industrial tariffs, usually ranging from 20–30 percent on average.

At the meeting of the G-4 in Potsdam, Germany, in July 2007, the United States and European Union asked India and Brazil to reduce their tariffs on manufactured goods in exchange for the trans-Atlantic offers on agricultural products. Even though China was not invited to the meeting, all fingers started to point to China this time. For example, according to Brazilian Foreign Minister Amorim, acceding to the requests presented by the United States and European Union would risk "deindustrializing Brazil" in key industrial sectors.[25] Instead, he argued that Brazil needed to maintain its right to impose high tariffs on manufactured goods so it would have "policy space for dealing with China." Similarly, Indian Trade Minister Kamal Nath was also reluctant to "pay for someone else's ride" as China stands to reap most of the benefits of lowering industrial tariffs.[26]

While these statements are obviously motivated by self-interests, they have also highlighted the unmistakable truth that China, as the largest exporter of manufactured goods, will gain most from any NAMA package. Therefore, after the Potsdam meeting, the United States and European Union started to push China into the center of the negotiating stage. To carry out their strategy, they employed both "carrots" and "sticks": on the one hand, they argued that China, with its phenomenal growth record, has been the biggest beneficiary of the multilateral trading system. Moreover, China will reap huge gains from a successful Doha Round. Thus, it is in China's self-interest to make more contributions. On the other hand, they kept pressuring China on specific areas. For example, they accused China of providing the largest amount of subsidy among

WTO members to its cotton farmers and requested China to scrap its cotton subsidy.[27] On NAMA, they asked China to lower tariffs in specific sectors that are of interests to the United States, such as industrial machinery, chemicals, and electronics.[28]

In summary, they called for China to "take more responsibility" in the multilateral trading system. Such responsibility takes the form of the coveted membership in the core decision-making group of the WTO, when China was invited to join the G6 to form the G7 at the July 2008 Mini-Ministerial in Geneva.

However, by then, China has become well-versed in the craft of trade negotiations. As noted by Dr Zhang Xiangcheng, the former director-general of the Division on WTO Affairs of MOFCOM and current deputy permanent representative of China's WTO mission, it is naive to simply draw its interests along developing country lines.[29] Instead, China shall try to form alliances with different countries on an issue-by-issue basis.[30] It is hard to blame China for being selfish, as many other developing countries do not view China as true friends either. For example, in anticipation of the expiration of the Agreement on Textile and Clothing (ATC), a group of forty-seven developing countries led by Mauritius adopted the "Istanbul Declaration" in mid-2004 petitioning the WTO to extend the ATC for another three years. As the justification for their request, they cited various alleged "trade distorting practices" by China, which "have allowed China to drop prices for textile and apparel products by as much as 75 percent, and have given China an unassailable and unfair advantage in world markets for textiles and clothing." Thus, unless the ATC is extended, "global textile and clothing trade will be monopolized by a few countries such as China" and this will lead to "massive job disruption and business bankruptcies in dozens of countries dependant [*sic*] upon textile and clothing exports."[31]

Thus, China started to adopt a practical approach to the negotiations. On the one hand, as the largest exporter, China shares many interests with developed countries. One example is trade facilitation. While many developing countries are against the inclusion of the issue, given its position as one of the top exporters in the world, it is actually in China's interest to push for the inclusion of trade facilitation in the WTO framework to make the customs processes of its exporting destinations more efficient and cheaper. On the other hand, as a country with a large low-income population, China also sympathizes with the concerns of many developing country members. This is why China supports the demand by India that developing countries should be entitled to a list of special products that will be exempted from tariff cuts, as well as a special safeguard mechanism that can deal with surge on particular agricultural imports. As a country that straddles the North-South spectrum, China is well positioned to be an "honest broker" among developed and developing countries. In the words of Dr. Zhang, China should play "a balancing, bridging and constructive role" between developed and developing countries.

One example of China's bridging role is its proposal at the 2005 Hong Kong Ministerial that the members should try to reap some early harvest of the negotiating results before the conclusion of a comprehensive agreement. This proposal helped to maintain the momentum of negotiations and pushed the negotiation forward.

Sometimes, China is willing to sacrifice some of its own interests to generate momentum for the Round. For example, in 2005, China voluntarily offered to provide duty-free quota-free market access to imports from least developed countries (LDC) even though it is not a requirement for developing countries.

Of course, playing the bridging role does not necessarily mean that China would always have to sacrifice its interests. While it recognizes that it has special responsibilities as a large developing country, China resents being singled out in the negotiations. Therefore, China has been consistently opposing efforts by developed countries and some developing countries to differentiate among developing country members. Similarly, when the July 2008 meeting ran into an impasse due to India's refusal to give in on special products and special safeguard mechanism, China turned down the United States' request for China to provide additional concessions on special products in agriculture and sectoral negotiations on industrial goods. Part of the reason is domestic political difficulties, but an equally important reason is that China does not wish to be treated differently from India, which has rejected US demands on these issues.[32]

At the end of the July 2008 meeting, the United States started to accuse China of breaking the deal. According to the United States, "China wanted a seat at the big kids' table, . . . [t]hey got it, they agreed to the text, and now they are trying to walk that text back."[33] This prompted a rare angry response from Mr. Sun Zhenyu, the Chinese ambassador to the WTO:

> We have tried very hard to contribute to the success of the round. It is a little bit surprised that at this time the US started this finger pointing. I am surprised because they are now talking about cotton, sugar, rice of China as it seems that we are not going to make any efforts in the Round. Let me explain what China has contributed in the round.
>
> Because of our accession negotiations, our tariff in agriculture on average is 15.2% and bound at this level, which is lower than the average of European Union, lower than Canada, lower than Japan, lower than quite a number of other developed countries on average. But on that basis, we are committed in this round to cut further down our tariffs—the applied tariffs deeply. And in NAMA, our average tariff rate is 9, bound at that level. And in this round, we will cut about 30% in applied level. So we are making contributions of 50% of the total developing countries in terms of applied rate cut. So that is our contribution.
>
> . . .
>
> If you consider what the contributions that developed countries are going to make, in OTDS the US is spending $7 to 8 billion this year or last year, maybe a little bit more to 10 billion, but they are offering $14.5 billion with a lot of policy space for themselves. And in their tariff cut in agriculture, they are protecting their sensitivities through sensitive products while they are saying "well even if we have sensitive products for 5 or 4% of our tariff lines, we will have TRQ expansions." But they can never expand their TRQ to the level of China's TRQ quantities. In our case, our TRQ is 9 million tons for wheat, 7 million tons for corn, 5 million tons for rice. How about your quota, even after the expansion they will never pass half a million tons. Where is the new market access to the developed countries?

In NAMA, they are using erosion trying to cover their sensitivities, keeping their tariff peaks in textiles and garments for another 10 years. They will cover all their sensitivities through various measures while they are asking China to participate in sectors where we have great sensitivities, particularly in chemicals, in electronics, in machinery.[34]

The Chinese Proposals: Quantity and Quality

Given the substantial obstacles China faced at the beginning, its performance in trade negotiations to date has been quite satisfactory. While no indicator can accurately quantify a country's negotiating prowess, the number of submissions made in the negotiations can serve as a useful proxy. China did not make any submission in the Doha Round until June 20, 2002, when China made a proposal on fisheries subsidies. By February 2005, China has made more than ten submissions. The number further jumped to 67 in December 2007. By the time of the July 2008 meeting, China has made more than one hundred submissions.[35] Judging from the rapidly increasing number of submissions, China has been learning very fast.

Judging from the number of proposals submitted, China is one of the most active members of the Round. According to a study[36] based on the official records of the WTO in 2003, China made a total of twenty-nine written submissions to the Trade Negotiations Committee and its subsidiary bodies, the Ministerial Conference at Doha and the working groups on the four Singapore issues, making it the most active developing country participant and the fourth most active among all WTO members in the Doha Round.

However, numbers alone only tell part of the story. Most of the proposals by China focuses on either the procedural issues or the special and differential treatment for developing countries and do not touch on the substance of the negotiations.

One reason for this is China's lack of experience in multilateral trade negotiations, while the other reason is China's awkward position on the substantive issues. As both the largest exporter in the world and a country with millions still struggling on the poverty line, China often finds it hard to define its own interests. For example, along with other developing countries, China has been asking the developed countries to liberalize agricultural trade. At the same time, China also feels the need to protect its highly vulnerable domestic agricultural sector. The only way to protect both interests is through the adoption of a double-standard, which in the WTO is achieved through special and differential treatment provisions for developing countries. Another example on the conflict of interests is in the area of trade remedies, where China is both the biggest victim and a major user. Take antidumping measures for example, as China has been the favorite target of antidumping investigations and actions for many years, we would think that China has an incentive to push for stricter disciplines on antidumping in the Doha Round.

On the other hand, as one of the major users of antidumping actions in recent years, it also seems right for China to argue for more discretion to be given to the investigating authorities. Two other factors further complicate the picture: First, as noted by Messerlin, China is much more targeted by developing countries, especially if the number of antidumping actions is adjusted for trade size, that is, the average number of cases by each country per thousand USD of exports from China to such country. However, as I noted above, it is politically awkward for China to confront developing countries. Second, because China is not treated as a market economy in antidumping investigations, it does not matter much if the general rules under the Antidumping Agreement are improved or not, unless, of course, if China argues for the clarification of the rules on the treatment of non-market economies in the Antidumping Agreement. But this is going to be a difficult task for two reasons: first, as very few countries are in the non-market economy club, most WTO members would not be sympathetic to China's request; second, even if the relevant rules in the main Antidumping Agreement were revised, it is unclear whether or not China would benefit from this at all as the China-specific provision is regulated by the Accession Protocol, which legally speaking is an entirely different agreement from the Antidumping Agreement.

Implications of the Chinese Experience for Global Trade Governance

From the above overview of China's experience in the Doha negotiations, we can draw some interesting lessons about the nature of global trade governance in general and China's approach to global trade governance in particular.

The first lesson is that the idea that world trade is governed under a unique model is largely a myth. According to the Marrakesh Agreement, the default decision-making rule in the WTO is supposed to be consensus. This appears to be quite different from the institutional arrangements in most other international organizations, which explicitly grants more power to the bigger countries. Examples include the veto powers of the five permanent members of the UN Security Council and the weighted voting powers of the IMF members. Thus, at least in theory, it seems that even the smallest members may single-handedly block the formation of consensus in trade negotiations. However, the reality is quite different because eventually, the organization is still controlled by the inner-group of the biggest and most powerful countries.

Second, how are powers allocated in the WTO? As the WTO is an organization that focuses on trade issues, one would assume that the powers in the organization would be distributed according to trade shares of each Member. However, as we can see from China's experience, while trade volume is important, it is by no means the determining factor in the allocation of power. Instead, India and Brazil, two countries with much lower trade volumes, seem to command more power than China, at least during the first seven years after China's accession. There are many possible reasons for the asymmetry between the trade shares and bargaining powers, but the main reason is that, on the one hand, these countries had a long history of participating in the GATT and thus were able to set the agenda in a way that maximizes their influences; while on the other hand, China lacked familiarity with the ways the game is played in the WTO and had to learn on the job.

This brings us to the last point: how did China and the WTO interact with each other? The short answer is that both took time to adjust to the changing reality. For the WTO, while the status quo powers might be uncomfortable with the rapid rise of China, they have finally granted China a seat at the key players' table, albeit only after seven years. On the other hand, China seems, until very recently, to be a bit uneasy with its newly-acquired major player status and unsure how to use such power. While this might appear to be bizarre in the WTO, it would be easier to understand if we compare China's behavior in the WTO with its approach in other international institutions. In the UN, for example, China has rarely exercised its veto power. Thus, at least for the next few years, it's reasonable to assume that China will continue to be a system-maintainer in the WTO and will not attempt to take extreme positions that might undermine the system.

CONCLUDING THOUGHTS

In summary, during its first decade in the WTO, while China has been an active participant in the WTO negotiations, it has never been a high-profile participant, and it emerged as a key player only very recently, that is, after 2008. While this might seem puzzling at first, as the discussions above have illustrated, China's decision to keep a low profile in the current Round actually makes great sense. Unless there are substantial changes in these factors, it is unlikely that China will voluntarily assume a leading role in the talks.

NOTES

1. China's dubious honor of being the WTO Member with the longest accession process has been overtaken by Russia, which is in its seventeenth year of accession negotiation as of 2010.

2. Miaomiao Shi, *China's Participation in the Doha Negotiations and Implementation of Its Accession Commitments, in* China's Participation in the WTO 23, 28–29 (Henry Gao and Donald Lewis eds., 2005).

3. Aaditya Mattoo, "China's Accession to the WTO: The Services Dimension," 6(2) *J. Int'l. Econ. L.* 299, 300 (2003).

4. Nicholas Lardy, *Integrating China into the Global Economy*, Brookings, 2002, at 104–05.

5. World Trade Organization, Ministerial Conference, 5th Sess., Cancún, Statement by H. E. Mr Lu Fuyuan, Minister of Commerce of China, at 2, WT/MIN(03)/ST/12 (Sept. 10–14, 2003).

6. World Trade Organization, Ministerial Declaration of December 18, 2005, at 11, WT/MIN(05)/DEC (2005).

7. See, e.g., Susan Schwab, U.S Trade Representative, Remarks at the 40th Anniversary Gala Dinner of the National Committee on U.S.-China Relations (Oct. 12, 2006) (transcript available at http://www.ncuscr.org/files/2006Gala_SusanSchwab.pdf).

8. See, e.g., Martin Khor, "Trade: China and EU Clash over RAMs at NAMA Meeting," #6362 SUNS, Nov. 9, 2007, available at http://www.twnside.org.sg/title2/wto.info/twninfo110719.htm (last visited Feb. 16, 2011).

9. World Trade Organization, *The Legal Texts: The Results of the Uruguay Round of Multilateral Trade Negotiations* (1999).

10. See General Agreement on Tariffs and Trade 1994, art. 1(a)-(c), Apr. 15, 1994, Marrakesh Agreement Establishing the World Trade Organization, Annex 1, Legal Instruments—Results of the Uruguay Round, 33 I.L.M. 1125 (1994) [hereinafter GATT 1994].

11. Appellate Body Report, *Japan—Taxes on Alcoholic Beverages*, WT/DS8/AB/R, WT/DS10/AB/R, WT/DS11/AB/R (Oct. 4, 1996).

12. Ibid. ¶ 18.

13. For a review of the problems with the GATT/WTO decision-making rules, see Claus-Dieter Ehlermann & Lothar Ehring, *Are WTO Decision-Making Procedures Adequate for Making, Revising and Implementing Worldwide and 'Plurilateral' Rules?, in* Reforming the World Trading System Legitimacy, Efficiency, and Democratic Governance, 497–522 (Ernst-Ulrich Petersmann ed., 2005).

14. World Trade Organization, "Whose WTO is it anyway?," in *Understanding the WTO: The Organization* 101, 104 (2008), available at http://www.wto.org/english/thewto_e/whatis_e /tif_e/ understanding_e.pdf (last visited Feb. 16, 2011).

15. The author's interview with a senior WTO diplomat (anonymous).

16. As I will note below, due to China's unique position as both a developing country and a major trader, neither the developed countries nor the major developing countries regard China as one of their own and both view China more as a threat rather than a potential ally.

17. See John Croome, *Reshaping the World Trading System: A History of the Uruguay Round*, Kluwer, 1998, at pp. 7–20

18. Para. 12, Doha Declaration.

19. For the legal problems raised by these provisions, see Henry Gao, *China's Participation in the WTO: A Lawyer's Perspective,* 11 SING. Y.B. INT'L L. 1 (2007), at 15–17.

20. For example, when Mongolia acceded to the WTO in 1997, it committed to phase out and eliminate its export duty on raw cashmere within ten years. Due to both economic and environmental concerns, however, Mongolia found it unable to eliminate the export duty. It requested the Council for Trade in Goods (CTG) for a five-year waiver on its accession commitment on cashmere, which was approved by the CTG on 9 July 2007. WTO, "Goods Council Approves Waivers for Mongolia," *US,* WTO: NEWS ITEMS, July 9, 2007, http://www.wto.org/ english/news_e/news07_e/good_counc_9july07_e.htm. (last visited Jan. 20, 2011). The background of this case can be found in Damedin Tsogtbaatar, "Mongolia's WTO Accession: Expectations and Realities of WTO Membership," in Managing the Challenges of WTO Participation: 45 Case Studies, 409–419 (Peter Gallagher et al. eds., 2005).

21. See, e.g., GATT 1994, *supra* note 30, art. XXVIII; General Agreement on Trade in Services, art. XXI, Apr. 15, 1994, Marrakesh Agreement Establishing the World Trade Organization, Annex 1, Legal Instruments—Results of the Uruguay Round, 33 I.L.M. 1125 (1994).

22. As noted by Cattaneo and Braga in their comprehensive study on WTO accessions, while many other WTO Members that acceded to the WTO recently were also asked to assume obligations beyond the normal WTO disciplines, none of them are as onerous as those imposed on China, which remain a "particularly challenging and atypical case." See generally Olivier Cattaneo and Carols A. Primo Braga, *Everything You Always Wanted to Know about WTO Accession (But Were Afraid to Ask)* (World Bank, Policy Research Working Paper Series 5116, 2009).

23. The G-20 is the coalition of developing countries pressing for ambitious reforms of agriculture in developed countries with some flexibility for developing countries (not to be confused with the G-20 group of finance ministers and central bank governors, and its recent summit meetings). It currently has twenty-three members, i.e., Argentina, Bolivarian Republic of Venezuela, Bolivia, Brazil, Chile, China, Cuba, Ecuador, Egypt, Guatemala, India, Indonesia, Mexico, Nigeria, Pakistan, Paraguay, Peru, Philippines, South Africa, Tanzania, Thailand, Uruguay, Zimbabwe. See WTO, http://www.wto.org/english/tratop_e/agric_e/negoti_groups_e.htm (last visited Feb. 16, 2011).

24. ICTSD, "G-4 Talks In Potsdam Break Down, Doha Round's Fate In The Balance Once Again," *Bridges Weekly Trade News Digest*, Volume 11, Number 23, June 27, 2007, available at http://ictsd.org/i/news/bridgesweekly/6515/.

25. Paul Blustein, "Misadventures of the Most Favored Nations: Clashing Egos, Inflated Ambitions, and the Great Shambles of the World Trade System," *PublicAffairs*, 2009, at p. 244.

26. Ibid., at p. 245.

27. Statement by US Ambassdor to the WTO Michael Punke at the China WTO 10 conference by ICTSD (on file with the author).

28. ICTSD, "Doha: EU Bid to Break NAMA Sectoral Deadlock Receiving Cool Initial Response," *Bridges Weekly Trade News Digest*, Volume 15, Number 16, May 4, 2011, available at http://ictsd.org/i/news/bridgesweekly/105612/.

29. 21st Century Business Herald, "Zhongguo de Duoha Celue (China's Doha Strategy)," Nov. 30, 2005, available at http://finance.sina.com.cn/chanjing/b/20051130/09052159265.shtml.

30. Ibid.

31. "Istanbul Declaration Regarding Fair Trade in Textiles and Clothing," available at www.ncto.org/quota/Idec.pdf.

32. Blustein, *supra* at 25, at pp. 271–273.

33. Ibid., at p. 274.

34. Sun Zhenyu, H.E. Ambassador, permanent Mission P.R.C. to the WTO, Statement at the Informal Trade Negotiations Committee Meeting (Aug. 11, 2008), available at http://wto2.mofcom.gov.cn/aarticle/inbrief/200808/20080805717988.html (last visited Feb. 16, 2011).

35. Xiangchen Zhang, *Wuzi li de Daxiang* [*Elephant in the Room*], 7 CHINA WTO TRIBUNE (2008), available at http://www.wtoguide.net/Html/jsy/061225111611339980871612532682519 94.html (last visited Feb. 16, 2011).

36. Håkan Nordström, *Participation of Developing Countries in the WTO—New Evidence Based on the 2003 Official Records* 28–30 (National Board of Trade, Sweden, 2002), available at http://www.noits.org/noits06/Final_Pap/Hakan_Nordstrom.pdf.

4

Learning and Socialization in International Institutions: China's Experience with the WTO Dispute Settlement System

Xiaojun Li

In 2009, the eighth year since China joined the World Trade Organization (WTO), Beijing was involved in seven of the fourteen disputes filed at the Dispute Settlement Body (DSB), four times as defendant and three times as complainant. In addition, panels were established for five cases involving China from the previous years. These cases dealt with a variety of issues, involving products that ranged from steel fasteners to poultry. Increase in such activities at the dispute settlement system prompted some observers to dub 2009 as "WTO's China year."[1] This poses a stark contrast to China's first five years as a WTO member during which only two cases involving China were lodged at the WTO DSB—one filed by China alongside seven other members in 2002 against the United States and another settled by China with the United States during the bilateral consultation stage in 2004.

How can we explain China's abrupt change from a cautious observer to an active participant in the WTO's dispute settlement system? What was holding China back from participating more often than what would be predicted by its sheer market size and trade surplus? In this chapter, I review China's experience in managing frictions associated with its growing role in world trade through formal WTO dispute settlement proceedings over the past decade by using both case studies and quantitative data. I argue that China's absence from WTO litigation in the initial period following its 2001 accession can be attributed to the normative constraints and the concern for reputation in particular. The aversion to multilateral adjudication was later overcome through a learning and socialization process that led to an attitudinal shift in China's normative orientation toward the use of the WTO dispute settlement procedure to both defend its domestic industry and push for market access abroad.

This chapter is organized as follows. In the next section, I briefly review the extant literature on WTO dispute settlement system, focusing on the interest, power, and capacity constraints commonly offered to explain the lack of adjudication from developing country members. The following section surveys China's experience with the WTO's dispute settlement system in the past decade and highlights the abrupt increase in China's participation in the DSB since 2007 from a comparative perspective. I argue that the trade interest, market power, and capacity constraint arguments would all predict higher levels of participation in the WTO DSB than what was actually observed in the initial years of China's membership. The ensuing section discusses the normative constraint and factors reinforcing this constraint faced by China in the earlier years that prevented it from exercising its right to adjudication. I illustrate these factors by examining China's first WTO case as a respondent on the issue of semiconductors. Next, I show how learning and socialization facilitated the shift in normative orientation that led to China's embracement of the multilateral dispute settlement forum as a normal trade policy tool. I conclude by suggesting that China's expanded role and involvement in the DSB could strengthen the multilateral trade regime and generate positive externalities in other areas of regional and global governance.

DISPUTE SETTLEMENT SYSTEM IN THE WTO

The WTO dispute settlement is a multi-stage process that combines litigation and negotiation. When a country claims that a trading partner has instituted a WTO-inconsistent policy, it has a right to enter formal dispute resolution under the auspices of the WTO DSB. The dispute settlement procedure begins with a formal request for bilateral consultation with the respondent government. If consultations fail to resolve the dispute within sixty days, the complainant can proceed to request for the establishment of a panel. Three panelists are then selected by the disputing countries to review the facts and develop legal findings before providing a recommendation on the case.[2] The panel will go through several rounds of deliberation before making a final report for adoption by the DSB soon after its release, in the absence of an appeal or negative consensus. Appeals go to the seven-member Appellate Body which has the authority to uphold, modify, or reverse the legal conclusions of the panel. Appellate Body rulings are final and legally binding. When a policy measure is ruled illegal, the defendant must comply with the WTO's recommendations within a reasonable period of time. Otherwise the complainant can request for authorization to impose sanctions. The level of sanction and the suspension of concession are determined using the proportionality principle. At any time during the dispute resolution process, the disputants may resolve the case by reaching a mutually agreed solution.

Citing increased participation by developing countries as evidence, some scholars and policymakers have praised the WTO DSB for creating a more level playing field for all members, not just the large, rich, and powerful ones.[3] Others, however, argue that the raw numbers are misleading.[4] Except for a handful of active participants (e.g., Brazil and Thailand), the rest of the developing country members have had no dispute participation at all.[5] Empirical research on the WTO dispute settlements thus far seems to support the latter view. Scholars using various samples find that controlling for the likelihood of trade conflicts and a number of other factors, developing countries are less likely to engage in dispute settlement procedures under the WTO.[6]

Three types of factors are commonly offered to explain why states hold back from participating in the WTO dispute system: trade interest, power, and capacity. First, states with larger trade interests tend to adjudicate more than the ones that are marginalized from fully participating in the global trade system. Horn, Nordström, and Mavroidis, for instance, show that states with more exports more frequently use the dispute settlement system because they have more potential disputes.[7] To give a concrete example, the European Union and the United States, which have been responsible for setting up more than half of the panels completed by the end of 2006, have a combined share of about a third of the world trade in goods and services. Members with limited role in global trade, on the other hand, do not participate in the DSB simply because they have no interest in doing so.[8]

Second, member states may refrain from bringing up disputes against larger trading partners for fear of possible retaliatory actions from the would-be defendant, which may include withdrawal of aid or restriction of market access.[9] Chad Bown, for instance, finds that states with greater retaliatory power to restrict imports from the defendant in a dispute are more likely to initiate a dispute and gain larger trade liberalization outcomes.[10] Finally, member states, developing countries in particular, may lack the necessary financial, human, and institutional capital to participate fully. These capacity constraints include language barriers, inadequate legal expertise, and limited knowledge of increasing complexity of dispute settlement procedures and partners' trade barriers.[11]

In sum, larger, richer, and administratively and legally more capable members are generally more active users of the DSB compared to smaller, poorer and less capable members. Two questions arise from these analyses: Did China's post-accession behaviors in the WTO dispute settlement system converge to this general pattern? How has China, a developing country as well as one of the largest trading states, fared in the WTO DSB? The next section explores these issues.

CHINA'S CHANGING BEHAVIORS IN THE WTO DISPUTE SETTLEMENT SYSTEM

Between the time of its accession to the WTO in December 2001 and the end of 2010, China was involved in a total of twenty-eight disputes at the DSB, seven times as complainant and twenty-one times as defendant (see appendix for a brief description of these cases). In seven of these cases, China and the disputant reached a mutually agreed solution during the consultation stage. Another seven cases are still at the consultation stage. Panels have been established in the remaining fourteen cases, among which five reached the Appellate Body and one is being appealed. Given its share in world trade and the political sensitivity of the sectors involved in many of its traded products, China's involvement in the multilateral trade regime is expected to further expand.

Figure 4.1 shows all disputes initiated at the WTO DSB from 2002 to 2010 in three groups: disputes filed by China, disputes filed against China, and all other disputes. A couple of interesting patterns emerge from this picture. First, while the total number of new disputes has decreased steadily over the years, dropping by half from thirty-seven cases in 2002 to eighteen cases in 2010, cases involving China has multiplied, accounting for half of all disputes initiated in 2009. Second, China's increasing participation in the DSB is not a gradual process. Between 2002 and 2006, China was complainant in one case and defendant in four additional cases, or two disputes if multiple complaints for the same product are combined. Since 2007, however, China has appeared in nearly 40 percent of the all the cases brought to the DSB, more than any other member except for the United States (twenty-eight times).

China's change of heart in embracing the WTO dispute settlement system is all the more conspicuous from a comparative perspective. Table 4.1 lists all the countries that have served as either complainant or defendant in at least one dispute at the WTO for the two time periods, ranked by the number of appearances between 2002 and 2006, and between 2007 and 2010.

In the first period, forty-two of the then 149 members have sued or been sued at least once in the DSB, with the United States and the European Community leading the pack with fifty-five and forty-three times, respectively. China was the only state that showed up in the list among the eight new members that joined the WTO during this period[12] and ranked at the eleventh place with five appearances.

During the second period, only twenty-nine of the one hundred and fifty-three members have used the DSB, with the United States still leading the way, although its number of appearances has dropped by half to twenty-seven. China, on the other hand, soared to the second place with twenty-three appearances, overtaking the European Community and most other members by a large margin. China was also one

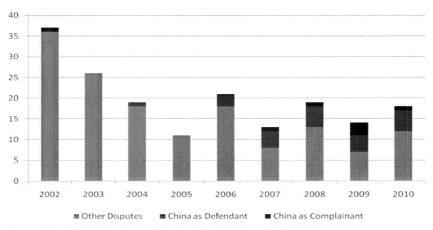

Figure 4.1.   WTO Disputes with and without China, 2002–2010
Source: WTO Dispute Settlement Gateway, http://www.wto.org/english/tratop_e/dispu_e/dispu_e.htm, last accessed March 10, 2011.

Table 4.1. WTO Disputes by Country 2002–2010

Country	2002–2006	Rank	2007–2010	Rank
USA	55	1	28	1
EC	43	2	20	3
Mexico	13	3	5	5
Canada	12	4	7	4
Argentina	11	5	2	12
India	9	6	4	6
Korea	9	6	3	8
Brazil	7	8	3	8
Chile	7	8	1	18
Japan	6	10	2	12
China	5	11	23	2
Australia	5	11	1	18
Thailand	4	13	3	8
Dominican Republic	3	14	4	6
Norway	3	14	1	18
Turkey	3	14	0	N/A
Philippines	2	17	3	8
Guatemala	2	17	2	12
Pakistan	2	17	2	12
Honduras	2	17	1	18
Peru	2	17	1	18
Chinese Taipei	2	17	1	18
Ecuador	2	17	0	N/A
Egypt	2	17	0	N/A
France	2	17	0	N/A
Germany	2	17	0	N/A
Hungary	2	17	0	N/A
Spain	2	17	0	N/A
UK	2	17	0	N/A
Indonesia	1	30	2	12
Costa Rica	1	30	1	18
New Zealand	1	30	1	18
South Africa	1	30	1	18
Antigua and Barbuda	1	30	0	N/A
Bangladesh	1	30	0	N/A
Croatia	1	30	0	N/A
Czech	1	30	0	N/A
Nicaragua	1	30	0	N/A
Poland	1	30	0	N/A
Switzerland	1	30	0	N/A
Uruguay	1	30	0	N/A
Venezuela	1	30	0	N/A
Netherlands	0	N/A	2	12
El Salvador	0	N/A	1	18
Ukraine	0	N/A	1	18
Vietnam	0	N/A	1	18

Note: This table lists all the countries that have served as either complainant or defendant in at least one dispute at the WTO for the two time periods: 2002–2006 and 2007-2010. The countries are ranked by the number of their appearances between 2002 and 2006.

Source: *WTO Dispute Settlement Gateway*, http://www.wto.org/english/tratop_e/dispu_e/dispu_e.htm, last accessed April 17, 2011.

of the eight countries[13] that experienced an increase in dispute participation. While the explosion of disputes concerning China since 2007 could be partly driven by the end of the initial phase-in period stipulated in China's WTO accession package, the double-digit boost (+23) was still paralleled by none.

If China's degree of involvement at the WTO dispute settlement system in the past four years matches its position in international trade, its behaviors in the earlier years would seem to be at odds with the predictions of the trade interest and market power arguments for dispute participation. At the time of China's formal accession to the WTO in 2001, China already ranked fourth in the world with almost US$700 billion USD in total exports and imports of goods and services (see Table 4.2). Since 2004, China has replaced Japan as the third largest trading state in the world. Given its huge market and export oriented trade policies, many expected China would soon become a frequent user and target in the DSB. Some observers even worried that China's accession would open the floodgate of disputes that could "overwhelm the already over-burdened [dispute settlement] system."[14]

On the contrary, China has been quite reluctant to utilize the dispute settlement system at the beginning. For over six years after China joined the WTO, the US Steel Safeguard case has remained the only instance that China complained against one of its trading partners. Even this case was unique as there were a number of other factors that prompted China's decision to adjudicate, such as the assistance of a strong team of co-complainants led by the European Community and Japan, bad publicity against US protectionism from the get-go, and the political calculations underlying the case.[15] It was not until 2007 that China, as the sole complainant, challenged US antidumping and countervailing duties on coated free sheet paper exported from China.

In comparison, Vietnam, a country with similar export-oriented trade policy yet economically much weaker, filed its first dispute against the United States only three years after it joined the WTO.[16] On the defensive side, China was doing no better, conceding to US demands in the dispute over tax rebates on semiconductors before the establishment of a panel. In addition, there were at least four instances of China being implicitly or explicitly threatened by one or more of its trading partners to take the potential disputes to the WTO DSB between 2004 and 2006.[17] In all of these cases, China settled the disputes through bilateral negotiations without leaving any trail on the official DSB casebook.

China's initial restraint from litigation on the surface seems to go well with the capacity argument. Like many new members upon accession, China lacked the legal, financial, and human resources to deal with the complexity of the WTO dispute settlement system. The shortage in human capital was particularly acute due to China's underdeveloped legal system and language barrier. China, however, has been catching up fast. The Chinese WTO delegation in Geneva has mushroomed over the years, with five Chinese listed on the roster of panelists by the end of 2006. There was also strong support from Beijing. By 2006, the Department of WTO Affairs under the Ministry of Commerce (MOFCOM) has sent over one hundred officials, scholars, and lawyers for training in the United States and Geneva on WTO affairs. In addition, a number

Table 4.2. Major Traders in the World (Billion USD), 2002–2009

Year	2002	2003	2004	2005	2006	2007	2008	2009
Brazil	134.52	149.51	192.31	235.09	281.31	344.38	448.48	355.90
Canada	578.27	627.60	719.66	815.10	891.91	968.04	1033.66	790.20
China	693.41	933.93	1262.37	1548.98	1914.45	2376.94	2814.56	2446.50
EC	6415.19	7665.07	9193.29	10039.46	11437.53	13340.52	14728.53	11510.80
India	151.99	185.24	265.95	344.58	433.70	557.79	637.09	600.58
Japan	839.37	947.00	1136.36	1241.81	1351.38	1469.41	1705.24	1256.93
US	2433.20	2586.10	2979.10	3332.90	3711.30	4037.40	4397.20	3543.10

Source: World Development Indicators, http://data.worldbank.org/data-catalog/world-development-indicators, last accessed March 10, 2010.

of research centers such as the China National Institute of WTO in Beijing and the Shanghai Consulting Center for the WTO have been set up on the eve of China's WTO accession, providing research and assistance to both the government and the industries. Furthermore, China has participated most actively as an interested third party in over half of the cases (56 out of 109) by the end of 2006, gaining valuable experience by observing and commenting on the disputes even before it joined the WTO (see Figure 4.2).[18] Given such effort and progress in capacity building, it is surprising that China had not been more assertive in filing and responding to disputes if only to gain some practical experience in the litigation process.

Indeed, during its first five years of membership, China had a number of opportunities to try out the dispute settlement system. One such case was the European Union's imposition of antidumping duties on polyester staple fibers on March 17, 2006, after which the China Chamber of Commerce for Import and Export of Textiles (CCCT) filed a petition to the MOFCOM, asking Beijing to challenge the European Union at the WTO DSB. The dispute was publicized as potentially being China's first dispute as a sole complainant, with an official from the MOFCOM quoted saying that the MOFCOM was "highly likely" to take the case to the WTO.[19] A lawyer involved with this case revealed that a team of experts for the case was already being assembled and foreign law firms contacted in April and that people "felt ready to go for the real thing."[20] Nevertheless, the dispute did not reach the WTO and China once again opted for bilateral negotiation.

In short, the trade interest, market power, and capacity constraint arguments would all predict a higher level of participation in the WTO DSB than what was

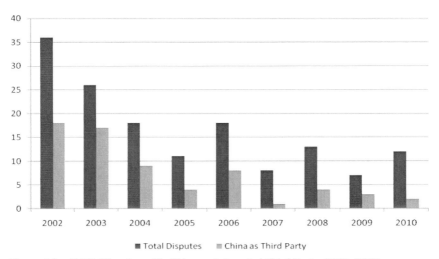

Figure 4.2. WTO Disputes with China as Interested Third Party, 2002–2010

Source: WTO Dispute Settlement Gateway, http://www.wto.org/english/tratop_e/dispu_e /dispu_e.htm, last accessed March 10, 2011.

actually observed. What then deters China from initiating and responding to more disputes in the earlier years of its WTO membership?

NORMATIVE CONSTRAINTS ON WTO ADJUDICATION

The foregoing arguments regarding the propensity to participate in the WTO dispute settlement system all focus on material and functional constraints faced by its member states. In contrast to these explanations, the social constructive argument stresses socially constructed ideas and therefore focuses on the normative constraints. Sociological approaches in international relations treat institutions as social environments and shift the focus to the non-material—psychological, affective, ideological—effects on behaviors generated by the interaction with other members of the institutions.[21] These normative concerns suggest that even in the absence of material constraints, states may restrain from certain behaviors in order to avoid social sanctions such as status loss, shaming, and humiliation.[22] From the social constructive perspective, therefore, China's reservation to adjudicate at the WTO DSB (despite improvement in its legal and human capacity) can be largely attributed to the normative constraints as illustrated in China's responses to its first WTO dispute.

On March 18, 2004, after becoming a member of the WTO for a little more than two years, China faced its first legal challenge when the United States filed a complaint with the DSB concerning Beijing's preferential value-added tax (VAT) for domestically produced or designed semiconductors. The American government claimed that all semiconductors sold in China were subject to a 17 percent VAT, but domestic producers—including both Chinese and foreign-invested firms—were eligible for an 11 percent tax rebate, rising to 14 percent if the products were designed and fabricated in the country. Imported semiconductors, on the other hand, did not qualify for any rebate.[23] The American government argued that the tax rebate for domestic producers violates the cardinal WTO principles of non-discrimination and national treatment in the General Agreement on Tariffs and Trade (GATT).[24] According to US official estimates, the cost of this discriminatory tax for American producers was as much as US$344 million a year.[25]

One day following the US formal request for consultations, Mr. Chong Quan, then spokesperson for MOFCOM, announced in a press release that China was confused by the US action.[26] He further revealed that China and the United States had held several rounds of bilateral consultations on the Integrated Circuits (IC) VAT rebate issue in the past three years. According to him, China felt baffled at the United States' abrupt change of course in bringing the case to the multilateral forum considering that the two parties were making some progress on the issue.[27]

The dispute was resolved without escalating to the panel stage. On July 14, 2004, China and the United States notified the DSB that they had reached an agreement on the matter raised by the United States in its request for consultations. According to the notification, China agreed to amend or revoke the measures at issue to eliminate the availability of VAT refunds on ICs produced and sold in China and on ICs designed in China but manufactured abroad by November 1, 2004, and September 1, 2004, respectively. On October 5, 2005, China and the United States informed the DSB that they agreed that terms of the agreement had been successfully implemented, and had reached a mutually satisfactory solution to the matter raised by the United States.[28]

The speed at which China settled the case is surprising, considering that over three years of prior bilateral negotiations on the issue failed to yield any meaningful results. Additionally, given that the WTO dispute process usually lasts for years, members tend to take advantage of the prospective remedy rule by choosing to go through the dispute settlement process while keeping the disputed policy for the domestic industries they aim to protect.[29] Since the Chinese government has made it a national strategy to promote China's overall competitiveness in the burgeoning semiconductor industry,[30] the decision to settle without taking this widely exploited option also seemed strange. The key factor that prevented China from litigation was the government's concern for potential reputation costs associated with defending its protectionist measures at the formal WTO dispute resolution system amid a global free trade community. Interviews with the Chinese negotiators on the VAT issue suggested that they were given explicit instruction from Beijing to avoid escalating the case to the panel stage by all means.[31]

This fear for reputation loss strengthened Beijing's belief that adjudication at the DSB would be a bad idea. Four factors account for this fear.

First, the aversion to litigation can be traced to the fact that Chinese are generally reluctant to use the court as a means of dispute resolution. According to the Confucian philosophy rooted deeply in the Chinese as well as other Asian societies, litigation would cause irreparable harm to normal relations and should be avoided as much as possible or serve as a last resort.[32] Taking this rationale to the international level, the Chinese leadership often finds it difficult to disentangle the legal issues from the political and reputation concerns and views the initiation of legal disputes in the WTO as tantamount to setbacks in diplomatic relations with the other countries.[33] In the case of polyester staple fibers mentioned earlier, for instance, one of the reasons that prevented China from challenging the EC was allegedly due to concerns for damaging the relationship between China and Europe as that year marked the thirtieth anniversary of the normalization of relations between the two.[34]

Second, the post-Deng leadership has been documented as being much more sensitive to China's international image and, by extension, their own.[35] Thus reputation loss (e.g., being sued and losing cases) at the international stage and actions that caused China to "lose face" would be detrimental to the central leader's political legitimacy back at home.

Third, from the social constructive perspective, social pressures should be particularly strong on novices facing uncertainty in a new environment.[36] China at the time of the VAT dispute can be clearly categorized as a novice in the WTO system. Merely into its third year as a formal WTO member after decades of negotiations and promises of abiding by the international rules, Beijing was keen on steering clear of any behaviors that might cause it to be stigmatized as protectionist and tarnish its image as a "responsible power."

Finally, when institutions are treated as social environment, the effect of social pressures is positively correlated with the size of the group that can bestow social rewards and punishments.[37] The cost of reputation loss at a multilateral forum such as the DSB thus will be much greater than at the bilateral level which has been China's preferred channel of negotiation and dispute resolution.

LEARNING AND SOCIALIZATION IN INTERNATIONAL INSTITUTIONS

The fact that China has now become one of the most frequent users of the DSB suggests that it has overcome the fear of reputation and status loss associated with multilateral adjudication. As part of a normal rule of the game in international trade governance, it has also embraced the WTO dispute settlement system as nothing more than a trade policy tool. This shift in normative orientation was a result of the learning and socialization process, a central concept of the social constructivist argument.

Socialization in the broadest sense is defined as a "process of inducting actors into the norms and rules of a given community."[38] In the social context of international institutions where member states interact on a regular and sustained basis, socialization leads states to endorse the expected ways of thinking and acting, and adopt behaviors accepted and practiced by the ongoing system.[39] This adoption is sustained over time and is quite independent from a particular structure of material incentives or constraints. In time, states take on new identities and interests, and ultimately change their behaviors to conform to the norms of the system.

The agent or target of socialization can include both individual policymakers and states. Socialization in the original social psychology literature refers to the internalization of norms and preferences by individual actors.[40] However, these norms and preferences can also affect larger social aggregates, including political parties and states. For constructivist IR theories, socialization effects emerge at both the individual and the state level. Individuals operating as agents of the state may transform their international experiences and interactions into national policy outcomes.[41] In this way, states are socialized.

Checkel identifies two different yet interrelated types of socialization in international institutions. On the one hand, agents may behave appropriately by "acquiring the knowledge that enables them to act in accordance with what is socially accepted in the system as well as what is expected of their roles, irrespective of whether they agree with these norms or not."[42] In this Type I socialization, conscious instrumental calculation is replaced by conscious role playing. On the other hand, following the logic of appropriateness may go beyond role playing and imply that agents accept community or organizational norms as "the proper thing to do." In the Type II socialization, agents adopt and ultimately internalize the norms of the community of which they are a part. Conscious instrumental calculation in this case is replaced by "taken-for-grantedness."[43]

There was evidence of both types of socialization in China's evolving attitude toward the multilateral dispute settlement system at the WTO. Agents instrumental in facilitating the revision of China's belief system regarding multilateral adjudication include diplomats and officials based in Geneva and lawyers and scholars working on various WTO cases and legal issues. Through interaction with foreign delegates (particularly large developing countries such as Brazil and India) and third-party participation in disputes, they realized that members of all sizes and polities commonly practiced the following: using the DSB properly, sometimes even taking advantage of the institutional loopholes of the WTO rules to defend and push for trade interests both at home and abroad. An official who had served on China's WTO delegation and attended training courses in Geneva, upon reflecting on China's membership experience in the first few years, made a very pertinent comment:

> We came to the WTO having a lot of reservations about using the dispute settlement system. We made a lot of commitments in the negotiations leading up to the signing of the [accession] agreement and do not want to be seen as breaking our promises. That's why we only adjudicated when we felt 100% sure that we were going to prevail such as the US Steel case. As we became more familiar with the system by learning and observing actual disputes, however, we found that our reservation was totally unnecessary. Countries as large as the US win and lose WTO cases all the time and it's all part of the game. China needs to be playing the same game.[44]

Evidence for Type II socialization was less clear. Nevertheless, there were signs of gradual internalization of norm in the official discourse on China's position on WTO dispute settlement. In a press conference on trade issues of textile products held on May 5, 2005, Mr. Bo Xilai, then Minister of Commerce, responded to a question about the possibility of resorting to the WTO DSB by saying that while China "reserved the right to take the issue to the WTO, whether China would exercise that right is a decision that needs to be based on a variety of considerations."[45] This point was reiterated in the *White Paper on China's Peaceful Development Road* published by the State Council on December 12, 2005,[46] hinting that China would not actively engage in the WTO dispute settlement system. Incidentally, one month later, the MOFCOM lifted the antidumping duties on Kraft linerboard from the United States, settling a potential dispute bilaterally two months after the United States threatened to bring the issue to the WTO.[47] The same thinking is also reflected in the decision not to challenge the European Union on polyester staple fibers a few months later, as previously discussed.

The official discourse began to change first in the *2006 Government Work Report* released in March which announced that China would "employ the multilateral dispute settlement mechanism to properly handle trade disputes in the future."[48] In January 2008, the minister of commerce, Mr. Chen Deming, addressing the National Working Conference on Commerce and Finance, added that China should "make good use of the multilateral rules for trade disputes . . . strive for the most favorable outcomes for China in responding to WTO disputes and actively challenge policies of other members that damage Chinese interests using the multilateral dispute resolution system."[49]

Such attitudinal shift in the normative orientation was reflected in China's third official WTO case, that is, China's response to the dispute on auto parts. On March 30, 2006, the United States, along with the European Community and Canada, rejected China's formal request for consultation regarding Chinese imposition of higher tariffs on imported auto parts when the value of these parts amounts to 60 percent or more of the cost of a car made in China. In the United States' opinion, although China bound its tariffs for auto parts at rates significantly lower than its tariff bindings for complete vehicles, these measures in effect allowed China to assess a charge on imported auto parts equal to the tariff on complete vehicles, if the imported parts were incorporated in a vehicle that contains imported parts in excess of threshold. Therefore, the complaining countries argued, China violated the national treatment principle in Article III of the GATT.[50]

Initially, it was widely speculated that China would settle the auto part case before full-blown litigation in the DSB, as it did for the semiconductor case and a number of other potential disputes.[51] However, this time, Beijing was determined to go through the entire process of the DSB, from the establishment of a panel all the way to appealing to the Appellate Body. After nearly three years of painstaking legal deliberations, the Appellate Body upheld the panel's finding and concluded that the charge imposed under the measures were inconsistent with Article III of GATT 1994 by according imported auto parts less favorable treatment than like domestic auto parts and requested China to bring its measures into conformity with its obligations under that agreement. Although China expressed regret over the WTO ruling, it informed delegations that it intended to implement the rulings within a reasonable period of time.[52] While this case was dubbed by the press as "China's first major defeat at the WTO,"[53] the MOFCOM seemed unperturbed, claiming that the case was successful in the sense that it bought time for the domestic industry and helped China gain valuable experience in using the WTO dispute settlement system.[54]

This case shares a couple of similarities with the VAT case two years ago. First, in both instances, China was challenged for violations of the National Treatment Principle of the GATT—it was widely believed that the semiconductor case would be an "easy win" for the United States should it escalate to the panel stage.[55] Second, the market size of the semiconductor and the auto parts industries were similar at the time of the challenge. Both industries while developing rapidly were facing strong competition from abroad, and the challenged measures were intended to protect and help them catch up with foreign competitors.

From the functional and economic perspectives, China's different approaches in managing these two cases may be explained by growing legal capacity and the ending of the phase-in period.[56] Nevertheless, the auto case probably would not have materialized if the normative constraint against litigation was as strong as that in the IC VAT case, or even in the more recent Kraft linerboard dispute. Lingering normative concerns for reputation and status might still exist, but could no longer override China's determination to bring its trade disputes to the WTO DSB.

CONCLUSION

In reviewing China's experience with the multilateral dispute settlement system since its accession to the WTO, I showed that, in addition to the lack of legal and administrative capacity, normative constraints, and the concern for reputation and status in particular were crucial in explaining Beijing's absence from WTO litigation in the initial period. Over time, however, a learning and socialization process led to an attitudinal shift in China's normative orientation regarding the use of the WTO dispute settlement procedure. Now that China has overtaken Japan and Germany as the world's second largest economy and second largest exporter, it can be expected that China will continue to be one of the most frequent users of the WTO DSB to further defend its domestic industry and increasingly push for market access abroad.

A number of implications can be drawn from China's evolving role in the WTO DSB. First, the multilateral trade regime as a whole should gain from Beijing's embracement of the dispute settlement procedure. Earlier concerns that increased Chinese engagement with the DSB would overwhelm and cripple the system have been largely debunked by a well-behaved China in the recent cases. On the contrary, should China prefer a bilateral, diplomatic approach to dispute resolution and opt out of the multilateral dispute system, the authority and legitimacy of the DSB would likely suffer from a de facto two-track system.

Second, China's changing view of the multilateral dispute settlement could generate positive externalities for other areas of global and regional governance. At the time of China's accession negotiation, then director-general of the WTO Mike Moore commented that "the most difficult move China needs to make as a new member is the transition from bilateralism to multilateralism,"[57] an apt characterization of China's traditional aversion to multilateral means of dispute resolution such as international arbitration, particularly in the security areas.[58] However, as China becomes more familiar and comfortable with the DSB and its multilateral forum for dispute settlement, similar attitudinal shifts may also occur in other areas that require multilateral efforts such as environmental protection and terrorism, especially if Chinese leaders could internalize the norm of multilateralism.

Finally, the socialization and learning process that prompts the evolution of China's behaviors in the WTO DSB suggests that social and normative (dis)incentives may sometimes be more effective than material (dis)incentives to elicit behavioral change in international institutions, particularly for new members like China. This suggests that western policymakers calling for China to become a responsible stakeholder in the international community may need to first set good examples themselves.

APPENDIX

Table 4.3. WTO Disputes Involving China, 2002–2010

Case ID	Name (DSB Abbreviation)	Start Date	Result
	China as Complainant (Defendant in Bracket)		
DS252	Steel Safeguards (US)	March 26, 2002	AB report adopted
DS368	Preliminary Anti-Dumping and Countervailing Duty Determinations on Coated Free Sheet Paper from China (US)	September 14, 2007	Terminated
DS379	Anti-Dumping and Countervailing Duties (US)	September 19, 2008	Panel report appealed by China
DS392	Poultry (US)	April 17, 2009	Panel report adopted
DS397	Fasteners (EC)	July 31, 2009	Panel report adopted
DS399	Tires (US)	September 14, 2009	Panel report adopted
DS405	Footwear (EC)	February 4, 2010	Panel composed on 5 July 2010
	China as Defendant (Complainant in Bracket)		
DS309	Value-Added Tax on Integrated Circuits (US)	March 18, 2004	Mutually Agreed Solution
DS339	Auto Parts (EC)	March 30, 2006	AB report adopted
DS340	Auto Parts (US)	March 30, 2006	AB report adopted
DS342	Auto Parts (Canada)	April 13, 2006	AB report adopted
DS358	Taxes (US)	February 2, 2007	Settled on December 19, 2007
DS359	Taxes (Mexico)	February 26, 2007	Settled on February 7, 2008
DS362	Intellectual Property Rights (US)	April 10, 2007	Panel report adopted
DS363	Audiovisual Services (US)	April 10, 2007	AB report adopted
DS372	Measures Affecting Financial Information Services and Foreign Financial Information Suppliers (EC)	March 3, 2008	Settled on December 8, 2008
DS373	Measures Affecting Financial Information Services and Foreign Financial Information Suppliers (US)	March 3, 2008	Settled on December 8, 2008

(continued)

Table 4.3. *(Continued)*

Case ID	Name (DSB Abbreviation)	Start Date	Result
DS378	Measures Affecting Financial Information Services and Foreign Financial Information Suppliers (Canada)	June 20, 2008	Settled on December 8, 2008
DS387	Grants, Loans, and Other Incentives (US)	December 19, 2008	In consultation
DS388	Grants, Loans, and Other Incentives (Mexico)	December 19, 2008	In consultation
DS390	Grants, Loans, and Other Incentives	January 19, 2009	In consultation
DS394	Raw Materials Exports (US)	June 23, 2009	Panel composed on March 29, 2010
DS395	Raw Materials Exports (EC)	June 23, 2009	Panel composed on March 29, 2010
DS398	Raw Materials Exports (Mexico)	August 21, 2009	Panel composed on March 29, 2010
DS407	Provisional Anti-Dumping Duties on Certain Iron and Steel Fasteners (EC)	May 7, 2010	Panel report appealed by EC
DS413	Certain Measures Affecting Electronic Payment Service (US)	September 15, 2010	In consultation
DS414	Countervailing and Anti-Dumping Duties on Grain Oriented Flat-rolled Electrical Steel (US)	September 15, 2010	In consultation
DS419	Measures concerning wind power equipment (US)	December 22, 2010	In consultation

NOTES

1. This comment was made by Li Chenggang, deputy director of the MOFCOM's Department of Treaty and Law, at the annual conference of the Shanghai Consulting Center for the WTO in December 2009. See also Naigen Zhang, 2009. *Dispute Settlement of WTO, the Year of China.* Shanghai: People's Press.

2. The appointment of panelists can be blocked once. But after twenty days, either side can ask the director-general to appoint the panel within ten days.

3. See, for instance, Robert E. Hudec, *Essays on the Nature of International Trade Law* (London: Cameron May, 1999); Pretty Elizabeth Kuruvila, "Developing Countries and the GATT/WTO Dispute Settlement Mechanism," *Journal of World Trade* 31 (1997): 171–208; Christina R. Sevilla "Explaining Patterns of GATT/WTO Trade Complaints," Working Paper 98–1 (1998), Weatherhead Center for International Affairs, Harvard University.

4. Constantine Michalopoulos, *Developing Countries in the WTO* (New York: Palgrave, 2001).

5. Roderick Abott, "Are Developing Countries Deterred from Using the WTO Dispute Settlement System?" ECIPE Working Paper No. 01 (2007).

6. See, for instance, Marc Busch and Eric Reinhardt, "Developing Countries and GATT/WTO Dispute Settlement," *Journal of World Trade* 37 (2003); Christina Davis and Sarah Bermeo, "Who Files? Developing Country Participation in WTO Adjudication," *Journal of Politics* 71 (2009): 1033–1049; Moonhawk, Kim, "Costly Procedures: Divergent Effects of Legalization in the GATT/WTO Dispute Settlement Procedures," *International Studies Quarterly* 52 (2008): 657–686.

7. Henrik Horn, Håkan Nordström, and Petros C. Mavroidis, "Is the Use of the WTO Dispute Settlement System Biased?" CEPR Discussion Paper 2340 (1999), Centre for Economic Policy Research.

8. See, for instance, Todd Allee, "Developing Countries and the Initiation of GATT/WTO Disputes" (paper presented at the Annual Meeting of the International Studies Association, Honolulu, 2005); Gregory Shaffer, "How to Make the WTO Dispute Settlement System Work for Developing Countries: Some Proactive Developing Country Strategies," ICTSD Resource Paper 5–I (2003), International Centre for Trade and Sustainable Development; James Smith, "Inequality in International Trade? Developing Countries and Institutional Change in WTO Dispute Settlement, *Review of International Political Economy* 11 (2004): 542–573.

9. Andrew Guzman and Beth Simmons, "Power Plays and Capacity Constraints: The Selection of Defendants in WTO Disputes," *Journal of Legal Studies* 34 (2005): 557–598.

10. Chad Bown, "On the Economic Success of GATT/WTO Dispute Settlement," *The Review of Economics and Statistics* 86 (2004): 811–823; Chad Bown, "Participation in WTO Dispute Settlement: Complainants, Interested Parties and Free Riders," *World Bank Economic Review* 19 (2005): 287–310.

11. See, for instance, Chad Bown, "Developing Countries as Plaintiffs and Defendants in GATT/WTO Trade Disputes," *The World Economy* 27 (2004): 59–80; Marc L. Busch, Eric Reinhardt, and Gregory Shaffer, *Does Legal Capacity Matter? Explaining Dispute Initiation and Antidumping Actions in the WTO* (Geneva: International Centre for Trade and Sustainable Development, 2007); See also Abott 2007; Davis and Bermeo 2009; Horn, Nordström, and Mavroidis 1999; Kim 2008; Shaffer 2003; and Smith 2004.

12. The other seven countries were Armenia, Cambodia, Lithuania, Macedonia, Moldova, Nepal, and Saudi Arabia.

13. The other seven countries were the Dominican Republic (+1), Indonesia (+1), Netherlands (+2), Philippines (+1), El Salvador (+1), Ukraine (+1), and Vietnam (+1). Ukraine and Vietnam were new members during this period.

14. Sylvia Ostry, 2001. "WTO Membership for China: To Be and Not to Be: Is that the Answer?" in *The State of Economics in Canada: Festschrift in Honour of David Slater*, ed. Patrick Grady and Andrew Sharpe (McGill, Canada: Queen's University Press, 2001), 263.

15. Henry Gao, "Aggressive Legalism: The East Asian Experience and Lessons for China," in *China's Participation in the WTO*, ed. Henry Gao and Don Lewis (London: Cameron May, 2005).

16. Vietnam joined the WTO on January 11, 2007 and requested for consultation with the United States on February 1, 2010, regarding its antidumping measures on certain shrimp from Vietnam. A panel was subsequently established on July 26, 2010.

17. Henry Gao, "Taming the Dragon: China's Experience in the WTO Dispute Settlement System," *Legal Issues of Economic Integration* 34 (2007): 369–392.

18. A number of scholars (e.g., Bown 2005; Busch and Reinhardt 2006; Davis and Bermeo 2009) have highlighted third-party participation as a cheap solution to the capacity constraint problem faced by developing countries. China's first participation as an interested third party occurred on November 18, 1997, for DS108, United States of America—Tax Treatment for "Foreign Sales Corporations."

19. *Zhongguo Qiye Bao*, March 29, 2005.

20. Author's interview, December 2010.

21. Alexander Wendt, "Collective Identity Formation and the International State," *American Political Science Review* 88 (1994): 384–397.

22. Alastair Iain Johnston, *Social States: China in International Institutions 1980–2000* (Princeton, NJ: Princeton University Press, 2008).

23. WTO DS309, China—Value-Added Tax on Integrated Circuits, http://www.wto .org/english/tratop_e/dispu_e/cases_e/ds309_e.htm. For a more detailed narration of the case background and the negotiation process, see Liang (2007).

24. Article III of the GATT requires WTO members to apply the same tax treatment to imports as they do to domestic products.

25. USTR Press Release March 18, 2004. Accessed March 10, 2011, http://www.ustr.gov/ Document_Library/Press_Releases/2004/March/US_Files_WTO_Case_Against_China_ Over_Discriminatory_Taxes_That_Hurt_US_Exports.html.

26. *People's Daily*, March 20, 2004.

27. Ibid.

28. WTO DS309.

29. Rachel Brewster, "Shadow Unilateralism: Enforcing International Trade Law at the WTO," *University of Pennsylvania Journal of International Economic Law* 30 (2009): 1133–1147.

30. Wei Liang, "China's WTO Commitment Compliance: A Case Study of the US-China Semiconductor Trade Dispute," in *China's Foreign Trade Policy: The New Constituencies*, ed. Ka Zeng and Andrew Mertha (London: Routledge, 2007).

31. Ibid., footnote 41.

32. Neil Diamant, "Conflict and Conflict Resolution in China beyond Mediation-Centered Approaches," *Journal of Conflict Resolution* 44 (2000): 523–546.

33. Gao 2007.

34. Author's interview, December 2010.

35. Johnston 2008.

36. Jeffrey Checkel, "International Institutions and Socialization in Europe," *International Organization* 59 (2005).

37. Xiaojun Li, "Social Rewards and Socialization Effects: An Alternative Explanation to the Motivation behind China's Participation in International Institutions," *Chinese Journal of International Politics* 3 (2009): 347–377.

38. Checkel 2005, 804.

39. Martha Finnemore, *National Interest and International Society* (Ithaca, NY: Cornell University Press, 1996).

40. David Bearce and Stacy Bondanella, "Intergovernmental Organizations, Socialization, and Member-State Interest Convergence," *International Organization* 61 (2007): 703–733.

41. Johnston 2008.

42. Checkel 2005, 805.

43. Checkel 2005, 804–805.

44. Author's interview, December 2010.

45. Xinhua News, May 30, 2005. http://news.xinhuanet.com/fortune/2005–05/30/content_3021731.htm.

46. http://www.china.org.cn/english/2005/Dec/152669.htm.

47. Gao 2007.

48. Government Work Report, 2006. http://www.chinadaily.com.cn/china/2006–03/15/content_538753.htm.

49. http://chendeming.mofcom.gov.cn/aarticle/speeches/200801/20080105345233.html.

50. WTO DS340. China—Measures Affecting Imports of Automobile Parts. http://www.wto.org/english/tratop_e/dispu_e/cases_e/ds340_e.htm.

51. Gary Hufbauer, Yee Wong, and Ketki Sheth, *US-China Trade Disputes: Rising Tide, Rising Stakes* (Peterson Institute for International Economics: Policy Analyses in International Economics 78, 2006).

52. WTO news, "China informs DSB of Its Intention Concerning Implementation of Auto Parts Rulings," February 11, 2009.

53. See, for instance, the feature report at Sina. http://auto.sina.com.cn/z/wtolbj/index.shtml.

54. Ibid.

55. Hufbauer et al. 2006.

56. Xiaowen Zhang, "China's Experience in the WTO Dispute Settlement System as Defendant—A Close Examination of the *Auto Parts* Case" (paper presented at the annual meeting of the International Studies Association, New York City, 2009).

57. Da Chen, "First Hand Experience with the WTO Negotiation: Who Can Serve the WTO?," *Beijing Youth Daily*, September 23, 2001.

58. Keyuan Zou, *China's Legal Reform: Towards the Rule of Law* (Leiden, the Netherlands: Martinus Nijhoff Publishers, 2006), 245.

5

The Politics and Economics of the Renminbi-Dollar Relationship

Yale H. Ferguson

A prominent feature of present-day discourse regarding the world economy in such international institutions as the G8, G20, and IMF is the need to correct serious "imbalances." Simply stated, the main idea is that all major economies would benefit if those who typically have unusual trade surpluses and foreign currency reserves (e.g., China) would increase imports and invest more abroad, while those with persistent trade deficits (e.g., the United States) would increase exports and spend less profligately on imports. In effect, the call to address imbalances is a plea for a greater measure of economic global governance, however reluctant the governments of leading states are to embrace that term. What is missing, of course—as in so many issue-areas of international affairs—is any effective mechanism of an institutional mechanism for the effective exercise of global governance beyond that of voluntary compliance by sovereign nation-states, which is almost always difficult to achieve in concert. Yet, as this chapter focusing on the renminbi-US dollar relationship demonstrates, even governments like China that are super-sensitive about guarding their sovereign autonomy are buffeted by larger forces in the world economy that are substantially beyond their control and may find themselves uncomfortably pressured by international criticism. Moreover, global issues like monetary imbalances *and* governments' calculations of "self-interest" in responding to them *both* continue to evolve. Thus, a measure of "governance" or "order" can arise from what might otherwise appear to be "anarchy" in the global system.[1]

CHIMERICA: A FAILED MARRIAGE

Correcting imbalances has not always been the watchword in global economic discourse. In February 2007, two prominent economic historians, Niall Ferguson

(Harvard) and Moritz Schularick (Free University in Berlin) invented the term "Chimerica" to describe the "combination" of the Chinese and United States economies, which then in their view "had become the key driver of the global economy."[2] Subsequently in his 2008 best-selling book *The Ascent of Money*[3] Ferguson famously proclaimed, "Welcome to the wonderful dual country of 'Chimerica'—China plus America." As he and Schularick explained, the symbiotic relationship appeared at the time "like a marriage made in heaven." "Chimerica accounted for around 13 percent of the world's land surface, a quarter of its population, more than a third of its domestic product, and around two fifths of global economic growth from 1998 to 2007"[4]

Chimerica—"an improbable financial marriage between the world's sole superpower and its most likely future rival"[5]—seemed at first to have important advantages for both sides. The relationship had been developing steadily for some years. China attracted foreign direct investment from the United States and elsewhere, although most of the investment that funded that country's remarkable economic growth came from domestic savings as well as the Chinese overseas diaspora.[6] Americans acquired a growing appetite for inexpensive Chinese goods, and US manufacturing firms enjoyed lower labor costs by outsourcing to China. The People's Bank of China bought billions of dollars of United States bonds and thus helped keep US interest rates down. China achieved unprecedented export-led development and entered the World Trade Organization in 2001, while the United States indulged in historic levels of over-consumption. China quadrupled its GNP after 2000, increased exports by a factor of five, imported western technology, and created tens of millions of manufacturing jobs for its rural poor. Meanwhile, the United States spent 45 percent more than its total national income, and Chinese imports constituted about a third of that over-consumption.[7] In fact, argued Ferguson, "Chimerica . . . was the underlying cause of the surge in bank lending, bond issuance and new derivative contracts that Planet Finance witnessed after 2000."[8] That, in turn, fed a housing bubble and encouraged wildly irresponsible financial speculation.

From the outset, the Chimerica marriage was fundamentally, as Ferguson notes, a "marriage between a saver and a spender" and thus "always likely to end in tears."[9] If Americans were profligate, Chinese policies were resulting in increasingly severe economic imbalances. China devalued its currency in 1994 and welcomed FDI, albeit with major restrictions. As exports rapidly increased, so did China's current account surplus, to nearly $400 billion by the end of 2008. China consistently bought dollars to keep the value of its currency down and promote the competitiveness of Chinese exports. In the beginning, accumulating more and more dollar-denominated securities in the reserves of the People's Bank of China and the State Agency for Foreign Exchange (SAFE) also might have seemed like a prudent hedge against the volatile capital outflows experienced by many other countries during the 1997–1998 Asian financial crisis. In due course, however, it became evident to most observers that China's giant foreign currency reserves—$2.4 trillion by the end of 2009, equivalent to more than 50 percent of China's annual output—far exceeded the dictates of simple prudence.[10] By March 2011 China's reserves stood at over $3 trillion, equivalent to around $2,250 per head for the entire population of China.[11]

The global financial collapse that hit in mid-2008 forced all affected countries, not least the United States, to focus in on all factors affecting their position in the world economy. Especially with the benefit of hindsight, it became obvious that China had been following and was continuing to pursue neo-mercantilist policies. China for some years had been blatantly exploiting the (relatively) free trade global environment symbolized by the WTO regime while behaving only selectively, as suited its perceived interests, like free-market country. As Ferguson explains, "In a standard macroeconomic model, exchange rate intervention should lead to monetary expansion, which in turn drives up domestic prices, nullifying the real effect of intervention. China's financial system, however, is owned and managed by the government"[12] Until external pressures fairly recently began to mount, China only allowed its currency to appreciate at close to an annualized rate of 10 percent during the years 2005–2008, and then firmly pegged the exchange rate at 6.83 RMB to the US dollar. Partly for that reason, while the global financial crisis and subsequent deep recession afflicted much of the world, China weathered most of the storm and its trade surpluses and reserves continued to mount. Independent analysts, depending on the particular method they adopted, calculated the extent of the renminbi's undervaluation to be as high as 50 percent.[13]

Ferguson and Schularick coined the term Chimerica to combine the two country names, but also to capture their belief that "this relationship was a chimera—a monstrous hybrid like the part-lion, part-goat, part-snake of legend." As the global financial crisis worsened, the relationship appeared to have been really more of a "chimera" (dictionary definition: "something totally unrealistic or impractical"). In any event, the two analysts suggested, "Now we may be witnessing the death throes of the monster." The question facing policy-makers seemed to be "whether to slay it or try to keep it alive."[14] Returning to the metaphor of marriage, the question was now whether there would be an "amicable divorce" or a bitter "currency war."[15]

POTENTIAL CURRENCY WARS AND
CONFLICT MANAGEMENT: 2004–MID 2011

A US law first enacted in 1988 still requires the US Treasury Department to report to Congress twice annually on international economic conditions and exchange-rate policies, with particular attention to which countries might be unfairly manipulating their currency. The treasury was to engage in direct talks with any offending country and also seek redress through the International Monetary Fund (IMF). In fact, until recently, the last country labeled a currency manipulator was China in 1994, although no major consequences then ensued.

Debate about China's exchange rate arose yet again in the US Senate in 2004, when the US trade deficit with China reached the largest amount that had ever been recorded with a single country. Senators Charles Schumer (D-NY) and Lindsey Graham (R-SC) introduced legislation that would have imposed a 27.5 percent tariff on Chinese goods. The measure became less compelling when China allowed the renminbi to appreciate from 2005–2008. However, in 2007 two bipartisan bills, together foreshadowing later proposals, were introduced in the Senate; neither advanced to passage. One (Schumer-Graham) would have enabled the Commerce Department to apply antidumping laws to currency manipulators. The second, co-sponsored by senators Debbie Stabenow (D-MI), Sherrod Brown (D-OH), and Olympia Snowe (R-ME), would have had Commerce apply countervailing duties.

While the global financial system remained on the verge of complete collapse in late 2008 and early 2009, the primary concern of most market-economy policymakers was halting the downward spiral, restoring investor and consumer confidence, stimulating flagging economies, and perhaps beginning to fashion reform measures to avoid a repeat crisis both in the near and longer-term. The United States, along with most of the world, was experiencing the most severe recession since the Great Depression of the 1930s. World trade contracted over 12 percent. Especially given fierce domestic partisan divisions, the George W. Bush and Barack Obama administrations were in remarkably one accord about policies with regard to the financial crisis. To the extent that China factored into their initial thinking, it was mainly a hope that that country's previously rising prosperity might escape the worst of the turmoil and that China and others less-affected might help to resuscitate the global economy. China, on the other hand, was concerned not only about reduced demand for its exports but also about the future of its huge investment in US debt. In fact, the dollar briefly spiked upward in value, reflecting its traditional role as a haven currency in the midst of widespread uncertainty. Soon, however, the increasing US budget deficit and its potential inflationary effects (which did not materialize) brought the dollar back into its more traditional relationships to the British pound, Euro, and Japanese Yen.

After Obama took office in mid-January 2009, there was already substantial hope that global financial panic had been averted and—if a second sharp downturn could be avoided—that gradual recovery might be anticipated. Attention then shifted to factors hindering US recovery and especially those that might be contributing to an unemployment rate of nearly 10 percent. The spotlight began to fall on China's huge dollar reserves and now once-again fixed exchange rate. In June 2009 senators Schumer, Brown, Graham, and John Rockefeller (D-WV) introduced the Currency Exchange Rate Oversight Reform Act of 2009, echoing the 2007 Schumer-Graham bill. Ferguson and Schularick began to write about serious strains in the Chimerica relationship in November 2009. They expressed concern that there were early signs of "defensive moves" by other countries, recalling the "currency games" that occurred during the disastrous 1930s: Brazil had recently imposed a "hot money" tax to curb volatile exit flows of foreign investment, and several Asian countries had intervened to weaken their currencies against the dollar.[16] That same month President Obama's first state visit to China ended with little progress on outstanding issues, including sanctions to deter the Iranian nuclear program. The year 2009 ended with an acrimonious mid-December climate change meeting in Copenhagen, when China found itself supported by a number of other developing countries and successfully resisted US and other developed-country demands for more stringent emissions control measures.

Tensions in US-China relations concerning a wide range of problems markedly increased during the first three months of 2010. On January 29 Beijing denounced the Obama administration's decision to allow $6.4 billion sales of sophisticated arms to Taiwan, suspended US-China military cooperation (which had only been restored the previous February), cancelled a planned February visit of the US aircraft USS Nimitz to Hong Kong, and threatened to impose sanctions against US companies participating in the sales. On February 18 China protested President Obama's relatively low-key meeting with the Dalai Lama. On March 23 a long-simmering dispute between the Internet company Google and the Chinese government dramatically worsened when Google announced it would no longer allow censorship of its search engine and was planning to pull its operations out of China.

Meanwhile, the continuing matter of China's exchange rate seemed to gain new momentum. Part of the context was a gradual emphasis on the woeful unemployment statistic in the run-up to the November mid-term congressional races and a looming April 15 deadline for a new Treasury Department report on currency manipulators. On January 29 Senior Fellow John Williamson of the highly respected center-left Peterson Institute of International Economics issued a widely noted assessment that "the renminbi was about 25 percent undervalued in effective terms and about 40 percent in bilateral terms vis-à-vis the US dollar, so very substantially undervalued." Williamson also bluntly commented on China's position: "There has been a lot of pressure, and the Chinese are being extremely obstinate about it; they regard the exchange rate of the renmibi as their own business and nobody else's. I think that is an untenable position when exchange rates inherently are the relationship between two currencies, and so no one country has the right to regard its exchange rates as only its business. It's inherently an international question, and the Chinese are not accepting that. But nobody is prepared to warn them to change."[17]

China's Premier Wen Jiabao sharply defended his country's currency and trade policies in a Beijing news conference on March 14. He decried foreign "finger-pointing" at China and suggested it was time for the United States to get its own financial house in order, so as to "reassure investors." He said what he didn't understand "is the practice of depreciating one's own currency and attempting to force other countries to appreciate their own currencies, just for the purpose of increasing their own exports." That, he insisted, was a form of trade protectionism. That same day, a well-known Chinese economist, Bai Chong-En of Tsinghau University, commented in an interview that the renminbi was not seriously undervalued and cautioned that criticism of China would not be productive: "The greater the outside pressure, the more difficult it is for the Chinese government to raise the exchange rate, and the more difficult it is for the Chinese people to accept a revaluation of the Chinese currency. People don't like to be forced to change things. They have to be willing to do it."[18]

A week later Chinese minister of commerce Chen Deming further complained that the US government's "obsession" with China's exchange rate could not be taken seriously until the United States stopped blocking exports of such high-tech products as supercomputers and satellites to China. "The reason our trade balance with the United States is skewed" is that the United States "has strict export controls to China." China could not be expected simply to do without affected goods. "We're a nation of 1.3 billion people. We graduated 7 million university students a year. We'll either make it ourselves or buy it from somewhere else." Moreover, he warned, it would be US companies, accounting for 60 percent of US exports to China, that would suffer the most in any US-China "trade war." "You're not going to get [the Chinese people] to change by insulting them." "Could it be related to upcoming elections. I don't know. Because economically it makes no sense." Chen noted that his deputy Zhong Shan would soon be arriving in Washington for conversations with the Department of Commerce and the office of the US Trade Representative. He advised that both sides should "stay cool" and "sit down and talk."[19]

While China was thus stridently expressing its own impatience and intransigence, pressures in the United States continued to mount. On March 15, the *New York Times* respected columnist, Nobel Prize–winning Keynesian economist, Paul Krugman, reacted to Mr. Wen's press conference by insisting, "something must be done." The "US Treasury Department must stop fudging and obfuscating" and plainly declare that China is engaging in currency manipulation, setting the stage for special import duties on Chinese goods of about 25 percent. He downplayed any fears that China might retaliate by "dumping its dollar assets," suggesting that the US Federal Reserve could cushion any effect on long-term interest rates by buying more long-term bonds. Also, in his view, any resulting decline in the US dollar would only cause China huge losses on its dollar holdings and help US exports. "America has China over a barrel, not the other way around." Krugman exhorted, "It's time to take a stand."[20]

Two days after Mr. Wen's rejection of calls for reform, as its sponsors pointedly noted, a bipartisan group of fourteen senators (including Republicans Graham, Samuel Brownbeck [D-KS], and Snowe proposed the Currency Exchange Rate Reform Act of 2010. This bill combined two earlier proposals and provided both for levying tariffs against an offending country's exports and for a ban on its companies receiving any US government contracts. Senator Schumer stated, "We are sending a message to the Chinese government: if you refuse to play by the same rules as everyone else, we will force you to. China's currency manipulation would be unacceptable even in good economic times. At a time of 10 percent unemployment, we simply will not stand for it. There is no bigger step we can take to promote U.S. job creation, particularly in the manufacturing sector, than to confront China's currency manipulation. This is not about China bashing; it's about defending the United States."[21]

On March 24, Ferguson gave his testimony on "The End of Chimerica" to the House Committee on Ways and Means. He readily acknowledged that China had pegged its currency "at a strongly undervalued rate" and urged the US Treasury to cite China for "currency manipulation" in its April 15 report. Ferguson also observed that some critics of China had been proposing retaliatory tariffs and others "point to the effectiveness of the import surcharge imposed by the Nixon administration in 1971 which encouraged the Germans and Japanese to revalue their currencies upwards against the dollar." Moreover, "the threat of tariffs was sufficient to prompt Chinese revaluation in 2005." However, Ferguson argued, the "situation is very different today," given increased calls for protectionism at a time of "such economic fragility," the rising threat of "a race to the bottom among fiat currencies" ("currency wars"), and Beijing's "more combative mood" now that the global financial crisis had taken "the shine off the 'Washington Consensus.'" Hence, in his opinion, the best course of action was to address the problem on a multilateral basis at the G20.

So matters stood in April 2010 when both the United States and China backed away from immediate confrontation. President Obama had an hour-long telephone conversation with President Hu Jintao in which they discussed outstanding issues, including Washington's desire for Chinese cooperation in dealing with Iran and North Korea. On April 2, the Obama administration announced that it would defer the Treasury report until well after President Hu Jintao's visit to Washington to attend a summit on nuclear security and a possible extension of UN sanctions against Iran. When President Obama met personally with him on April 12, President Hu Jintao reportedly promised at least some adjustment in the renminbi peg to the dollar in the relatively near future. A *New York Times* editorial supported the administration's decision to postpone the Treasury report and suggested that the next G20 meeting in Toronto would offer an opportunity to continue currency negotiations. Wrote the editorialist, "The Chinese bureaucracy is clearly split. Central bank officials have been arguing for some time that a stronger currency would help them combat rising inflation. The Commerce Ministry is adamantly opposed. Ministry officials latched on the fact that China recorded its first monthly trade deficit in six years in March."[22]

On June 19, a week before the Toronto G20 meeting, the Chinese central bank finally announced an important, if tentative, shift in policy. It pledged to introduce a more "flexible" exchange-rate policy. A subsequent statement from the bank warned that a substantial appreciation in the renminbi was "not in China's interest" and that the rate would remain "basically stable."[23] The actual exchange rate initially rose only about half a percentage point, and critics remained highly skeptical. Krugman, for example, termed the Chinese move the "renminbi runaround" and scoffed that "all indications are that watching the future movement of the renminbi will be like watching paint dry." He predicted a rise of about 2 percent by the end of the year, which in his opinion was "basically a joke."[24]

In fact, the summer of 2010 was generally a troubled one. The Toronto G20 concerned itself mainly with competing financial recovery strategies and reforms and unpleasant clashes with local protestors. China began to claim an extension of its sovereignty over the South China Sea. There were widespread expressions of concern from China's neighbors, including Japan, and the United States both about lingering territorial disputes in the region and an increase in China's military capabilities and assertiveness. South Korea insisted that it had established proof that North Korea had torpedoed its naval vessel the previous May, and, to China's discomfort, the United States held military exercises with the South Koreans off the Korean peninsula. The United States filed two WTO cases against China for its duties on US steel and discrimination against US suppliers of electronic payment services. In early August came the news that China's July trade surplus had risen to an all-time high of $28.7 billion, more than the record $27.9 billion in October 2008.

That announcement and the nearing mid-term congressional elections set the stage for renewed confrontation in the US-China bilateral relationship, although there were still some efforts to defuse the situation. Lawrence Summers, then the director of the National Economic Council, and Thomas Donilon, Deputy National Security Adviser, had quiet talks with President Hu Jintao and other Chinese officials, but made little visible progress on key issues. On September 14 the conservative American Enterprise Institute and Heritage Foundation held a high-profile public event in which AEI China economic experts, Walter Loman and Phillip Levy, Linda Manghetti of the Emergency Committee for American Trade (ECAT), and Heritage Foundation economist Derek Scissors all strongly cautioned against precipitous congressional legislative action on the China front. The video of the seminar is well worth viewing as an expression of the opinions of many large US companies (e.g., in ECAT) with business interests in China.[25] The speakers argued that China's currency was slowly on the rise and that, in any event, the exchange rate has minimal actual impact on U.S. unemployment. China's losses from a higher renminbi would be a gain in competitiveness for even lower-wage countries in Southeast Asia, and few jobs would return to the US economy. China does not respond well to threats from the United States, nor are countervailing duties a legal remedy for currency imbalances under current WTO rules. Those rules were not in place in 1971 when the Nixon administration so successfully used a tariff surcharge as a bargaining tool. Were the United States to levy new tariffs on currency grounds, China would complain to the WTO, perhaps rightly label the United States a trade offender, and retaliate by curbing US exports to China. In fact, far worse than the currency matter are Chinese practices detrimental to foreign business investment, such as limitations on the economic sectors in which foreign companies can operate, preferences and subsidies given to domestic firms, lack of protection for intellectual property, and so on. These and other complaints can be best addressed in multilateral forums and by insisting that China live up to its WTO accession agreement to become a full-fledged "market economy."

Not surprisingly, US Treasury Secretary Timothy Geithner faced difficult questioning from the Senate Banking Committee on September 16 about China's trade and finance policies, and Geithner responded with uncharacteristic frankness. Regarding the renminbi, he said, "the pace of appreciation has been too slow and the extent of appreciation too limited." His department "will take China's actions into account as we prepare the next Foreign Exchange Report," due October 15. He also complained about China's support for "indigenous innovation," "rampant" and "unacceptable" violations of intellectual property rights, and pending requirement that only certain accredited products could be sold to the Chinese government. Geithner promised the United States would work to correct these problems through the G20 and International Monetary Fund and not hesitate to use the full set of trade remedies available in the WTO. Indeed, the United States was also at present "reviewing carefully" a complaint by the United Steelworkers Union about various Chinese policies in the renewable energy sector. The senators greeted Secretary Geithner's testimony with considerable skepticism. Committee Chair Senator Christopher J. Dodd (D-CN) commented: "I've listened to every administration, Democrats and Republicans, from Ronald Reagan to the current administration, say virtually the same thing." "And China does basically whatever it wants, while we grow weaker and they grow stronger." "It's clearly time for a change in strategy."[26]

When major legislative action on US-China currency finally came, it was not from the Senate but the House of Representatives, which on September 29 (just before adjournment for final electoral campaigning) voted by an overwhelming bipartisan margin of 348–79 to authorize import duties against a country having a substantially undervalued currency. Despite the preelection context, the vote precipitated warnings from Brazil's finance minister, Guido Mantega, about a looming "currency war," echoed by the IMF managing director Dominique Strauss-Kahn. The warning had some credibility since several governments including Brazil, Japan, South Korea, and Switzerland had all recently intervened or were in the process of doing so to keep their currencies from appreciating. The Institute of International Finance, representing more than 420 of the world's prominent bank and finance houses, called for a new currency pact to help rebalance the global economy.[27]

Despite all the furor, very little of substance happened when the world's financial leaders gathered in Washington on October 9 for the annual meetings of the IMF and World Bank. The meeting produced a weak pledge to "work toward a more balanced pattern of global growth, recognizing the responsibilities of surplus and deficit countries" and to "address the challenges of large and volatile capital movements, which can be disruptive." Strauss-Kahn remarked, "The language is ineffective. The language is not going to change things. Policies have to be adopted." If anything, the meeting revealed growing recognition of a structural shift n the global economy and exposed a widening rift between the European and US positions. One European official commented, "We have come to the end of a model where seven advanced economies can make decisions for the world without the emerging countries. Like it or not, we simple have to accept it." France's Minister of Finance Christine Lagarde said, "It's not helpful to use bellicose statements when it comes to currency or trade."[28]

Attention in mid-October shifted briefly to other concerns in the US-China relationship—Chinese war games with the Australians in the Yellow Sea, a relatively mild exchange over South China Sea disputes between US Defense Secretary Robert Gates and Beijing's delegation at a forum of Asian defense ministers in Hanoi, and the highly embarrassing (for China) announcement from Oslo that the Nobel Committee had selected jailed dissident Liu Xiaobo to be the recipient of the Nobel Peace Prize. Then it was back to a focus on currency issues, symbolized by *The Economist's* choice of "Currency Wars" for the cover of its October 16–22 issue. The US Trade representative Ron Kirk agreed to investigate the United Steelworkers complaint that China had violated WTO rules by subsidizing its manufacturers of clean energy products like wind and solar devices, advanced batteries, and energy-efficient vehicles.[29] September economic statistics again were dramatic: China reported a $16.9 billion monthly trade surplus, with exports up 25 percent and imports 24 percent. Foreign exchange reserves climbed $194 billion to a record $2.65 trillion, still by far the largest reserve holdings in the world. The US trade deficit with China stood at 20.6 percent above the 2009 rate. However, on October 15 the Treasury Department again delayed its report on currency manipulators, looking ahead to the November G20 meeting in Seoul.

As it happened, the Seoul G20 meeting November 11–12 proved to be less about Chinese policy than developments in the United States. Although it was not officially on the discussion agenda, the Obama administration had clearly suffered major reversals in the November 3 midterm congressional elections, losing control of the House of Representatives and having its already slim majority further eroded in the Senate. The assessment of most observers was that the new Congress would be more sensitive to business fears about the possible consequences of tough measures against China—and possibly deadlocked on practically everything anyway. The media was beginning to make much of the contrast between China's "rise"—along with that of other leading developing countries like Brazil and Turkey—and the "decline" of a debt-saddled, politically paralyzed United States, as well as troubles with sovereign debt and sluggishness in much of the Euro zone.

Most economic discussion at the G20 was about the US Federal Reserve's November 3 announcement that it would be pursuing a second round of "quantitative easing" (soon dubbed QE2), including the purchase of $600 billion of Treasury securities by the end of the second quarter 2011. Although Fed policymakers vigorously denied any intent beyond promoting a stronger recovery,[30] China and others criticized the move as a blatant attempt to drive down the value of the US dollar that could also have dangerous inflationary consequences. (It might be noted that by February 18, 2011, US inflation remained minimal, while the dollar was only very slightly weaker against the British pound and Japanese yen and was actually stronger against the Euro). In any event, the G20's pronouncement related to currency was yet again bland, mentioning only the goal of "moving toward more market-determined exchange rates systems, enhancing exchange rate flexibility to reflect underlying economic fundamentals, and refraining from competitive devaluation."[31]

Early in January 2011, free-market-oriented Chile and Peru joined Brazil in intervening to prevent appreciation of their respective currencies. Continuing as finance minister under Brazil's new president Dilma Rousseff, Mantega warned that what had begun as a currency war was rapidly "turning into a trade war." He singled out both the United States and China for criticism and said Brazil would be raising the issue at the WTO. There were also upward spikes in the Australian dollar and the Swiss franc as investors moved funds from the United States and Europe.[32]

However, before, during, and after President Hu Jintao's mid-January visit to Washington, there were subtle signs of changes in economic fundamentals and more conciliatory postures on both sides of the relationship. For some time in China there were concerns about labor shortages and strikes—and associated rising labor costs—but the most recent fear has been rampant inflation and general "overheating" of the economy. Statistics released in January indicated that year-to-November consumer prices had risen 5.1 percent, the fastest increase for twenty-eight months, offering a striking contrast to deflationary tendencies the previous year.[33] Subsequent figures showed that the national economy grew 10.3 percent in 2010 and the inflation rate dropped to 4.6 in December.[34] The inflation figure for January, based on a somewhat different index, was 4.9 percent. Food prices rose but also did the cost of many other goods and services.[35] Another significant statistic was China's much lower trade surplus in December, $13.1 billion compared with $22.9 billion in November. The $154.2 billion value of China's total trade was a record high, but in December imports grew 25.6 percent and exports only 17.9 percent.[36] The US December trade gap with China declined to $20.7 billion in December from $25.6 billion in November.[37]China's trade surplus in January fell to a nine-month low of $6.5 billion; exports increased 38 percent over the previous January, while imports were up 51 percent.

There were other interesting economic trends. At the end of 2010 China replaced Japan as the world's number two economy, valued at $5.88 trillion versus Japan's 5.47 trillion.[38] China and Russia were the main sellers of US Treasury paper in November, moves analysts attributed to "post QE2 profit-taking" when bond yields rose. China's portfolio shrank to $895.6 billion.[39] Then in February it was revealed that, only halfway through its latest round of quantitative easing, the US Federal Reserve's $1108 billion had surpassed China in its holdings of Treasuries. China continued to hold $896 billion, while Japan was a close third with $877 billion.[40]In a small but noteworthy step toward the renminbi's becoming a global currency, Cheung Kong Holdings, a large property company owned by a Hong Kong businessman, became the territory's first renminbi-denominated public offering.[41] China has also been loosening some of its tight currency controls. The People's Bank of China announced that Chinese companies may soon be allowed to use domestic currency to buy foreign assets and companies. Foreigners are currently permitted to hold deposits in renminbi and buy and sell goods.[42] US companies like McDonald's and Caterpillar have been able to finance China projects by selling renminbi-denominated bonds in Hong Kong. Some cross-border trades with Russia, Vietnam, and Thailand now take place using the Chinese currency. China has even allowed its New York branch of the Bank of China to accept deposits in renminbi,[43] and Wall Street giants Goldman Sachs and Morgan Stanley have both announced their own plans for renminbi-denominated private equity funds.[44]

On January 12, 2011, shortly before President Hu Jintao's Washington visit, US Treasury Secretary Geithner gave a well-publicized speech at Johns Hopkins School for Advanced International Studies (SAIS) on "The Path Ahead for the U.S.-China Economic Relationship."[45] According to *New York Times* reporters in the audience, Geithner "hinted that jockeying for power and a coming leadership transition have degraded China's ability to set consistent policies."[46] (In fact, at about this same time, US Defense Secretary Gates was meeting in Beijing with President Hu Jintao, who was apparently unaware that the Chinese air force had just conducted a test of a stealth fighter.) In any event, Geithner's address stands as a sophisticated analysis of Chinese policies, politics, strengths, and constraints—and a summary of shifting US thinking on the exchange rate issue. Geithner stated that China's currency indeed did remain "substantially undervalued," which he argued "is not a tenable policy for China or for the world economy." "If China does not allow the currency to appreciate more rapidly, it will run the risk of seeing domestic inflation accelerate and face greater risk of a damaging rise in asset prices, both of which will threaten future growth. And sustaining an undervalued currency will undermine China's own efforts to rebalance growth toward domestic consumption and higher-value-added production." Then in what would prove to be an especially important comment, Geithner said, although the renmibi still needed to appreciate faster, it was now doing so at "about 6 percent a year in nominal terms, but significantly faster in real terms because inflation in China is much higher than in the United States."

In the end, President Hu Jintao's actual visit was almost an anti-climax. Talks were generally cordial and low-key. At their joint press conference, President Obama urged the Chinese to end discrimination against US companies, adopt a market-oriented currency, and pay more respect to human rights, including in Tibet. Mr. Hu stressed China's desire for close ties with the United States based on "mutual respect,"[47] and asserted at a separate meeting with a business audience that Chinese imports had helped create 14 million jobs around the world.[48] On Capitol Hill Senator Brown and others reintroduced familiar legislation to allow the United States to restrict imports from countries on grounds of currency misalignment, but with even less chance of eventual passage into law than in previous years. Dave Camp, the new Republican chair of the House Ways and Means Committee, voted for a resolution backing a similar bill in the House, but indicated that neither he nor the Republican leadership regarded currency legislation as "a priority."[49] The *Financial Times* headline "Renminbi Issue Is Put on the Back Burner"[50] seemed to capture the situation precisely. Then late on Friday afternoon February 4, the US Treasury quietly issued its long-postponed report, declining to label China a currency manipulator. Echoing Geithner's earlier assessment, the report stated that, factoring in inflation, the renminbi's real exchange rate was appreciating at an annualized rate of about 10 percent.[51]

There remained the February 18–19 G20 meeting in Paris. In the days before the meeting, the US Fed upgraded its outlook for US economic growth, but acknowledged that high unemployment could be expected for a lengthy period. Secretary Geithner indicated his hopes for more pressure on China to allow the renminbi to accelerate at a faster pace and flew to Brazil to try gain support for that position.[52] Brazil, for its part, called for an entirely new monetary system, including expanded use of special drawing rights from the IMF—with both China's renminbi and the Brazilian real in the SDR basket mix, along with the US dollar, Euro, Yen, and British pound. Fred Bergsten, director of the Peterson Institute for International Economics, argued for a similar system that would emphasize three "global currencies"—the US dollar, Euro, and China's renminbi. All too predictably, the Paris G20 discussed nothing so sweeping, limiting itself largely to toning down US proposals for clear market-oriented targets for both currencies and size of reserves. At the close, the delegates were only willing to promise future efforts to draw up "indicative guidelines."[53] Two months later, this initiative reduced to asking the IMF to look at levels of public debt and budget deficits as well as external balances and make recommendations in the light of historical norms and economic theory.[54]

EPILOGUE

For a brief period in mid-2011, the dollar/renminbi issue thus seemed at last to be evolving into a somewhat less contentious one in the US-China bilateral relationship. Prior to the Eurozone sovereign debt crisis, China appeared to be diversifying its reserve holdings by buying more European government (primarily German) debt than US dollar assets, the Chinese government's fiscal stimulus policy gave a modest boost to imports, and the renminbi continued its gradual rise.[55] Then the political context for global monetary policies shifted yet again. The Eurozone debt situation suddenly escalated, Europe appealed to China for urgent investment support, and Wen Jiabao responded with firm warnings that Europe must first get its own financial house in order by addressing key countries' deficit spending.[56] Meanwhile, the WTO upheld US unilateral action in blocking China tire imports. US Federal Reserve Chairman Ben Bernanke criticized the undervaluation of the renminbi in a high-profile public address, and the Senate passed the long-pending currency bill threatening China with retaliatory tariffs by a comfortable 63–35 majority, including several influential Republicans. Although the legislation still had inadequate support from a Republican majority in the House, the currency issue was clearly heating up yet again. Mitt Romney, the Republican 2012 presidential nominee, also condemned China's manipulation of the exchange rate and vowed to get tough with China on that and several other fronts.[57] In February 2012 President Obama and Vice President Joe Biden welcomed Chinese Vice President Xi Jinping (presumptive heir to Hu Jintao), but used the occasion to insist that "mutual respect" in the US/China relationship depends, in substantial part, upon China's improving its trade and monetary practices.[58]

At this writing in mid-February 2012, the official exchange rate stands at 6.29509 to US$1, an appreciation in the renminbi of a mere 5 percent from the beginning of 2011. Although inflation in China has made the appreciation effectively somewhat higher, there is widespread opinion in expert circles that the Chinese currency remains moderately to hugely undervalued. A slowing of Chinese growth rates as a result of the global recession and especially slump in the Eurozone have, in fact, put downward pressure on the renminbi, caused China's imports to fall by 15.3 percent, and increased China's trade surplus to a six-month high of $27.3 billion.[59]

To be sure, the currency manipulation by China that the United States and others have been decrying, persists. Yet, despite the latest complaints, this author and some other analysts believe that, for all practical purposes, the political acrimony over this issue has now become essentially ritualistic in nature. There is every reason for the public debate to continue, but neither side expects any major changes in policy for the foreseeable future.

Most of the reasons for the current truce about the exchange rate are domestic politics and economic realities on both sides. From the outset, China has faced real concerns about the fragility underlying its remarkable rise: an aging autocratic system severely intolerant of political dissent, a transition to a new president in 2012, bureaucratic contests like the one we have noted between the People's Bank and central administration policymakers, an increasingly independent military establishment, dangerous inflation coupled with global-recession-induced slowdown in exports and growth rate that could portend social instability, labor shortages and the related need to relocate industries from coastal regions to the interior, the absent transportation infrastructure to move goods from the interior to the coast, rising labor costs that threaten competitiveness, high university graduation rates without adequate prospects for employment, serious corruption throughout the political/economic system, environmental conditions reaching life-threatening proportions in some cities, and a shocking income gap between urban elites and the poor in both cities and the countryside. All China has needed at a time of global economic turbulence was to invite a major shock to its relative prosperity by too quickly abandoning its carefully crafted neo-mercantilist policies.

As for the United States, President Obama assumed office with what many journalists called an "inbox from hell." There were ongoing conflicts in Iraq and Afghanistan, the worst global financial crisis since the 1930s, persistent terrorist threats, probable nuclear weapons programs in Iran and North Korea, a stalemate in Israeli-Palestinian negotiations and then violent regime change in several Middle Eastern countries, increasing repression and expansive nationalism in Russia, a bloated national debt, out-of-control budget deficits, furor over illegal immigration, continuing confrontation over health care—all accompanied by bitter partisan disputes that made for legislative gridlock even before the midterm elections that brought the Tea Party movement to national prominence. However important, the US-China relationship was only ever just one of numerous critical issues. The US urgently needs China's help with North Korea and Iran, and Europe, with its sovereign debt problem. Moreover, there has always been an uncomfortable recognition by some policymakers that taking on China over the renminbi might not only further open up a Pandora's box of currency/trade wars in the unstable global economy, but also bring few tangible benefits to the United States. Yes, China had profited outrageously by violating the rules, but undercutting China's competitiveness would only cause the jobs to go to other low-income countries. It has thus seemed wiser to focus on negotiating better access to the Chinese market for US companies and pursue whatever limited remedies might be had from multilateral institutions like the G20 and WTO. Meanwhile, there was some hope from the fact that, as in China, throughout the emerging world economies, growing inflation fears seemed to suggest that an appreciating national currency might not be altogether a bad thing.[60]

Three further observations might be made in closing: First, what started as a bilateral issue over exchange rates and foreign currency reserves has now morphed into other global issues. One such issue is early, yet significant calls for a new international monetary system that will not rest exclusively on the US dollar. China is rightly interested in seeing the renminbi in the mix, but no such inclusion will be possible until it is an unrestricted market currency.[61] Another concern, not least for the US—in the be careful what you wish for category—is China's increasing interest in diversifying its immense foreign exchange reserves and actively investing them abroad. For example, prominent Chinese economist Li Yining recently suggested that, rather than holding so many foreign bonds, China should be buying foreign land, mines, forests, and stock equities and lending to domestic enterprises to invest abroad and buy advanced equipment, raw materials, and fuels.[62] An upsurge in Chinese FDI and purchases could be a boon to economic growth in particular countries, but are they prepared to accept a much greater Chinese presence within their borders?[63]

Second, it is important to stress that there are few secure predictions in political life. However unlikely, a Tea-Party dominated United States, ultra-nationalistic and in many respects hostile to government and suspicious of big banks and companies, could be aggressive both militarily and economically. China has been hypersensitive about its sovereignty, but others could also play that tune. Although much has also been said about WTO constraints, the serious lacunae in them invites and may even necessitate unilateral action. It should be recalled that when the Nixon administration in 1971 suspended the convertibility of dollars into gold and levied a 10 percent surcharge on all imports, its actions all too plainly declared that the existing monetary system was hopelessly dysfunctional.

Third and finally, the fascinating dollar/renminbi issue also invites us to explore much broader questions. As mentioned in the introduction to this chapter, the controversy tells us much about the continued relevance of state sovereignty as well as the degree to which state autonomy is limited by bilateral relations as well as system-wide constraints. It also testifies to the importance of multilateralism as well as the palpable weaknesses of same. It speaks to the influence of shifting power structures, the differences between military and economic power, and the importance of the soft power of image, reputation, and good diplomacy. There are potential insights too about how issues are constructed ("understood") and have their own dynamics, waxing and waning and changing their "frame" over time. Certainly we are further reminded of the amazing complexity and interconnected nature of even the most apparently straightforward issues in global affairs. Even if we could agree on the most appropriate economic indices for the dollar/renminbi, for example, that would be only a beginning and perhaps a misleading one at that. But these important subjects are beyond the scope of the present chapter.

NOTES

1. The classic statement of this proposition was by Hedley Bull in his *The Anarchical Society* (New York: Columbia University Press, 1977).

2. See by Niall Ferguson and Moritz Schularick, "Chimerical? Think Again," *Wall Street Journal*, February 5, 2007; and "'Chimerica' and Global Asset Markets," *International Finance* 10, 3 (2007), pp. 215–239. [Citations from Niall Ferguson, "The End of Chimerica: Amicable Divorce or Currency War?" Testimony before the Committee on Ways and Means, US House of Representatives (March 24, 2010), p. 1, footnote 1.]

3. Niall Ferguson, *The Ascent of Money: A Financial History of the World* (New York: Penguin, 2008), p. 235

4. Niall Ferguson and Moritz Schularick, "The Great Wallop," *New York Times*, November 16, 2009, accessed November 17, 2009, http://www.nytimes.com/2009/11/16/opinion/16ferguson.html?scp=1&sq=the%20great%20wallop&st=cse.

5. Ferguson, "The End of Chimerica," p. 3.

6. Ferguson, *The Ascent of Money*, p. 333.

7. Niall Ferguson, "The End of Chimerica," p. 2.

8. Ferguson, *The Ascent of Money*, p. 336.

9. Ferguson, "The End of Chimerica," p. 3.

10. *Ibid.*, pp. 3–4.

11. http://www.Chinability.com/Reserves.htm, accessed May 23 2011.

12. Ferguson, "The End of Chimerica," p. 3.

13. Ferguson argues that "the most illuminating approach focuses on the united labor cost based real exchange rate between the renminbi and the dollar," making for a 25 percent underevaluation (*ibid.*, pp. 5–6).

14. Ferguson and Schularick, "The Great Wallop."

15. Ferguson, "The End of Chimerica."

16. Ferguson and Schularick, "The Great Wallop."

17. http://www.iie.com/publications/interviews/pp20100129williamson.pdf.

18. Micheal Wines, "Chinese Leader Defends Currency and Policies," *New York Times*, March 14, 2010, accessed March 14, 2010, http://www.nytimes.com/2010/03/15/world/asia/15china.html?scp=3&sq=wen+jiabao++march+15%2C+2010&st=nyt.

19. John Pomfret, "China's Commerce Minister: U.S. Has the Most to Lose in a Trade War," *Washington Post*, March 22, 2010, accessed March 22, 2010, http://www.washingtonpost.com/wp-dyn/content/article/2010/03/21/AR2010032101111.html.

20. Paul Krugman, "Taking on China," *New York Times*, March 15, 2010, accessed March 15, 2010, http://www.nytimes.com/2010/03/15/opinion/15krugman.html?scp=1&sq=Krugman%20March%2015,%202010&st=cse.

21. http://www.schumer.senate.gov/record.cfm?id=323135. Comments of twelve other Senators who were sponsors are also on Senator Schumer's website.

22. "Editorial: Mr. Obama and Mr. Hu," *New York Times*, April 14, 2010, accessed April 14, 2010, http://www.nytimes.com/2010/04/14/opinion/14wed1.html?scp=1&sq=Mr.%20 Obama%20and%20Mr.%20Hu&st=cse.

23. Geoff Dyer and Alan Beattie, *Financial Times,* June 19, 2010, accessed June 20, 2010, http://www.ft.com/intl/cms/s/0/ac0ca08e-7ba7–11df-aa88–00144feabdc0 .html#axzz1NO4keyCL.

24. Paul Krugman, "The Renminbi Runaround," *New York Times*, June 24, 2010, accessed June 24, 2010, http://www.nytimes.com/2010/06/25/opinion/25krugman .html?scp=1&sq=Krugman%20The%20renminbi%20runaround&st=cse.

25. http://www.heritage.org/Events/2010/09/Targeting-China-on-Currency?query=Target ing+China+on+Currency:+Is+Congress+Serious+This+Time?

26. Sewell Chan, "China Hinders U.S. Recovery, Senators Tell Geithner," *New York Times,* September 16, 2010, accessed September 17, 2010, http://www.nytimes.com/2010/09/17/ business/17geithner.html?ref=sewellchan.

27. Alan Beattie,Tom Braithwaite, and Joshua Chaffin, *Financial Times*, October 4, 2010, accessed October 4, 2010, http://www.ft.com/intl/cms/s/0/96d8b886–cfe1–11df-bb9e -00144feab49a.html#axzz1NO4keyCL.

28. Sewell Chan, "Cuurency Rift With China Exposes Shifting Clout," *New York Times*, October 10, 2010, accessed October 10, 2011, http://www.nytimes.com/2010/10/11/ business/economy/11currency.html?scp=1&sq=chan,%20October%202010.

29. Sewell Chan and Keith Bradsher, "U.S. to Investigate China's Clean Energy Aid," *New York Times*, October 15, 2010, accessed October 15, 2010, http://www.nytimes .com/2010/10/16/business/16wind.html?scp=1&sq=U.S.%20Plans%20Inquiry%20on%20 China's%20Subsidies%20of%20Clean%20Energy&st=Search.

30. See the spirited defense of the Fed's QE2 by the *Financial Times* expert, Martin Wolf, in the issues of November 9 and November 17, 2010.

31. http://www.g20.org/Documents2010/11/seoulsummit_declaration.pdf.

32. Jonathan Wheatley and Joe Leahy, "Trade War Looming, Warns Brazil," *Financial Times,* January 9, 2011, accessed January 10, 2010, http://www.ft.com/intl/cms/ s/0/6316eb4a-1c34–11e0–9b56–00144feab49a.html#axzz1NO4keyCL.

33. "Inflated Fears," *Economist,* January 8, 2011, 71–2.

34. Cardiff Garcia, "Fears Grow That China Is Overheating," *Financial Times,* January 20, 2011, accessed January 20, 2011, http://ftalphaville.ft.com/thecut/2011/01/20/465131/ fears-grow-that-china-is-overheating/.

35. Sharon LaFraniere, "Inflation Hits Nearly 5 Percent in China, with Food Costs Soaring, *New York Times,* February 14, 2011, accessed February 14, 2011, http://www.ny times.com/2011/02/15/business/global/15chinaecon.html?scp=1&sq=Inflation%20Hits%20 Nearly%205%20Percent%20in%20China&st=cse.

36. "London Headlines," *Financial Times,* January 10, 2011, accessed January 10, 2011, http://blogs.ft.com/beyond-brics/2011/01/10/188671/.

37. Alan Rappeprt, "US Trade Gap Widens in December, *Financial Times*, February 11, 2011, accessed February 11, 2011, http://www.ft.com/intl/cms/s/0/88ab2f78–35e9–11e0 –b67c-00144feabdc0.html#axzz1NO4keyCL.

38. Hiroko Tabuchi, "China Replaced Japan in 2010 as No. 2 Ecnomy," *New York Times,* February 13, 2011, accessed February 13, 2011, http://www.nytimes.com/2011/02/14/ business/global/14yen.html?scp=1&sq=Tabuchi,%20China%20Replaced%20Japan%20 in%202010&st=cse.

39. Michael Mackensie, "China and Russia Main Sellers of US Treasuries," *Financial Times,* January 18, 2011, accessed January 18, 2011, http://www.ft.com/intl/cms/s/0/5fb213a6 –2325–11e0–b6a3–00144feab49a.html#axzz1NO4keyCL.

40. Michael Mackensie, "Fed Passess China in Treasury Holdings," *Financial Times,* February 2, 2011, accessed February 2, 2011, http://www.ft.com/intl/cms/s/0/120372fc -2e48–11e0–8733–00144feabdc0.html#axzz1NO4keyCL.

41. "Another Breach in the Wall," *Economist,* January 8, 2011, 75.

42. "Looser Renminbi," *New York Times,* January 18, 2011, B2.

43. David Barboza, "In China, Tentative Steps Toward Global Currency," *New York Times,* February 10, 2011, accessed February 10, 2011, http://www.nytimes.com/2011/02/11/busi-ness/global/11yuan.html?scp=1&sq=In%20China%20Tentative%20Steps%20Toward%20 Global%20Currency&st=cse.*New York Times,* February 10, 2011.

44. Jamil Anderlini, "Wall St. Banks to Launch Renminbi Funds," *Financial Times,* May 12, 2011, accessed May 12, 2011, http://www.ft.com/intl/cms/s/0/919a5e4e-7c7d-11e0 –b9e3–00144feabdc0.html#axzz1NO4keyCL.

45. See full text on US Department of Treasury website, Press Releases for January 12, 2011, http://www.treasury.gov/press-center/press-releases/Pages/tg1019.aspx.

46. David E. Sanger and Michael Wines, "China Leader's Limits Come into Focus as US Visit Nears," *New York Times,* January 16, 2011, accessed January 16, 2011, http://www .nytimes.com/2011/01/17/world/asia/17china.html?scp=1&sq=China%20Leader's%20 Limits%20Come%20into%20Focus&st=Search.

47. Richard McGreagor and Geoff Dyer, "Obama Toughens Line in Talks with Hu," *Financial Times,* January 19, 2011, accessed January 19, 2011, http://www.ft.com/intl/ cms/s/0/4ba1b6ac-23ff-11e0–bef0–00144feab49a.html#axzz1NO4keyCL.

48. Cardiff Garcia, "Hu Hails Creation of 14M Global Jobs,"*Financial Times*, January 20, 2011, accessed January 20, 2011, http://ftalphaville.ft.com/thecut/2011/01/20/465086/ hu-hails-creation-of-14m-global-jobs/.

49. Alan Beattie, "US Lawmakers Revive Cina Currency Bill," *Financial Times,* Febru-ary 10, 2011, accessed February 10, 2011, http://www.ft.com/intl/cms/s/0/0f705954–3566 –11e0–aa6c-00144feabdc0.html#axzz1NO4keyCL.

50. Alan Bettie, "Renminbi Issues Is Put on the Back Burner," *Financial Times,* January 19, 2011, accessed January 19, 2011, http://www.ft.com/intl/cms/s/0/4341d154–23f5–11e0 –bef0–00144feab49a.html#axzz1NO4keyCL.

51. US Department of the Treasury, *Report to Congress on International Economic and Exchange Rate* Policies, February 2011, 12, http://www.treasury.gov/resource-center/ international/exchange-rate-policies/Documents/Foreign%20Exchange%20Report%20 February%204%202011.pdf. *Financial Times,* February 5, 2011.

52. Joe Leahy, "US Seeks Brazil's Support on Renminbi," *Financial Times,* February 7, 2011, accessed February 7, 2011, http://www.ft.com/intl/cms/s/0/f3e63012–32ec-11e0 –9a61–00144feabdc0.html#axzz1NO4keyCL.

53. Ralph Atkins and Quentin Peel, "G20 Strikes Compromise on Global Imbalances," *Financial Times,* February 19, 2011, accessed February 20, 2011, http://www.ft.com/intl/ cms/s/0/1a12713e-3c56–11e0–b073–00144feabdc0.html#axzz1NO4keyCL.

54. Chris Giles, "G20 Agrees on Criteria for IMF Scrutiny of Countries," *Financial Times,* April 16, 2011, accessed April 16, 2011, http://www.ft.com/intl/cms/s/0/96d3ca1a -6794–11e0–9138–00144feab49a.html#axzz1NO4keyCL.

55. *The Economist,* October 15, 2011, p. 16.

56. Jamil Anderlini and Lifen Zhang, "Wen Sets Preconsitions to Help Europe," *Financial Times*, September 14, 2011, http://www.ft.com/cms/0/b234ad8a-de98–11e0–a228–00144 feabdc0.html.

57. "Understanding Romney on China, "*The Diplomat,"* http://the-diplomat.com/2012/ 02/01/understanding-romney-on-china/.

58. "US President Asks China to Follow 'Same Rules' in Trade," http://www.bbc.co.uk/ news/business-17036837.

59. www.bbc.co.uk/news/business-16977202.

60. See, for example, Stefan Wagstyl, "Currency Wars Fade as Inflation Hits Emerging World," *Financial Times*, April 13, 2011, accessed April 13, 2011, http://www.ft.com/intl/ cms/s/0/35055b74–65ef-11e0–9d40–00144feab49a.html#axzz1NO4keyCL.

61. See, for example, Sebastian Mallaby and Olin Wethington, "The Future of the Yuan: China's Struggle to Internationalize Its Currency," *Foreign Affairs*, Vol. 91, No. 1 (January/ February 2012), 135–46.

62. "China Should Diversify Foreign Exchange Reserves to Keep Safe: Leading Economist," *Xinhua News*, March 8, 2011, accessed March 8, 2011, http://news.xinhuanet.com/ english2010/china/2011–03/08/c_13767457.htm.

63. See, for example, David Barboza, "As China Invests, U.S. Could Lose," *New York Times*, May 4, 2011, accessed May 4, 2011, http://www.nytimes.com/2011/05/04/busi-ness/global/04yuan.html?_r=1&scp=1&sq=As%20China%20Invests,%20U.S.%20Could%20 Lose&st=cse; and "Who Wants to Be a Triple Trillionaire," *The Economist*, April 16, 2011, p. 81.

6

Coping with the Dollar Hegemony: China's New Monetary Strategy and Its Implications for the Regional Monetary Governance

Wei Li

Over the past three decades, as a financially weak state, China has largely followed a "free-riding" strategy in the U.S. dollar–centered international monetary system, relying on the dollar as the international currency in its economic engagement with other countries. China showed very little willingness to expand the use of its own currency abroad due to its concern over unpredictable financial risks. This strategy has gone together with the process of China's integration into the U.S.-led world market, and China has stayed quiet and acquiesced to the existing hierarchy of the international monetary system, which dates from the collapse of the Bretton Woods System in 1973.

However, this situation has been changing rapidly since the financial crisis of 2008. China is no longer satisfied with being a junior partner and staying silent in the international monetary structure. Instead, it is becoming increasingly concerned with the negative effects of the dollar dominated system, and has begun to take steps to internationalize its own currency. Furthermore, its voice on the reform of the international monetary system is becoming louder and louder. China, which has already overtaken Japan as the world's second-largest economy in 2010, is trying to flex its monetary muscles in the global arena for the first time. This will definitely reshape the global and regional monetary order.

Why is the Chinese government trying to shift from its traditional monetary strategy of bandwagoning with the U.S. dollar to instead balancing against the global monetary hegemony?[1] Faced with two different strategic choices, building a regional multilateral currency union or expanding its own currency unilaterally, which one will China take? How will China's new monetary strategy affect East Asian regional monetary order building at present and in the future?

This chapter attempts to answer these questions and is structured into four sections. The first section surveys the so-called "dollar trap" that China confronts, and

115

how it presses the Chinese government to change its previous international monetary strategy. The second section elaborates on China's new monetary move in detail, discussing both its diplomatic and domestic policy changes. The third section reviews Germany and Japan's experiences, and analyzes how they handle the dollar hegemony when they realized their period of economic rise in the 1970s and 1980s. This section also reviews the experiences of East Asian monetary cooperation during the past decade. The final section discusses China's present and future monetary strategic choice and its implications for the regional monetary order building.

THE GLOBAL FINANCIAL
CRISIS AND CHINA'S "DOLLAR TRAP"

Discord, disputes, and even conflicts have been ubiquitous in the Sino-U.S. relationship after the establishment of bilateral diplomatic relations in 1979.[2] Even though there have been many instances of Sino-U.S. confrontation in the political, economic and even militarily arenas, China has never taken substantial measures to reduce its economic dependence on the United States, particularly its monetary dependence. Keohane and Nye pointed out early in the late 1970s that asymmetric interdependence brings about certain power relations,[3] but China did not seem to take this seriously, which remains a big puzzle in the history of China's foreign policy making.[4]

On the monetary front, it is surprising how little the *renminbi* (RMB) is currently used outside of China's borders. China is now the second-largest economy and trading nation worldwide, the largest exporter of manufactured goods and holds the largest volume of foreign exchange reserves in the world. Yet the amount of its currency held and circulating overseas is negligible—the result of China's strict capital controls and restrictions on currency trade. Since its reform and opening movement in the 1980s, China has been relying heavily on the dollar to conduct its foreign transactions, be it in international trade settlements or transnational financial dealings. Earning more foreign exchanges, especially the U.S. dollar, had been one of China's main strategic aims in its foreign economic relations.

The massive depreciation of RMB in 1994 and the entering into the WTO in 2001 continually strengthened the import-oriented economic development model of economic development.[5] In the past decade, China began running larger and larger trade surpluses and also began attracting substantial inflows of foreign capital. The Chinese government chose to keep the value of the *yuan* in terms of the dollar more or less fixed on a depreciated level.[6] To do this, it had to buy up dollars as they came flooding in. As the years passed, those trade surpluses just kept growing—and so did China's hoard of foreign assets. According to the data at the end of 2011, China's foreign assets have reached $3,200 billion, of which more than two-thirds are dollar-denominated.[7]

China now is the largest foreign reserve holder in the world, far more than the second largest holder, Japan. These huge foreign exchange reserves offend economic logic, since they mean that China, still a developing country in terms of per-capita income, should have abundant investment opportunities domestically, but in fact is lending cheaply to richer countries, mainly the United States.

China's holding of a huge volume of U.S. dollar denominated financial assets is currently the fundamental feature of Sino-U.S. financial relations. Theoretically speaking, this kind of financial relationship has increased the possibility for the two states to exercise financial statecraft—the use financial instruments to realize strategic aims.[8] As the creditor, China can use the financial assets as "debt weapons"; as the debtor, the United States can use it as hostage. The former U.S. Treasury Secretary and now Harvard Economics Professor Lawrence Summers describes this situation as the "balance of financial terror"—neither one can hurt the other without hurting itself.[9] However, in the real world, the advantage has tilted largely to the U.S. side rather than the Chinese side.

At first, the U.S. government indeed worried about this type of huge indebtedness and its dependence on China's holding of T-securities,[10] as they feared that the Chinese government could try to wreck the American economy by dumping U.S. T-securities, and thus influence U.S. policy on sensitive political issues—like Taiwan. While an increasing number of serious studies and past practice have shown that in reality China's huge holding of U.S, securities cannot be a source of power,[11] there are evidences that suggest otherwise.

Nicholas R. Lardy, a Chinese economy expert, agreed that the Chinese government had little incentive to begin any large sell-off of U.S. securities and probably could not find a market to buy them even if it did. He said, "If it was known they are beginning to sell their holdings, prices would come down and they'd take bigger losses. They'd be shooting themselves in the foot . . . they're in the dollar trap, and there is no easy way out of it."[12] Nobel Laureate Paul Krugman also pointed out explicitly that "there's nothing to keep China from diversifying its reserves away from the dollar . . . for the fact that China now owns so many dollars that it can't sell them off without driving the dollar down and triggering the very capital loss its leaders fear."[13]

The vulnerability of China's financial security was exposed in the U.S.-triggered global financial crisis of 2008, during which the United States could defer or even deflect its adjustment costs to others by virtue of its monetary hegemony, while China's huge amounts of dollar-denominated reserves, including the T-securities and large fraudulent agency securities, were at risk of shrinking. After Krugman's famous article titled "China's Dollar Trap," China's "dollar trap" has become a very popular term in China and the world to describe this kind of vulnerability.

Thus, the dominant role of the dollar has increasingly aroused China's concern and fear. When U.S. Treasury Secretary Timothy Geithner tried to relieve the widespread concern at Peking University's lecture in June 2009 insisting that "Chinese financial assets are very safe," it drew peals of laughter from the audience.[14]

Moreover, China's lack of an international currency precludes it from benefiting from the efficiency gains and the seigniorage that are associated with the use of a

Table 6.1. Major Foreign Holders of U.S Treasury Securities (Billions of Dollars, October 2010)

Country	Amount
China, Mainland	906.8
Japan	877.4
United Kingdom	477.6
Oil Exporters*	213.9
Brazil	177.6
Hong Kong	139.2
Carib Bnkng Ctrs**	133.7
Russia	131.6
Taiwan	131.2
Canada	125.2
Switzerland	101.3

*Oil exporters include Ecuador, Venezuela, Indonesia, Bahrain, Iran, Iraq, Kuwait, Oman, Qatar, Saudi Arabia, the United Arab Emirates, Algeria, Gabon, Libya, and Nigeria.
**Caribbean Banking Centers include Bahamas, Bermuda, Cayman Islands, Netherlands Antilles and Panama. Beginning with new series for June 2006, also includes British Virgin Islands.
Source: http://www.treasury.gov/resource-center/data-chart-center/tic/Documents/mfh.txt

country's own currency in international transactions.[15] What's more important is that China suffers more and more from the dollar's devaluation, which has threatened its financial security.

Yu Yongding, a former member of the Central bank's monetary policy commission, is a renowned figure in China who speaks loudly about the so-called "dollar trap."[16] He advocated with passion to stop increasing dollar bonds, diversify, and even decrease China's foreign exchange reserves. China's economists held heated debates in 2009 regarding China's policy on foreign exchange reserves and possible methods of defending China's financial security.[17]

In addition, as Chinese young IPE expert Song Guoyou has argued, China's "dollar trap" also implies another more important political and strategic outcome. If China and the United States quarrel in the future, China's large volume dollar assets could be held hostage by the United States as leverage to change China's foreign policy.[18] There are more than a few precedents for the United States using its monetary power for coercive diplomacy, for instance pressing the United Kingdom to retreat from Egypt during 1956 Suez Crisis.[19] The dilemma China faces is similar to that faced by France in the 1920s, as it sought to reduce its massive sterling reserves. The Bank of France found itself in a "sterling trap" in which it "could not continue selling pounds without precipitating a sterling collapse and a huge exchange loss for itself."[20]

According to some realist scholars, the structural confrontation between the two states is inevitable.[21] However, China is passively and ironically becoming the largest sponsor of the U.S. dollar in what has been one of the worst financial crises in modern history with potential strategic conflicts looming between China and the United States in 2010. This is surprisingly contradictory to what traditional International Relations and International Political Economy theories predict.

China's failures in preventing the U.S. government initiatives—from selling arms to Taiwan, Obama's meeting with Dalai Lama in the White House, criticism of RMB issue, State Secretary Hilary Clinton's involvement in South China Sea, and U.S. Quantitative Easing Monetary Policy—may explain why Obama seems humble to China in 2009,[22] but tough in 2010 and thereafter.

The global financial crisis led China to feel the burden of growing political and economic costs for its over-reliance on the dollar. These concerns stimulated China to strategically review and change its international monetary strategy of following the dollar hegemony over the past three decades.

BEYOND THE DOLLAR: CHINA'S
NEW MONETARY MOVE

A hot debate on China's "dollar trap" and the storm of criticism about the Chinese government's unreasonable monetary strategy,[23] together with the real threat posed by the dollar, have prompted the central government to make some amendments through several new monetary diplomatic overtures, as well as a set of massive domestic policy adjustments in the last three years in order, to reduce the international role of the dollar and to seek a greater international role for its own currency.

New Monetary Diplomacy

During the period of the global financial crisis, China's financial and monetary issues have topped the international diplomatic agenda. China's monetary diplomacy has been in the world media's spotlight for the first time. The fundamental aim of China's financial and monetary diplomacy has been to defend its financial security and interest, and push back against a dollar-dominated monetary system.

First, China's senior leaders have overtly expressed their serious dissatisfaction with the dollar-centered monetary system to the whole world in order to win some allies for the reform of the existing international monetary system. In March 2009, Prime Minister Wen Jiabao told reporters that he was concerned about China's financial investments in the United States: "We have lent a huge amount of money to the U.S. Of course we are concerned about the safety of our assets. To be honest, I am definitely a little worried."[24] Zhou Xiaochuan, the head of the People's Bank of China, and Wang Qishan, the vice premier, followed up with papers suggesting a shift from the dollar as the world's dominant reserve currency, before the G20 summit in London.[25] Mr. Zhou caused a stir in March 2009 when he argued that the special drawing rights (SDR) should become a true global reserve asset to replace the dollar.[26] These calls elicited quick responses of support from Russia and Brazil. Although they also declared that the world needed new reserve currencies to break up the dollar monopoly, only China's voice received much attention around the world.

More importantly, prior to Hu Jintao's state visit to Washington in January 2011, the Chinese president gave a direct and considered response to a question about the dollar's status in the written interview with the *Wall Street Journal* and the *Washington Post*. Hu said, "The current international currency system is the product of the past," "The monetary policy of the United States has a major impact on global liquidity and capital flows and therefore, the liquidity of the U.S. dollar should be kept at a reasonable and stable level."[27] Although these words were modest and measured, China's highest leader clearly called on the United States to take up a more responsible monetary policy.

In addition, China and France have come together with regard to the international monetary system reform under the framework of the G20. In November 2010, when President Hu Jintao arrived in Paris for a three-day state visit on the eve of France assuming the presidency of the G20; he paid much attention to international currency affairs in discussion with his counterpart Nicolas Sarkozy. The two leaders shared very similar objectives, paths, and methods for the reform. Sarkozy wants to put international monetary reform at the top of the group's agenda for the next year, which is also in China's interest, and Hu readily expressed his appreciation and support.[28] Throughout the history of the modern international economy, France has traditionally been one of the most politically sensitive nations with regard to international monetary affairs. France's sensitivity to currency affairs dates back at least as early as the era of Napoleon, who attempted to gauge the success of the "continental system" directed against Britain's sterling system.[29] After the establishment of Bretton Woods system, it is also France that has fought most actively against dollar hegemony. In the wake of the eruption of the global financial crisis, China is siding with France against the dollar-dominated international monetary system.

Although China's proposals and diplomatic gestures are largely symbolic, it has succeeded in placing the United States under great pressure by raising doubts over the dominant role of the U.S. dollar. Furthermore, behind the scenes, China's consistent investment in the European debt market has won European Union support for its monetary stances.[30] In a joint press conference with European Union President Herman Van Rompuy in Beijing on February 15, 2012, Chinese Premier Wen Jiabao promised that "China's willingness to support Europe to cope with sovereign debt problems is sincere and firm" and that "China is ready to get more deeply involved in participating in solving the European debt issue." Besides, the People's Bank of China Governor Zhou Xiaochuan echoed comments by Premier Wen in Beijing on the same day: "China will always adhere to the principle of holding assets of EU sovereign debt. . . . We would participate in resolving the euro debt crisis."[31] Wen and Zhou are giving the best support China can offer now, which is to send out positive messages such as promising not to cut Euro assets and to buy European bonds to help bolster market confidence.

By promising to bailout these states in overcoming the debt crisis, China is sending a signal to the world that China is trying to support the euro in order to hedge against the U.S. dollar, and then promote a multicurrency system. And this approach has won domestic support, as many commentators believe that, in order to curb U.S. monetary privilege, China should help the euro through the current financial mess, because there is no other currency can counter balance against the U.S. dollar at present or in the near future; if the euro collapses, U.S. monetary policy will become even less disciplined. Here, assisting the euro is part of China's grand strategy, not solely a commercial consideration.[32]

Second, China has tried its best to increase its IMF and World Bank quotas and voting rights on the G20 platform. While the global financial crisis again sparked outrage and criticism among the international community toward the existing international financial institutions, China has successfully made use of the renewed momentum for reform to advance its own ambition of power expansion in these institutions.

At nearly every G20 meeting, reform of the IMF was on the top of the agenda. According to the agreed reform plan, China, taking 6.39 percent voting share at the fund, will overtake Germany, France, and Britain as the fund's third-largest holder after the changes are implemented, second only to the United States and Japan.[33] The agreement will help to revitalize the IMF's outdated governing structure, created just after World War II. What's more, Chinese officials have already called for the *renminbi* to be included in the International Monetary Fund's basket of main currencies.

With the help of Chinese government, the Chinese economist Zhu Min was elevated to the position of deputy managing director of the IMF on July 26, 2011. Zhu thus became the second Chinese to take on a senior position in a top international financial institution after Justin Yifu Lin, who was appointed vice president of the World Bank in 2008. Both of the promotions are considered as China's success in financial diplomacy.

Third, China had signed a collection of bilateral currency swap agreements with a number of states that enjoy good relations with China since the end of 2008. So far, the Central Bank of China has inked currency swap agreements with the central banks or monetary authorities of South Korea, Hong Kong SAR, Malaysia, Belarus, Indonesia, Singapore, Argentina, and Iceland. These moves aim to promote bilateral trade and direct investment, and to provide short-term liquidity for the stabilization of financial markets in China and these states.

In order to avoid the risks posed by the dollar, the bravest cooperative action occurred between China and Russia, considered by some as the two largest political and military balancers to the United States. The two countries have been traditionally accustomed to using other currencies instead of their own currencies, especially the dollar, for bilateral trade. Since the financial crisis, however, high-ranking officials on both sides have begun to explore alternatives to using the U.S. dollar. During Premier Wen Jiabao's visit to Russia in November 2010, Wen and his Russian coun-

Table 6.2.   Bilateral Currency Swaps Agreements (Billon, RMB)

Date	Country	Scale
2008.12.12	South Korea	180
2009.1	Hong Kong	200
2009.2.8	Malaysia	80
2009.3.11	Belarus	20
2009.3.23	Indonesia	100
2009.3.29	Argentina	70
2009.6.9	Iceland	35
2009.7.23	Singapore	150
2011.4.18	New Zealand	25
2011.4.19	Uzbekistan	0.7
2011.5.6	Mongolia	5
2011.6.13	Kazakhstan	7
2011.11.22	Hong Kong	200
2011.12.22	Thailand	70
2011.12.23	Pakistan	10
2012.2.21	Turkey	10
2012.3.22	Austria	200

Source: Central Bank of China

terpart Vladimir Putin announced that China and Russia have decided to resort to gradually use their own currencies for settling bilateral trade. Putin said at a joint news conference with Mr. Wen in St. Petersburg, "the Yuan has now started trading against the Russian Ruble in the Chinese interbank market, while the *renminbi* will soon be allowed to trade against the Ruble in Russia."[34] The ruble has became the seventh foreign currency (the other six are the U.S. dollar, Hong Kong dollar, yen, euro, sterling, Malaysia ringgit) listed for trading in China's foreign exchange market, which will enhance RMB's proportion and reduce the dollar's role in China's foreign economic transaction.

Fourth, China made an effort to promote the financial and monetary cooperation among emerging markets under the framework of BRICS.[35] Born during the period of global financial crisis, the BRICS summit has become an important platform for discussing global monetary system reform, and an active advocate for a "diversified, stable and predictable currency system" and wider use of SDR. It aims at promoting greater use of local currency in trade settlement, taking place of the third currency vehicle, mainly the U.S. dollar, as well as advocating for emerging economies in international financial institutions. At present, the five emerging states are collectively committing to sign currency swap agreements and even establishing a common development bank. While the idea of a common development bank is still at the initial stages of discussion, its purpose would be extending loans denominated in their respective currencies: "A common development bank could be an important tool for China, however, in its quest to promote the renminbi, which it is trying to build into an international currency that could one day rival the dollar or euro."[36]

On the monetary front, although IPE scholar Daniel W. Drezner insisted that Chinese rhetoric about international monetary system reform and its criticism on dollar hegemony were largely bluffing and gained little actual effect,[37] Chinese actions have pressed U.S. officials to issue multiple public reassurances about the safety of U.S. Treasury bonds. In addition, China has successfully increased its shareholding in international financial institutions. Partly with China's efforts, the G20 has replaced the G7 as the core platform of global financial governance, marking a new era where emerging countries can participate more actively in the global financial arena.

New Monetary Policies

In addition to the active monetary diplomacy, a set of domestic policy adjustments has noticeably emerged, proceeding on two parallel tracks.[38] The first track aims to increase the bilateral and regional use of the RMB, with policies focusing on its use as vehicle currency for invoicing and settling cross-border trade. The second track approaches the convertibility of the RMB through the development of an RMB-offshore market in Hong Kong, with policies focusing on providing instruments for hedging the currency risk and making RMB holdings more attractive to non-residents.

For the first track, Beijing launched policy measures aimed at cross-border RMB trade settlements in July 2009, in order to improve the use of the RMB among non-residents and expand the scope of RMB business outside China. The scheme, originally limited to five pilot cities, was broadened in June 2010 and expanded to include whole countries since August 23, 2011. Encouraging the use of RMB in cross-border trade settlements in large extent indicates China's ambitions of pushing forward the internationalization of the yuan.

The scheme began slowly, but has picked up momentum since the beginning of 2010. The cross-border transactions totaling 2,080 billion Yuan were settled under the scheme in 2011, four times that of 2010, including 110.87 billion RMB settlements in its foreign financial transactions.[39] However, compared to its total foreign trade in 2011, the amount is still minimal, only accounting for about 10 percent. And given that China has about 9 percent share of the world trade and most of it is currently settled in dollars, the scope for increasing the use of the RMB is potentially huge, especially in cross-border trade.

For Chinese companies, the attractions of settling cross-border trade in their own currency are clear. If the scheme works and continues, the *renminbi* would become the main currency for commercial transactions in East Asia, the world's most economically dynamic region, in the next decade.

With regard to the second track, the Chinese central government is strengthening Hong Kong's role as the *renminbi*'s offshore market, which is also a very important part of China's new international monetary strategy. China has acknowledged that, as a world-famous financial center, Hong Kong is a precious resource for China's financial rise, especially for RMB internationalization. Hong Kong can serve a role for the RMB going abroad, similar to London's support for the dollar's Euromarket in 1960s, when the capital account regulations in the United States had not been lifted.[40]

Even if the RMB cross-border transactions are to be limited to trade, companies and banks still need to be able to hold and invest *renminbi* offshore. Hong Kong's role as *renminbi*'s offshore market started to become much clearer from July 2010 when the authorities allowed *renminbi*-denominated financial markets to spring to life in Hong Kong.

On September 28, 2010, The Ministry of Treasury of China issued 6 billion T-bonds in Hong Kong. What makes these bond issues important is that the offshore *renminbi* market is much more than just a new avenue for debt financing—it is one of the core components in China's plan to internationalize the Chinese currency. While the offshore market is still its infancy, foreign interest is growing quickly. Caterpillar, the U.S.-based maker of earthmoving equipment, launched a RMB 1 billion ($150 million) bond issue in November, 2010, making it the second multinational corporation to tap the market, following an August issue by the fast-food chain McDonald of 200 million Yuan. Besides private corporations, a select group of institution investors, including international organizations and foreign central banks, were given access to China's offshore bond market. The Asian Development Bank has thrown its weight behind Hong Kong's fledgling *renminbi*-denominated bond market, raising 1.2 billion RMB ($180 million) in October 2010 in the first deal of its kind by a supranational agency.[41] This bond will act as a useful benchmark for other potential borrowers, helping to develop the offshore *renminbi* bond market into an important source of funding for borrowers as well as an investment destination. Also, in January 2011, the World Bank issued its first-ever bond denominated in China's currency, priced at 500 million yuan, which will offer investors the chance to diversify their currency holdings and promote the internationalization of the Chinese currency.[42] Malaysia is believed to have become the first central bank to hold mainland *renminbi* assets in its reserves. The Manila-based central bank is planning a series of *renminbi* bond sales in the coming years.

China is trying to use Hong Kong as a laboratory where it can encourage international companies and investors to hold and trade *renminbi*-denominated products and assets.[43] And international investors' strong interest in issuance of *renminbi* bonds will promote Hong Kong, the Asian financial center, as a platform for international banking in the yuan.

In sum, China is making concerted effort to counterbalance the dollar hegemony and has already taken important steps in this direction both externally and internally. Indeed, the process is a slow one, having taken more baby steps than giant leaps, and it is also by no means assured that the RMB will immediately forge a decisive international role. But it is one that could have a huge long-term impact on global trade, the global financial system, and even international politics.

Yet while China is beginning to flex its financial and monetary muscles as described above, in terms of its long-term international monetary strategy, China is still vacillating between the choices of a multilateral union like Germany and unilateral expansion like Japan, due to the regional security dilemmas and its ambiguous national grand strategy, which make the reform of the East Asian monetary order full of uncertainty.

REGIONAL MONETARY GOVERNANCE: DIFFERENT PRACTICES

The dilemma China is now facing is quite similar to Germany and Japan's situation since the early 1970s. Having been exposed repeatedly to U.S. predatory and coercive monetary policy and diplomacy, both European and Japanese authorities embarked on projects to deploy countermeasures; the European Monetary Union (EMU) was an early example of this. But the two countries, Germany and Japan, have taken totally difference approaches, and thus offered different lessons for China's monetary strategy in the future.

The closure of the "gold window" in 1971 ushered in a new era, when the dollar delinked with gold and the United States is no longer bound by any rules in the international monetary system. The global role of the dollar has created further fear and concern for monetary policymakers around the world. As Treasury Secretary John Connally was alleged to have told his European counterparts in 1971, "The dollar is our currency, but it's your problem."[44] The late IPE founder Susan Strange later put it, "to decide one August morning that dollars can no longer be converted into gold was a progression from exorbitant privilege to super-exorbitant privilege; the U.S. government was exercising the unconstrained right to print money that others could not (save at unacceptable cost) refuse to accept."[45]

As early as the 1960s, French President Charles de Gaulle complained about the "exorbitant privilege" that the United States gained as a result of the use of the dollar as a key currency.[46] In order to cope with what they saw as America's economical exploitation and political coercion through its unbinding monetary power, Germany and Japan, as two economically rising states at that time, changed their previous international monetary strategy of relying on the dollar for the international currency, and tried their best to promote a multicurrency world, in the hope of constraining the United States from abusing its exorbitant monetary privileges. Yet their strategies were very different.

Germany adopted the strategy of building a multilateral monetary union, combining with its regional ally—France, and three decades later, the regional common currency—the euro—was born.[47] As the second most important international currency, the euro's struggle for international position with the dollar had reduced the U.S. "power to deflect." As a hedge against the U.S. dollar, the creation of the euro has provided an alternative, and is now the dominant reserve currency in most European countries and remains a potential challenger to the dollar as the world's leading reserve currency.[48]

Table 6.3. The Amount and Share of Euro as Foreign Reserve

Year	Amount ($ Billion)	Share (%)
2001	301.0	19.2%
2002	427.3	23.8%
2003	559.2	25.2%
2004	658.5	24.9%
2005	683.8	24.0%
2006	831.9	25.1%
2007	1082.3	26.3%
2008	1112.2	26.4%
2009	1245.8	27.3%

Sources: IMF, COFER database.

However, the situation at the time was totally different in the East. Japan had been on the road of unilateral monetary expansion since the mid-1980s, trying to build a yen zone in East Asia, only to fail after two decades of working to promote the yen's internationalization. In spite of Japan's status as the second largest economy and a major trading power in nearly four decades, the yen is relatively little used for international transactions and accounts for less than 10 percent of the world's foreign-exchange reserves.[49]

Prior to the global financial crisis, efforts to promote East Asian economic integration were mainly launched by private sectors, while governments showed little serious interest in regional economic cooperation. Japan wants to be the leader of East Asia, through industrial attraction rather than diplomacy. The so-called Flying Geese Paradigm is one such embodiment.

While the European economy has been de-linking itself from the dollar gradually, Japan can hardly insulate its economy from U.S. influences. Japan's unilateral road to internationalize its currency and expand its economic power regionally has largely proved unsuccessful.

The financial crisis of 1997 marked a turning point for Japan to change its previous unilateral monetary strategy to multilateral strategy. According to Korean scholar Hyoung-Kyu Chey's study, the political dynamics of East Asian financial cooperation have changed in the wake of the financial crisis of 1997 and were a key factor behind the development of the regional financial and monetary order building.[50] Japan has become more active in providing regional initiative, while China has become more willing to support East Asian financial cooperation. Like Germany and France in the Europe, collaboration between Japan and China constitute the mainstay of East Asian regional monetary order building since 1997.

Due to weak government participation, the East Asian regional economic governance lacked the formal institutionalization, lagging far behind the rest of the world.[51] The scenario has partly changed since the 1997 crisis as the East Asian monetary governance is approaching a new stage.[52]

In December 1997, to deal with the sudden financial crisis, ASEAN+3 was established and then institutionalized in 1999.[53] This was the first summit mechanism in the region, opening the door of regional economic cooperation. Under this framework, member states have gradually promoted financial regionalism in several major areas, for instance, the emergency liquidity provision through the Chiang Mai Initiative (CMI), and the development of regional bond markets.

Insulation from monetary hegemony will be a central motivating factor in advancing financial regionalism. The financial and monetary cooperation projects mentioned above have clearly aimed, at least partly, at reducing dependence on the United States and the dollar. The core of East Asian financial cooperation achievement is the Chiang Mai Initiative, a network of bilateral swap arrangements established in May 2000 to provide short-term liquidity assistance.

The development of the CMI has been largely driven by Sino-Japanese cooperation. Japan was the initial leader in East Asian financial cooperation during the interim of the two crises of 1997 and 2008. Japan's unique position in East Asian political economy offers it the opportunity to be a leader in financial regionalism. And Japan has been enthusiastic in promoting regional financial cooperation after 1997, in the hope of establishing a regional institution representing Asian voices, facilitating internationalization of the yen, and bolstering its own leadership.[54] More importantly, Japan wants to use regional means to reduce economic exposure to unilateral changes in U.S. economic policies, and cooperate with China and other East Asian economies to counter the power of the United States in international finance and currency issues, such as reducing reliance on the dollar.[55]

In addition to Japan's efforts to promote CMI development, China has increasingly participated in East Asian financial cooperation since the late 1990s. In sharp contrast to its negative reaction to the AMF (Asian Monetary Fund) proposal in 1997, China supported the CMI, a key factor in guaranteeing its success. China's key role in East Asia became apparent for the first time during the Asian financial crisis of 1997–98. Since then it has been actively involved with regional monetary arrangements. China is an important fund supplier for the Bilateral Swap Arrangements within the Chiang Mai Initiative framework.

CHINA'S NEW MONETARY ASPIRATIONS AND IMPLICATION FOR THE FUTURE

Although East Asian monetary cooperation is proceeding, in general, the moves toward greater financial and monetary governance in the past 10 years have proceeded more roughly and slowly than expected; and an effective regional monetary order has not yet been established.

The existing mechanism of regional monetary governance in East Asia, including CMI, is only a partial solution to the liquidity problems, and it does not address the other two fundamental problems of East Asian monetary governance: the lack of an anchor currency and the lack of exchange rate arrangements. The U.S. dollar is still the anchor currency in the region to date, serving as an external anchor and foreign exchange reserve. The dollar standard in East Asia is an asymmetric monetary system which most East Asian countries heavily rely on.[56] This may bring some benefits in the short term, but the inherent risks are high in the long term. During the global financial crisis, the inflation caused by the two rounds of U.S. quantitative easing monetary policies further aggravated the adjustment costs in many East Asian countries.

Grand Debates on China's Monetary Strategy

Heated debates on the type of international monetary strategy China should adopt in the future have emerged, both in China's policy-making circles and in academia. It is unfortunate that the debates on the orientation of China's monetary strategy have occurred primarily within the economic community, and there are very few international relations experts participating in the debates. This is due in part to the relative weakness of China's International Political Economy group. Consequently, the present debate exhibits certain weaknesses in terms of its strategic considerations.

In summary, China is confronted with two possible paths. The two contending schools on the issue agree that China should expand its monetary influence and reduce its reliance on the dollar as soon as possible. Both schools propose that the RMB go abroad but differ in the concrete approaches.

The unilateral expansion school holds that expanding the use of the RMB as a means of payment in international transactions would help reduce both over-reliance on the dollar and the risk of liquidity crises. They claim that past evidence shows that the more limited the size of a country's economy, the more limited the scope for its currency to become fully internationalized. In this sense, scale and scope are set to play in China's favor. This school argues that RMB can realize a higher international status independently and directly, as long as China's economy keeps growing sustainably as it has done in the past three decades.

What's more, this school notes that East Asian monetary cooperation confronts various political obstacles. They also note that economically East Asia is far from being an optimum currency area, according to Robert Mundell's standards, because of its great diversities in economic development levels and economic policies. In their eyes, the regional monetary system is still something that exists only in our imagination, let alone a common regional currency.[57]

Therefore, the unilateral expansion school holds an optimistic view toward China's economic power growth, and and believes China can learn from Britain and America's experiences, respectively, in the nineteenth and twentieth centuries . They encourage RMB to be a kind of world currency, like the dollar at present and like the sterling in the past. Within this school, some analysts argue that if China wants to internationalize the RMB, it should increase the use of RMB in East Asia first. However, they do not think that the East Asian cooperation is indispensable or even possible. They argue that the currency competition in East Asia is in China's favor and that China should create a regional monetary system centered on RMB, not a basket of currencies.[58]

On the other hand, the multilateral union school holds that RMB's unilateral expansion means it has to "go head to head" with the dollar. They believe that RMB will face fierce competition with the dollar, the incumbent hegemonic currency. They think that establishing international credibility for the RMB, and making it acceptable in those parts of the world economy where the dollar dominates, will take many years. This school sticks to the opinion that under the current dollar system characterized by the America's powerful financial and political resources, it is impossible for the rising state to internationalize its currency on a global level, due in part to the path dependence of the incumbent dominant international currency. For this school, Japan's unsuccessful attempt to internationalize the yen in the 1980s and 1990s is an important lesson.[59] Therefore, they feel that the rising states like China should learn from Germany's experience, allying themselves with the states geographically nearby to create a regional monetary system. They believe that only a regional monetary union can serve as a balancer against dollar hegemony.[60]

The two different schools recommend different policies and strategic paths. If the path proposed by the unilateral expansion school is taken, the Chinese government should enhance its monetary status globally and unilaterally. Without getting involved in monetary policy cooperation, monetary sovereignty sharing and compromising, it should devote its economic and diplomatic resources toward global monetary system reform to build a *renminbi*-based system.

On the other hand, if the path proposed by the multilateral union school is taken, Chinese government should promote regional monetary cooperation, engage in regional monetary order building on the basis of multicurrency, and even seek to create a common regional currency in the long run.

The debate is ongoing, and steps to promote renminbi's internationalization continue. However, whether the unilateral expansion school or multilateral union school's approach will be taken is still unclear. Global and regional political dynamics always powerfully influence the academic debates. The uneasy progress of regional monetary cooperation to hedge against the U.S. dollars has been constrained by the competition and instability in regional politics. The rapid changes in the power distribution and political environment in East Asia bring about uncertainty in the regional monetary order building. The extreme lack of political trust hinders the growth of financial regionalism. Specifically, the future regional monetary order building is severely challenged by the power shift between China and Japan.

Japan's top concern is to retain its leadership in East Asian regionalism and governance; however, it has encountered severe challenge from China's rapid economic rise during the past decade. It appears that Japan's strategy for regional financial governance has shifted from cooperating with China to reduce the dollar's influence and to welcoming the United States back into East Asia to balance against China's growing economic and political power.[61]

Although China is being increasingly active in reforming the existing global monetary system and devoting more resources to monetary regionalism to curb the dollar's long-term dominance, Japan seems to be retreating somewhat from its previous stance and strengthening its alliance with the United States. Recently, Japan and ASEAN, due to their apparent desire to counter balance China's power, brought other big powers from outside the region to join in the East Asia's regionalization. They invited Austria, New Zealand, and India to attend the first East Asia Summit in 2005, and then invited the United States and Russia to be observers in 2010 and to become formal members in 2011. This further complicated regional cooperation. According to the conventional logic of collective action, "more members" equals "more troubles."[62] APEC, commonly considered as talk shop, is an instructive precedent. That is why Chinese Premier Wen Jiabao emphasized in the East Asia serial summits in Hanoi in 2010 that China would like to promote East Asian regional cooperation within the framework of "10+3."

ASEAN and Japan's actions deterred China's efforts to promote East Asian regionalism and also cast a shadow on the multilateral union school, which came to be seen as holding the weaker position in the debate.

China's Future Monetary Strategy

As China's financial rise and opening to the outside world continues, it is likely to have stronger interests in preventing regional financial volatility, enhancing its currency status, and insulating itself from the negative effects of future U.S. macroeconomic policies. The web of U.S alliances and quasi-alliances in the region in the future may constitute a stumbling block for China's regional monetary strategy. In the case of Japan's future, China may be in a position where it must choose either to seek to weaken that alliance or to isolate Japan in Asia.

For the United States, the continuation of the dominant status of the dollar and U.S. political and military presence in East Asia would be ideal. This means maintaining military alliances and quasi alliance with Japan, South Korea, and ASEAN states as a potential balancing coalition against China on the one hand, and preventing the construction of a new East Asia monetary order to be built centered on yen or RMB on the other hand. Financial regionalism in East Asia may be tolerable as long as it is nested in the dollar-dominant global financial system and it contributes to solving the global economic imbalances; however if it detracts from that goal or threatens dollar hegemony, U.S. hindrance and disruption would be assured.[63]

Facing this kind of complicated situation, to appease other countries' concern about China's rise, China itself has to constrain its power, and make some compromises to win others' support. It needs to continue to play a reassurance game with South Korean and the ASEAN states in order to prevent them from investing in a balancing coalition with Japan, the United States, and possibly India or Australia as well.

The issuer of an international currency has often been associated with the provision of international public goods. Britain in the nineteenth century and the United

States after World War II both defended the international position of their currencies by providing the public goods for international financial stability.[64] As a rising state, China, together with Japan, could provide regional public goods for the whole region, including an anchor currency. It could also act as a lender of last resort, and provide formal and informal architectures essential for fostering regional cooperation. The provision of public goods such as these is very important for the success of East Asian economic integration.

While the comprehensive strength of a rising state is still far inferior to that of the hegemon, it is hard to say China's effort to internationalize its currency unilaterally will be doomed to fail. Thus, a better strategy would be pushing for a multilateral union rather than a unilateral expansion. Just as in the international political arena, building soft power and credibility is of paramount importance for China's monetary strategy to succeed, so winning more friends in the region by compromising to some extent is the right path for China to take. In short, only monetary regionalism can hedge against dollar hegemony, and effective joint leadership by Japan and China constitutes an indispensable factor for its success.

In conclusion, just as a report issued in London has pointed out, "Possibly the most difficult of these challenges is that China has no roadmap or past experience to rely on. It is indeed the first emerging country to seek to establish a truly international currency. Most countries had fully developed before they started to internationalize their currency—and Germany and Japan did not even complete the internationalization of their currencies."[65] Whichever path it ultimately takes, China's new international monetary strategy will inevitably exert great influence on regional monetary order building.

CONCLUSION

Dollar hegemony has given the United States enormous privilege in setting rules, acting as a de facto leader in shaping financial globalization, and deferring or even deflecting the adjustment costs by running large-scale deficits and depreciating its currency. Those states that have been most burdened by these adjustment costs—including China, Japan, and key members of the EU—have an incentive to disengage from the dollar system or otherwise press the United States to bear more of those costs. Europe has collectively been moving in that direction since 1973; financial and monetary regionalism in East Asia raises the possibility that Japan and China will also be in a position in the future to reduce the U.S. "power to deflect."

Despite its prominent role on the international stage, both politically and economically, China's monetary strength is still limited. It does not have a currency that can be used as a unit of account, a medium of exchange and a store of value in international transactions, and also, it has not participated in a workable regional monetary arrangement to defend its financial security. China has found itself at risk for it has been significantly exposed to current unsafe monetary circumstances. Recent policy and diplomatic measures by China are aimed at overcoming such a disadvantaged position. Beijing is pursuing this goal in an unprecedented way, and no clear road map exists to guide this process, although it can learn lessons through the past experiences of other countries such as Japan and Germany.

To cope with the losses that the dollar hegemony may bring to all East Asian countries, ASEAN+3, and especially China and Japan, which share common interests in de-linking with the dollar and building an East Asian monetary order, should join hands to overcome the security dilemma. They should go beyond the idea of unilaterally internationalizing their currencies and work together to build a regional currency union. However, because of the complications of regional political factors, especially the power shift in East Asia, one must remain cautious and restrained in expectations about the future of regional monetary order building.

NOTES

1. Balancing and bandwagoning are, of course, terms used to describe international alliance strategy. See Stephen M. Walt, *The Origins of Alliances* (Ithaca, NY: Cornell University Press, 1987). Here, I make use of the two terms to describe international monetary strategy.

2. A famous Chinese expert describes China and the United States as sleeping in the same bed, but dreaming differently, see David Lampton, *Same Bed, Different Dreams: Managing U.S.- China Relations, 1989–2000* (A Philip E. Lilienthal book).

3. Robert O. Keohane and Joseph S. Nye, *Power and Interdependence: World Politics in Trans*ition (Boston: Little, Brown and Company, 1977).

4. Although the U.S. and Chinese economies—the world's largest and the fastest growing major economy, respectively—have become mutually intertwined, both in terms of trade and finance, the mutual interdependence is never symmetrical. As far as bilateral financial relations are concerned, America, with growing budget deficits and a massive national debt, depends on China as the main holder of U.S. Treasury securities; China, with larger and larger surplus, depends on dollar-denominated financial assets as foreign reserves.

5. Nicholas R. Lardy, *Integrating China into the Global Economy* (Washington, DC: Brookings Institution Press, 2002).

6. Morris Goldstein and Nicholas R. Lardy, eds., *Debating China's Exchange Rate Policy* (Washington, DC: Peterson Institute for International Economics, 2008).

7. The data is available at the website of Chinese State Administration of Foreign Exchange. Assessed March 10, 2012, http://www.safe.gov.cn/model_safe/tjsj/tjsj_detail.jsp?ID=110400000000000000,22&id=5.

8. For financial statecraft, see Benn Steil, Robert E. Litan, *Financial Statecraft: the Role of Financial Markets in American Foreign Policy* (New Haven: Yale University Press, 2008).

9. Lawrence H. Summers, *The United States and the Global Adjustment Process*, Speech at the Third Annual Stavros S. Niarchos Lecture Institute for International Economics, Washington, DC March 23, 2004. Assessed January 17, 2011, http://www.iie.com/publications/papers/paper.cfm?researchid=200.

10. Recent work includes Brad W. Setser, *Sovereign Wealth and Sovereign Power: The Strategic Consequences of American Indebtedness* (New York: Council on Foreign Relations Press, 2008). Recent work includes David M. Andrews, ed., *International Monetary Power* (Ithaca, NY: Cornell University Press, 2005); Helen Thompson, "Debt and Power:

The United States' Debt in Historical Perspective," *International Relations*, 21(2007): 305–323; Gregory Chin and Eric Helleiner, "China as a Creditor: A Rising Financial Power?" *Journal of International Affairs*, 62(2008): 87–102; and Herman Schwartz, *Subprime Nation: American Power, Global Capital, and the Housing Bubble* (Ithaca, NY: Cornell University Press, 2009).

11. Daniel W. Drezner, "Bad Debt: Assessing China's Financial Influence in Great Power Politics," *International Security*, 34 (2009): 7–45.

12. Keith B. Richburg, "China, U.S. Stuck in Mutual Reliance; Unease on Eve of Obama Visit 'In the Dollar Trap' There, and 'In Hock' Here," *Washington Post*, Nov 16, 2009.

13. Paul Krugman, "China's Dollar Trap," *New York Times*, April 2, 2009.

14. See http://int.nfdaily.cn/content/2009–07/20/content_5389072.htm.

15. For the seigniorage of an international currency, see Benjamin. J. Cohen, "The Seigniorage Gain of an International Currency: An Empirical Test," *Quarterly Journal of Economics*, 85(1971): 494–607.

16. Yu Yongding, Jianzheng Shiheng: Shuang Shuncha, Renminbi Huilv he Meiyuan Xianjing (Beijing: Sanlian Chubanshe, 2010). For other Chinese articles talking about the "dollar trap," see Song Guoyou, Meiyuan Xianjing, Zhaiwu Wuqi yu Zhongmei Jinrong Kunjing, *Guoji Guancha*, 4(2010): 72–79. Jiang Yong, Meiyuan Xianjing: Zhongguo Yuexianyueshen, *Shijie Zhishi*, 14(2009): 46–48.

17. For the detailed debate, see Li Wei, *Kongbu Pingheng de Zhongmei Jinrong Guanxi*, in Sun Zhe ed., Jinrong Weiji yu Zhongmei Guanxi Biange (Beijing: Shishi Chubanshe, 2010), 176–185.

18. Song Guoyou, Meiyuan Xianjing, Zhaiwu Wuqi yu Zhongmei Jinrong Kunjing, *Guoji Guancha*, 4(2010): 73.

19. Diane B. Kuntz, *The Economic Diplomacy of the Suez Canal* (Chapel Hill: The University of North Carolina Press, 1991).

20. Olivier Accominotti, "The Sterling Trap: Foreign Reserves Management at the Bank of France, 1928–1936," *European Review of Economic History*, 13(2009): 349–376. Also see, Olivier Accominotti, "China's Syndrome: The "dollar trap" in historical perspective," Assessed March 1, 2011, http://www.voxeu.org/index.php?q=node/3490.

21. John Mearsheimer, "The Gathering Storm: China's Challenge to U.S. Power in Asia," *Chinese Journal of International Politics*, 3(2010): 381–396; Yan Xuetong, "The Instability of China-U.S. Relations," *Chinese Journal of International Politics*, 3(2010): 263–292.

22. "China's Role as a Lender Alters Dynamics for Obama's Visit," *New York Times*, November 15, 2009.

23. This kind of criticisms can be heard in many conferences and seen in newspaper and websites.

24. Quoted in Michael Wines, Keith Bradsher, and Mark Landler, "China's Leader Says He Is 'Worried' over U.S. Treasuries," *New York Times*, March 14, 2009. Assessed March 1, 2011, http://www.nytimes.com/2009/03/14/business/worldbusiness/14china.html

25. Zhou Xiaochuan, "Reform the International Monetary System," People's Bank of China, March 23, 2009. Assessed March 17, 2011, http://www.pbc.gov.cn/english//detail.asp?col?6500&ID?178.

26. Zhou, "Reform the International Monetary System."

27. "President Hu Jintao's Interview with American Press," Assessed March 21, 2011, http://www.fmprc.gov.cn/eng/topics/hjtzxdmgfw/t787237.htm.

28. "Beyond Bretton Woods 2: Is There a Better Way to Organize the World's Currencies?"

29. Jonathan Kirshner, *Currency and Coercion: The Political Economy of International Monetary Power* (Princeton: Princeton University Press, 1995), 148–149.

30. Peggy Hollinger and Geoff Dyer, "Sarkozy to Meet Hu as France Takes G20 Lead," *Financial Times*, November 3, 2010. Assessed March 21, 2011, http://www.ft.com/intl/cms/s/0/063a9a94–e79f-11df-8ade-00144feab49a.html.

31. China Pledges Sustained Euro Holdings With Plan to Invest in Bailout Funds. Assessed March 21, 2011, http://www.bloomberg.com/news/2012–02–14/eu-s-van-rompuy -welcomes-china-s-interest-in-aiding-europe.html.

32. See one of my articles in newspaper, Li Wei, "Baowei Ouyuan Suan de Shi Zheng-zhizhang," *Huanqiu Shibao*, May 10, 2010.

33. Song Jung-a, "G20 Agrees to Historic Reform of IMF," *Financial Times*, October 23 2010. Assessed March 21, 2011, http://www.ft.com/intl/cms/s/0/816ee036–dea2–11df -9b4a-00144feabdc0.html.

34. "China, Russia Quit Dollar," *China Daily*, November 4, 2010, http://www.chinadaily .com.cn/china/2010–11/24/content_11599087.htm.

35. In economics, BRIC is a grouping acronym that refers to the countries of Brazil, Russia, India, and China that are deemed to all be at a similar stage of newly advanced economic development. Despite lagging behind the other members in terms of economic growth, South Africa was formally invited by China to join the BRICs in 2010, and so the acronym changes from "the BRICs" to "the BRICS." The acronym was coined by Jim O'Neill in a 2001 paper titled "Building Better Global Economic BRICs." The acronym has come into widespread use as a symbol of the shift in global economic power away from the developed G7 economies toward the developing world.

36. Joe Leahy in São Paulo and James Lamont, "Brics to Discuss Common Development Bank," http://www.ft.com/intl/cms/s/0/99ed485e-7209–11e1–90b5–00144feab49a .html#axzz1t0nGQUql.

37. Daniel W. Drezner, "Bad Debts: Assessing China's Financial Influence in Great Power Politics," *International Security*, 34 (2009): 7–45.

38. Paola Subacchi, "'One Currency, Two Systems': China's Renminbi Strategy," October 2010, see http://www.chathamhouse.org.uk/files/17670_bp1010renminbi.pdf.

39. See "Zhongguo Huobi Zhengce Zhixing Baogao Disijidu", 15, http://www.pbc.gov.cn/ publish/zhengcehuobisi/3679/2012/20120215170702347457349/20120215170702347 457349_.html.

40. Eric Helleiner, *States and the Reemergence of Global Finance* (Ithaca and London: Cornell University Press, 1994), 81–100.

41. Robert Cookson, "ADB Issues Landmark Renminbi Bond," *Financial Times*, October 19 2010.

42. "World Bank's First Yuan Bond Promotes Chinese Currency's Internationalization," http://news.xinhuanet.com/english2010/business/2011–01/05/c_13677915.htm.

43. Chinese officials admit, however, that while the offshore market in Hong Kong can help lay the groundwork for greater international use of the currency in trade, the renminbi cannot become a reserve currency until there is much greater access to the mainland bond markets and the renminbi is easier to trade on the foreign exchange market. See Robert Cookson and Geoff Dyer, "Currencies: Yuan Direction," *Financial Times*, December 13, 2010.

44. While the original source is obscure, this line has long been widely quoted (with some variations of wording) by reputable sources. See, for example, Barry Eichengreen, *Globalizing*

Capital: A History of the International Monetary System (Princeton: Princeton University Press, 1996), 136,

45. Susan Strange, "The Persistent Myth of Lost Hegemony," *International Organization*, Vol. 41, No. 4, 1987, p. 569.

46. Paul Volcker and Toyoo Gyohten, *Changing Fortunes: The World's Money and the Threat to American Leadership* (New York: Times Books, 1992), 42–43.

47. See Barry Eichengreen, Jeffrey A. Frieden, *The Political Economy of European Monetary Unification*, Second Edition (Boulder, Colorado: Westview Press, 2001).

48. Menzie D. Chinn and Jacob A. Frankel, "The Euro May Over the Next 15 Years Surpass the Dollar as Leading International Currency," *NBER Working Paper*, No. 13909, April 2008.

49. For yen internationalization, see William W. Grimes, "Internationalization of the Yen and the New Politics of Monetary Insulation," in Jonathan Kirshner, ed., *Monetary Orders: Ambiguous Economics, Ubiquitous Politics* (Ithaca: Cornell University Press, 2003), 172–194.

50. Hyoung-kyu Chey, "The Changing Political Dynamics of East Asian Financial Cooperation: The Chiang Mai Initiative," *Asian Survey*, 49(2009), 450.

51. Paul Bowles, "Asia's Post-Crisis Regionalism: Bring the State Back in, Keeping the (United) States Out," *Review of International Political Economy*, 9(2002), 245.

52. Heribert Dieter and Richard Higgott, "Exploring Alternative Theories of Economic Regionalism: From Trade to Finance in Asian Co-operation?" *Review of International Political Economy*, 10(2003), 430–454.

53. For more on the 10+3, see Markus Hund, "ASEAN Plus Three: Towards a New Age of Pan-East Asian Regionalism? A Skeptic's Appraisal," *Pacific Review*, 16(2003), 383–417; and Richard Stubbs, "ASEAN Plus Three: Emerging East Asian Regionalism?" *Asian Survey*, 42(2002), 440–455.

54. Hyoung-kyu Chey, "The Changing Political Dynamics of East Asian Financial Cooperation: The Chiang Mai Initiative," 450.

55. William W. Grimes, *Currency and Contest in East Asia: The Great Power Politics of Financial Regionalism* (Cornell University Press, 2009), 8.

56. For East Asia's dollar standard, see Ronald I. McKinnon, *Exchange Rates under the East Asian Dollar Standard* (Cambridge: MIT Press, 2005).

57. See Zhao Haikuan, "Lun Renminbi Keneng Chengwei Shijie Huobi Zhiyi," *Jingji Yanjiu*, 3(2003); Liu Qun, "Quyu Huobi yu Shijie Huobi: Renminbi Qianjing Panduan yu Jueze Fenxi," *Xueshu Lunkan*, 9(2006).

58. See Yao Zhizhong, "Buduicheng Jingzheng yu Renminbi de Yazhou Zhanlue," *Shijie Jingji Yu Zhengzhi*, 7(2004); Li Daokui, "Zhongguo Ying Jujue Yayuan," *Da Jingmao*, 6(2006).

59. Xu Mingqi, "Cong Riyuan Guojihua de Jingyan Kan Renminbi Guojihua Yu Quyuhua," *Shijie Jingji Yanjiu*, 12(2005); Li Xiao, "Riyuan Guojihua de Kunjing Jiqi Zhanlue Tiaozheng," *Shijie Jingji*, 6(2005).

60. See Li Xiao, Ding Yibing, *Renminbi Quyuhua Wenti Yanjiu* (Beijing: Qinghua Daxue Chubanshe, 2010); Zhang Bin, "Dongya Quyu Huilv Hezuo: Zhongguo de Shijiao," *Shijie Jingji*, 10(2004); Zheng Haiqing, "Yazhou Huobi Hezuo Jincheng: Zhongguo de Shijiao," *Yatai Jingji*, 4(2003).

61. Li Wei, "Dongya Jingji Diqu Zhuyi de Zhongjie," *Dangdai Yatai*, 4(2011), 23–25

62. Mancur Olson, *The Logic of Collective Action* (Cambridge: MA: Harvard University Press, 1965).

63. William W. Grimes, *Currency and Contest in East Asia: The Great Power Politics of Financial Regionalism* (Cornell University Press, 2009), 207. Also see Thomas J. Christensen, "Fostering Stability or Creating a Monster? The Rise of China and U.S. Policy toward East Asia," *International Security*, 31 (2006), 81–126.

64. David A. Lake, "British and American Hegemony Compared: Lessons for the Current Era of Decline," in Michael Fry, ed., *History, the White House and the Kremlin: Statesmen as Historians* (Printer Publishers Ltd., 1991), 106–122.

65. Paola Subacchi, "'One Currency, Two Systems': China's Renminbi Strategy," 10.

7

Bargaining for More: China's Initiatives for Regional Free Trade in East Asia

June Park

This chapter analyzes China's initiatives in bilateral free trade in the East Asian region by examining free trade and economic partnership agreements. Despite potential benefits of a multilateral regional free trade in East Asia, bilateral agreements have been the preferred method for trade agreements and investment treaties in the region. While trade negotiations are lagging at the multilateral level in the Doha Round, countries have found better alternatives to tackle with trade issues—via bilateral free trade agreements (FTA) and economic partnership agreements (EPA), which provide partnering states with the opportunity for bargains and options to protect specific industries and agricultural sectors. The research proceeds in the following four segments: This research will first account for the motives and the driving force behind China's active engagement in trade deals via EPAs, and provide detailed case studies of China's EPAs; the second section will analyze regional trade dynamics with comparative perspectives from neighboring economies of the region—Japan and Korea. The third section will focus on the dilemmas of China's trade policies, in which China's aggressive positioning in the WTO trade disputes and the abuse of trade policies may dim China's prospective role in global and regional governance by examining reciprocal responses from trading partners in the region and at the multilateral level. The chapter will conclude with the prospects of the two-faced dimensions of China's foreign economic policy via trade bargaining.

In uncovering the initiatives and dilemmas of China's regional expansion of free trade, this research uses a process-tracing method by providing economic and financial statistics to support the arguments raised throughout the chapter. The periodization of 1999–2012 (post–Asian Financial Crisis) will allow for a decade-long analysis including recent developments of China's initiatives in regional and global trade. This given periodization will encompass the time frame from post–Asian Financial

Crisis of 1997–1998 and the Global Financial Crisis of 2008–2010, which have served as critical junctures for East Asian economies, including China.

THE BACKGROUND OF CHINA'S
FREE TRADE AGREEMENTS

In the post–Cold War era, the profound impact of economic interdependence resulted in the expansion of regional trade networks across the neighboring countries in Northeast Asia, and the region benefited greatly from these changes. While the initial phase of East Asian economic integration was a reflection of state interests and pragmatic calculations that focused on growing intra-regional trade, a concomitant sense of community derived from mutual influence of states on one another. Such effects of internationalization on states' economic policies and institutional forms have been emphasized in the "second image reversed" literature of international political economy, which stresses the influence of international factors on domestic outcomes. Meanwhile, powerful economies still make the rules for the global economy and shape regional order. The roles of sovereign states and their responses toward internationalization remain significant, particularly in the case of East Asia, in which bilateral relations continue to be important.

Following the Reform Era that began under Deng Xiaoping's rule in 1978, China has had remarkable progress in economic development and has transformed itself into the world's biggest manufacturing house. The economic transformation that occurred under the highly centralized and controlled government initiatives of the Chinese Communist Party (CCP) allowed it to serve as an increasingly attractive market for trade and manufacturing, owing to the most favorable conditions in factors of production any country has enjoyed in the past two decades: abundance of low-cost labor, huge landmass, and the ability to absorb and attract huge inflows of capital via foreign direct investment. Despite abrupt changes in the factors of production as the demands for wage increases and requests for improvement of working conditions are gradually evolving into social unrest and demonstrations in many parts of China, the Chinese government has nevertheless persistently pursued the goals of economic development as a priority agenda.

China's foreign economic policies remain strongly based on the Chinese government's agenda of economic growth. In previous decades, the regional trade network in East Asia had expanded in tandem with the economic growth of Japan and the Four Asian Tigers, with the United States as the main targeted market for sales across the Pacific. During the phase of economic recovery just after the World War II, Japan took the lead and had been at the forefront of the exploration and construction of production networks throughout Southeast Asia. And from the late 1970s, Korea's big leap into the regional production network building followed suit. Now, China is in the forefront of intra- and extra-regional trade networks. Since China's engines for economic reform were started up, it was presented with several opportunities throughout the past three decades: the combination of economic opening and domestic economic reform in China from the 1980s, coupled with the accommodation of the opportunities created by East Asian economic restructuring and foreign investment in the 1990s, and normalized trade relations with the United States and the entering into the world economy via accession to the WTO in 2001.[1] While China's potential for finance and services has yet to be realized, it has indeed succeeded in low-cost manufacturing and expansion of trade networks in the past decade, with high economic growth rates second to none in the global economy, albeit at the cost of unavoidable high inflation.

It is also apparent that China's economic rise has provided an opportunity for China to gradually restructure power politics in East Asia. Cautionary warnings for its trading partners are sent out regionally and globally. At the regional level, the intensified triangular relationship among the United States, Japan, and China manifests itself in current East Asian political and economic affairs. Its East Asian neighbors have already become very weary of China's speed of growth. At the global level, in addition to the debate on global imbalances and pressures for the appreciation of the renminbi from the United States and the European Union, developing economies, particularly those in Southeast Asia and Latin America, continuously raise concerns about losing ground to China in global market shares.[2]

Nevertheless, the upsurge of China's economic power and the CCP's adjustment to market capitalization have brought about challenges and frictions in trade at home and abroad. Three decades after the economic reform had been launched, China's quest for continued growth has inevitably widened the income disparity gap, and brought about political demonstrations and an outcry from its trading partners around the world in response to China's reshaping of the global economy.

In an effort to identify where China stands in the quest for regional free trade in East Asia, this chapter intends to focus on China's initiatives and dilemmas regarding regional free trade in East Asia. In response to the changing dynamics of East Asian regionalism, this research aims to provide the linkage between China's interests in trade for domestic growth. Through examinations of China's trade deals that are bargaining for interests catered to its economic development, it finds that China's objectives of economic growth and its control of finance and investment are embedded in its initiatives for regional free trade. It also finds that China continues to expand this capability via foreign economic policy: via proliferation of the Chinese economic development model to other developing countries of Southeast Asia, massive investment in the economies of ASEAN member states, and rapprochement with its East Asian neighbors to secure factors of production and markets for export. Finally, the research also sheds light upon the current dilemmas of China's pursuit of economic regionalization that may not be resolved simply by increasing the number of EPAs and/or FTAs.

CHINA'S INITIATIVES IN TRADE POLICY: GOING BILATERAL AND TRILATERAL

Prevailing Bilateral and Trilateral Economic Interests

From a macroeconomic perspective, China's comparative advantage in factors of production renders it a complementary economy for the developed economies—i.e., the United States, Japan, and the EU—but poses a considerable threat for competition for emerging market economies (EMEs). As developed economies become strongly reliant on China's low-cost goods, the impact of the Chinese economy on theirs is no longer complementary but has become the source of domestic political debates on the loss of manufacturing jobs and trade imbalance. This is all the more the case at the regional level in East Asia, in which the United States has played a significant political role since World War II and a Sino-U.S. rivalry is conceivable in proposed regional trade cooperation schemes as the Chinese economy continues to rise.

China has pushed for stronger ties with its Southeast Asian trading partners, the economies of whom Japan has continued to build firm production networks with in pursuit of its own economic development. Politically, Japan still holds open the door for the United States to continue to play a crucial role in the region, while protecting its economic gains by maintaining a sound relationship in trade and investment with China. This trend has become more apparent in Japan's foreign economic policy making in recent years. Regarding security dynamics that may impact economic interests in the region, the Asia-Pacific military allies of the United States—Japan, South Korea, Australia, Singapore, Thailand, and the Philippines—continue to rely on their alliances with the United States for security back-up and stability. At the same time, however, their economic interests are also closely attached to China, as trade volumes with China have increased considerably during the past decade.

The bilateral interests of neighboring economies compel China to pursue likewise. For Japan and South Korea, the dependence on the China market for their exports of high-tech goods and imports of low-cost materials has become an unavoidable, albeit rational, choice regardless of their preferences in trade tactics. Furthermore, running trade surpluses with China has motivated them to seek further opportunities in the China market—such as the initiatives for a South Korea–China FTA, a Japan-China EPA, and/or a trilateral China-Japan-Korea FTA and investment treaty. The most recent achievement is the Trilateral Investment Treaty reached by China, Japan, and Korea in April 2012. It is the first economic treaty concluded by the three economies, which includes a provision stipulating that a phased investment made before the establishment of a corporation is not subject to the anti-discrimination provision designed to protect foreign investors, while a phased investment after a corporation's establishment is subject to the provision.

The trilateral treaty also includes the Investor-State Dispute Settlement provision, which allows investors covered by the provision to initiate dispute settlement proceedings against foreign governments in their own right under international law, as do China's bilateral investment treaties with Japan and Korea. The treaty is also expected to enhance investor rights in that it emphasizes the transparency of investment systems and protection of intellectual property rights and prohibits requirements for the transfer of technology belonging to foreign-invested companies. It is also anticipated that the signing of the China-Japan-Korea trilateral investment treaty will give boost to the possibility of a free trade agreement amongst the three economies in the longer future. Nevertheless, considering public opinions and domestic political dynamics in the three countries, regional initiatives for a trilateral trade agreement among the three countries would most likely be a long-term project.

Free Trade Agreements (FTA) and Economic Partnership Agreements (EPA)

In addition to the bilateral schemes that Japan and South Korea had been pursuing, China has also pursued extra-regional trade alternatives via trade agreements with the EU and India. The recent commitment that ASEAN countries have made through economic partnership agreements with China imply that U.S. economic influence in the region could decline significantly, in the midst of the weakening of the dollar and the increasing importance of the renminbi for transactions in the aftermath of economic recovery from the Global Financial Crisis. It is important to note that these new trade deals are pedestals for China's development strategies, in order to secure markets, energy, and resources from its Asian neighbors.

An additional source of pressure that adds to the prevalence of bilateral trade agreements is the relative stalemate in multilateral trade negotiations. Given the constraints in the current multilateral trade regime, China has been very active in pursuing bilateral free trade agreements outside the WTO framework. Within the past decade, it has succeeded in launching FTAs and EPAs with countries within the East Asian region and elsewhere. In principle, an FTA (Free Trade Agreement) is a legally binding agreement between two or more countries that allow the parties of the agreement to reduce or eliminate barriers to trade, and to facilitate the cross-border movement of goods and services between the territories of the parties. Technically, FTAs are in fact a part of (comprehensive) Economic Partnership Agreements (EPA), which were initiated by countries such as Japan and Korea in the turn of the century. The differences between FTAs and EPAs are in that EPAs are not necessarily limited to trade and investment, but also encompasses agreements on other components of the economy—that is, tourism, the standardization of regulations for businesses, and intellectual property, among many other sectors.[3] Accordingly, EPAs cover a wider range of economic relations than FTAs, but are also preferential in that parties to the agreement may choose to open certain sectors of the economy and keep other sectors protected. As for China, establishing FTAs within the region is a preliminary step in building economic trade networks in East Asia.

Table 7.1.   China's Participation in Bilateral and Regional Trade Agreement (May 2012 Present)

China's Free Trade Agreements	
China-ASEAN FTA (ACFTA)—includes the Philippines, Malaysia, Myanmar, Thailand, Brunei, Singapore, and Indonesia	Signed in November 2004
China-Pakistan FTA	Signed in November 2006
China-Chile FTA	Signed in 2005
China-New Zealand FTA	Signed in April 2008
China-Singapore FTA	Signed in October 2008
China-Peru FTA	Signed in April 2009
Mainland and Hong Kong Closer Economic and Partnership Arrangement	Signed in June 2003
Mainland and Macau Closer Economic and Partnership Arrangement	Signed in October 2004
China-Costa Rica FTA	Signed in November 2008
China's Free Trade Agreements under Negotiation	
China-GCC (Gulf Cooperation Council) FTA	Negotiations launched in July 2004
China-Australia FTA	Negotiations launched in October 2006
China-Iceland FTA	Negotiations launched in April 2007
China-Norway FTA	Negotiations launched in September 2008
China-SACU(Southern African Customs Union) FTA	Negotiations launched in June 2004
China's Free Trade Agreements under Consideration	
China-India Regional Trade Arrangement (RTA) Joint Feasibility Study	Study Group established in 2003
China-Korea FTA Joint Feasibility Study	Study Group established in November 2004
China-Japan-Korea Trilateral FTA Joint Study	Study Group established in August 2010
China-Switzerland FTA Joint Study	Study Group established in September 2010
China's Preferential Trade Agreement	
Asia-Pacific Trade Agreement (The Bangkok Agreement)	Signed in 1975

Source: Ministry of Commerce, the People's Republic of China (May 2012)

China's Trade Deals in East Asia

China has worked extensively on expanding its trade network not just in the East Asian region and the Asia-Pacific region, but also around the world. Its free trade agreement with Pakistan shows that China has reached out with a strong political appeal. It is a contrast from the stagnant procedures of the China-India Regional Trade

Agreement (RTA) Joint Feasibility Study Group which has prolonged the process since 2003, and this backwardness can be assessed as China's balancing on India as a potential, emerging rival economy of South Asia. Recent developments have shown India's reluctance toward signing of the RTA, notably owing to India's current trade imbalances with China, and continuous Indian requests to lower China's non-tariff barriers (NTB) to facilitate the increased movement of goods over the border. More importantly, political and security risk concerning India have influenced China's attitude regarding India's expanding role at the regional and international level. The proposal for the China-India RTA has been put on the back burner as the bilateral relationship has become tense.

Meanwhile, FTAs with Chile, Peru, and Costa Rica show that it is determined to actively engage with the Latin America and the Caribbean (LAC) region.[4] The China-Peru FTA was the first comprehensive FTA that China had signed with a Latin American economy. Amongst all LAC countries, Chile has been the most open to FTAs—it was the first FTA partner for South Korea in 2002 and an FTA with Japan followed suit in 2006. Chile's 2005 FTA with China extended zero duty treatment phase by phase to cover 97 percent of products over a span of ten years. China has also been closely engaged with signing FTAs with economies of the Asia-Pacific, specifically in the Oceanic region. Its FTA with New Zealand was the first that China had ever signed with a developed economy, and FTA negotiations with Australia have been ongoing since 2005—Australia has also engaged in FTA negotiations with Japan since 2007.

China's current negotiations underway for FTAs outside the region include those with the Gulf Cooperation Council (GCC: Bahrain, Kuwait, Oman, Qatar, Saudi Arabia, and United Arab Emirates) which started in 2004; negotiations with the Southern Africa Customs Union (SACU: South Africa, Botswana, Namibia, Lesotho, and Swaziland) which also started in 2004; and negotiations with Northern European economies such as Iceland and Norway. Also, a study group for an FTA with Switzerland is ongoing since 2010—Switzerland already signed an EPA with Japan in 2009. Iceland was the first developed European country to recognize China as a full market economy and the first European country to negotiate an FTA with China. A potential FTA with Norway is also pivotal in that it is one of China's main suppliers of fertilizers, aquatic products, and oil, with negotiations having been launched in 2008. While China's penetration into the economies of the Arab region and the African region are not a surprise given that these regions are abundant in natural resources, it is also not a surprise that China has yet to begin FTAs with MERCOSUR and the European Union, since the economies of these regions have mixed effects from Chinese imports.

China's most extensive regional FTA is the China-ASEAN FTA, which has evolved over a span of nearly a decade. China and the ASEAN Member States (AMS) first signed the Framework Agreement on China-ASEAN Comprehensive Economic Cooperation at the Sixth China-ASEAN Summit in November 2002. In November 2004, Chinese Premier Wen Jiabao and the leaders of AMS witnessed the signing of the Agreement on Trade in Goods of the China-ASEAN FTA, which entered into force in July 2005. In January 2007, the two parties signed the Agreement on Trade in Services, which entered into effect in July 2007. In August 2009, the two parties signed the Agreement on Investment. The establishment of China-ASEAN Free Trade Area was intended to enhance the close economic and trade relations between the two parties, and also to contribute to the economic development of Asia and the world at large. What appears to have been essential for China in launching the China-ASEAN FTA, is gaining further access to its geographically closest neighboring nations that are still in earlier phases of economic development, and establishing stable political relations through the process. In recent years, China's regional initiatives in Southeast Asia have been reflected in its gradual increase of FDI net inflows into ASEAN member state economies.

The most critical and recent development in China-ASEAN economic relations is the transactions held in renminbi (RMB). Since the ASEAN-China Free Trade Area came into force in January 2010, Thailand the ASEAN have increasingly requested RMB denominated transactions and trade settlements. The direct settlement of renminbi and respective local currencies of ASEAN economies has become possible via agreements by the Bank of China Hong Kong, the Bank Central Asia—Bangkok branch of the Bank of China, Manila Branch of the Bank of China, Jakarta Branch of the Bank of China, Singapore branch of the Bank of China, Malaysian branch of the Bank of China, which will become participating banks of RMB business in the ASEAN region. The clearing and settlement agreement of RMB-denominated trade transactions is a big leap toward making the Chinese yuan one of the world's top currencies, allowing Chinese exporters and importers to start settling trade in RMB rather than dollars.

Among the ASEAN member states, Singapore is the most open economy in trade with a positive stance toward FTAs. Since the signing of Singapore's first FTA under the ASEAN Free Trade Area (AFTA) in 1993, Singapore's network of FTAs has expanded to cover eighteen regional and bilateral FTAs with twenty-four trading partners—given its restraints in resources but advantages in geographical location, it is by far one of the most FTA-driven economies of the world. It was the first test option for an FTA for Japan (New-Age Economic Partnership Agreement: JSEPA) in 2002, and it was the one ASEAN state to sign a bilateral FTA with China in 2008. Although physically small in size, Singapore's per capita income, living standards, and strategic priorities resemble those of Japan. For China, Singapore's growing diplomatic profile in the Southeast Asian region was also enticing, as its influence with other ASEAN member states cannot be underestimated. The absence of a major agricultural sector in Singapore was also an important factor for the highly protected agricultural markets in the Japanese economy, if not for China.

China's EPAs with Hong Kong and Macao were crucial in building political and economic partnerships with these two areas. These EPAs were signed between the Chinese Central Government and the Special Administrative Region of Hong Kong in 2002, and also between China and the Special Administrative Region of Macao in 2003, which are separate customs territories. To note, these were the first FTAs to be fully implemented in the Chinese mainland. Given the political importance of these regions for China, these two agreements were a necessary foundation for the application of the "One Country, Two Systems" principle, for institutional cooperation between the mainland and the two SARs. Since the turnover of Hong Kong in 1997, it was a necessary and advantageous step for China to embrace the Hong Kong economy, as China's economic transformation from the 1980s owed much to the prepared legal institutions based in Hong Kong, which enabled mainland enterprises to start operations.

The most anticipated but elongated FTA in the region for China is the China-Japan-Korea Trilateral Free Trade Agreement. At the current stage, it is still in the status in which an established Joint Study and Research Committee status is holding meetings, with the first meeting launched in August 2010. The negotiations are prolonged in part due to Korea's willingness to negotiate a China-Korea FTA beforehand, but more because of Japan's careful approach toward a trilateral free trade agreement or any FTA—Japan's FTA negotiations with Korea had been stalled since 2003 and an FTA with China is an option that Japan should dwell upon when the Trans-Pacific Partnership (TPP) negotiations under the lead of the United States are ongoing. Korea, which has been strongly driven by FTA and EPA agendas in the past few years, has continuously showed keen interest in an FTA with China. The unofficial joint study group for a China-Korea FTA was launched in 2004 and the group was upgraded to a joint official study group with the participation of government officials, businessmen, and academics, although difficult issues remain that may halt the launch of negotiations.. However, just as in the course of KOR-US FTA negotiations, the incumbents of the Korean government must risk losing votes from upset farmers, fishermen, and small-and-medium-sized manufacturing companies in the event of a China-Korea FTA.

TRADE AGREEMENTS OF CHINA'S NEIGHBORING STATES IN THE REGION: COMPARATIVE PERSPECTIVES

Japan's Comprehensive Economic Partnership Agreements (CEPA)

As Japan's dependency ratio on trade with other economies as a percent of GDP (approximately 40 percent, 2012 percent) is far lower than China's (60 percent, 2012 present) and Korea's (approximately 85 percent, 2012 present), Japan has taken a relatively careful and gradual approach in terms of signing economic partnership agreements. Japan has maintained a highly protected agricultural market whilst opening manufacturing and high-tech industries to the world for parts and whole products. For a country like Japan that retains a large, self-sustaining domestic market and a slow and rigid decision-making process in which the Japanese bureaucracy primarily depends on precedence, opting for trade was the least favorable choice for Japan. However, changing trade dynamics with neighboring economies China and Korea and potential market losses have stirred debates on the Japanese government's unhurried approach in adding new EPAs to its agenda. The Japanese government therefore has taken very cautious steps toward EPAs—a noticeable characteristic of Japan's trade policy is reflected in the choice of wording "EPA" rather than using the term "FTA" in their agreements. Labeling most of the trade agreements as EPA instead of FTA lessens political burdens on the incumbent parties and ministries by not directly engaging the Japanese public's negative stance regarding trade.

Japan's EPA negotiations are prepared and conducted simultaneously by relevant ministries in the Japanese government: the Ministry of Foreign Affairs (MOFA), the Ministry of Finance (MOF), the Ministry of Agriculture, Forestry and Fisheries (MAFF), and the Ministry of Economy, Trade and Industry (METI). While the MOFA takes the initiative for scheduling and conducting the negotiations, other industries strive to see the potential benefits and losses of future EPAs through careful examinations and simulative discussions. Economic research institutions such as the Japan External Trade Organization (JETRO) and the Japan Chamber of Commerce and Industry (JCCI) also generate ideas on the future prospects of potential EPAs and assessments on current EPAs.

While Japan and China both exhibit their interests in regional trade with Southeast Asian economies, Japan's recent hurdles in regional trade are reflected in the ongoing negotiations for an EPA with Australia. Since the launch of negotiations in April 2007, the negotiations have been prolonged considerably due to unmet interests. An economic partnership with Australia and New Zealand also opens doors for Japan to join the Trans-Pacific Partnership Agreement, but coming to terms with strong agricultural producers such as Australia and New Zealand requires opening the agricultural market for Japan. The main causes of the stalemate process in Japan-Korea EPA negotiations are centered around the same reason—Japan's reluctance to agricultural market opening. Meanwhile, both Japan and Korea have managed to sign EPAs with an emerging economy that China has yet to sign an FTA with—India.

Korea's FTAs and EPAs

Korea is by far the most active country among the three Northeast Asian economies in terms of conducting FTA and EPA negotiations. Korea's free trade negotiations are conducted in a similar fashion to Japan's, with the Ministry of Foreign Affairs and Trade at the lead and relevant bureaus at the Korean Customs, the Ministry of Strategy and Finance (MOSF), the Ministry of Agriculture and Forestry (MAF), the Ministry of Culture, Sports, and Tourism (MCST). Final decisions for the signing of FTAs are also conducted at the presidential level and in the Korean National Assembly. Additionally, the Korea International Trade Association (KITA) and the Korea Institute for International Economic Policy (KIEP) conduct research on the potential benefits and losses of FTAs.

Table 7.2. Japan's Participation in Bilateral and Regional Trade Agreements (May 2012 Present)

Japan's Economic Partnership Agreements	
Japan-Singapore EPA	Signed in March 2007
Japan-Mexico EPA	Signed in September 2004
Japan-Malaysia EPA	Signed in December 2005
Japan-Chile EPA	Signed in February 2006
Japan-Thailand EPA	Signed in April 2007
Japan-Indonesia EPA	Signed in August 2007
Japan-Brunei EPA	Signed in June 2007
Japan-ASEAN EPA	EPAs signed with Singapore, Laos, Vietnam, Myanmar, Brunei, Malaysia, Thailand, Cambodia by July 2010. Indonesia is the only signatory of the EPA remaining to go into effect.
Japan-Philippines EPA	Signed in September 2006
Japan-Switzerland EPA	Signed in February 2009
Japan-Vietnam EPA	Signed in December 2008
Japan-India EPA	Signed in February 2011
Japan-Peru EPA	Signed in May 2012
Japan's Free Trade Agreements under Negotiation	
Japan-Korea EPA	Negotiations stalled since November 2004. Japan-Korea high-level meetings to restart negotiations have begun since May 2010; the second bilateral was held in May 2011.
Japan-GCC EPA (includes Bahrain, Kuwait, Oman, Qatar, Saudi Arabia, UAE)	Negotiations have begun since September 2006
Japan-Australia EPA	Negotiations have begun since April 2007

Source: Recompiled from "EPA/FTA Negotiations and Status," Ministry of Agriculture, Forestry and Fisheries, Japan, May 2012.

Korea's trade agreements are not necessarily labeled as "EPAs," with the CEPA with India being an exceptional case. Nevertheless, the processes of opening up additional sectors of the economy undoubtedly stirs political controversies, and strong public opinion regarding trade agreements is often times manifested in massive on-street demonstrations. Despite the political difficulties, the Korean Ministry of Foreign Affairs and Trade has spearheaded trade negotiations with a strategic approach—gaining markets ahead due to its high dependency-ratio on external trade, and simultaneously expanding free trade networks with multiple countries in a steadfast manner. In this respect, expanding free trade networks outside the WTO is an inevitable choice for Korea due to its heavy reliance on external trade. Currently, Korea lacks the room for policy space to improve the import-export structure.

Currently, Korea's FTAs with Chile, Singapore, EFTA, ASEAN, the European Union, Peru, and the United States and an EPA with India are in effect. Another

Table 7.3. Korea's Participation in Bilateral and Regional Trade Agreements (May 2012 Present)

Korea's Free Trade Agreements	
Korea-U.S. FTA	In effect since March 2012
Korea-Peru FTA	In effect since August 2011
Korea-EU FTA	In effect since October 2011
Korea-India CEPA	In effect since January 2010
Korea-ASEAN FTA	In effect with all ASEAN states
Korea-EFTA (European Free Trade Area: includes Switzerland, Norway, Iceland, Lichtenstein) FTA	In effect since September 2006
Korea-Singapore FTA	In effect since March 2006
Korea-Chile FTA	In effect since April 2004
Korea-Turkey FTA	Negotiations completed in March 2012
Korea's Free Trade Agreements under Negotiation	
Korea-Canada FTA	Under negotiations since May 2004
Korea-Mexico FTA	Under negotiations since May 2000
Korea-GCC FTA	Under negotiations since March 2007
Korea-Australia FTA	Under negotiations since December 2006
Korea-New Zealand FTA	Under negotiations since December 2006
Korea-Columbia FTA	Under negotiations since July 2008
Korea-Indonesia FTA	Under negotiations since May 2011
Korea-China FTA	Under negotiations since September 2004
Korea's Free Trade Agreements under Consideration	
Korea-Japan FTA	Under joint study since November 1998
Korea-China-Japan Trilateral FTA	Under joint study since 2003
Korea-MERCOSUR TA	Under joint study since 2005
Korea-Russia BEPA	Under joint study since 2007
Korea-Israel FTA	Under joint study since 2009
Korea-SACU FTA	Under joint study since 2009
Korea-Vietnam FTA	Under joint study since 2010
Korea-Mongolia FTA	Under joint study since 2008
Korea-Central America FTA	Under joint study since 2010
Korea-Malaysia FTA	Under joint study since 2011

Source: Recompiled from the FTA Portal, the Ministry of Foreign Affairs and Trade, Korea, May 2012.

FTA was signed with Turkey, which will soon come into effect within this year. Negotiations for trade agreements are currently ongoing with Canada, Mexico, the Gulf Cooperation Council, Australia, New Zealand, and Columbia. Korea's joint-study groups for FTAs are being conducted with China and Japan for a trilateral FTA and respective bilateral FTAs; MERCOSUR, Russia, Indonesia, Malaysia, Central America, Mongol, Vietnam, SACU, and Israel are also participating in joint-study groups for FTAs with Korea. After completing years of trade negotiations and renegotiations for the EU-KOR FTA and KOR-US FTA, an FTA with China had been a top priority agenda for Korea in terms of securing large markets, and its negotiation is likely to be launched in the immediate future.

DILEMMAS OF CHINA'S INITIATIVES IN ECONOMIC REGIONALIZATION

Frictions in Trade Disputes at the Multilateral Level and Responses from Trading Partners

One of the most debatable issues in policy agenda following the Global Financial Crisis was the discussion on global imbalances. Since the recovery from the Asian Financial Crisis and particularly from about 2005, there have been growing concerns on the issue of global imbalances, with a focus on trade imbalance between the United States and China. The increasing amount of U.S.-China trade imbalances had been the grounds for the Obama administration's continued pressures on China for renminbi appreciation. For the United States, the exchange rate pressures on China are in effect a preventive measure to avoid the U.S. being placed at a huge comparative disadvantage in trade with export-oriented trading partners.

Trade frictions at the government level through the WTO and private lawsuits by industries will continue as long as there is a losing ground for the United States to do business in China and a domestic pursuit of incentives and interests through lobbying that will foster industries in the United States (Refer to the list of China's WTO dispute settlement cases as complainant and respondent in the appendix section.) Similar policies with diplomatic pressures at a different angle have been placed on Japan and Korea's automobile industries, that is, in the hearings on Toyota Congressional Hearing in 2010 and the renegotiation process of the KOR-US FTA. The mounting trade imbalances with its Northeast Asian trading partners in the past decades remains unresolved, and the United States still seeks to remain engaged in the region to avoid being "decoupled" from the East Asian regional policy-making process. Looking back on the past exchange rate debates and pressures regarding the Japanese yen and the Korean won in the 1970s–1980s, the U.S. claims on China's manipulation of its currency is highly likely to be repeated over time in the course of future U.S.-China trade relations. Though the yuan has been appreciated slightly following the currency debate in the G20 in 2009, China's fixed exchange rate pegged to the U.S. dollar will remain for the time being, and political confrontations over monetary policy are here to stay.

China's economic growth has now become a prominent issue for U.S.-China bilateral relations as well as for countries closely linked with China in the region. Despite the U.S. interests in maintaining a stable relationship with China and Japan to retain its influence in Asia, the relative gains of China in the region are compelling the United States and neighboring nations to engage in competitive bilateral relations. This in turn creates a constant power game and instability in the region. The intra-regional competition dynamics can be summarized as the "U.S.-China-Japan Triangle" and is quite straightforward: while Japan's economic stagnation has been

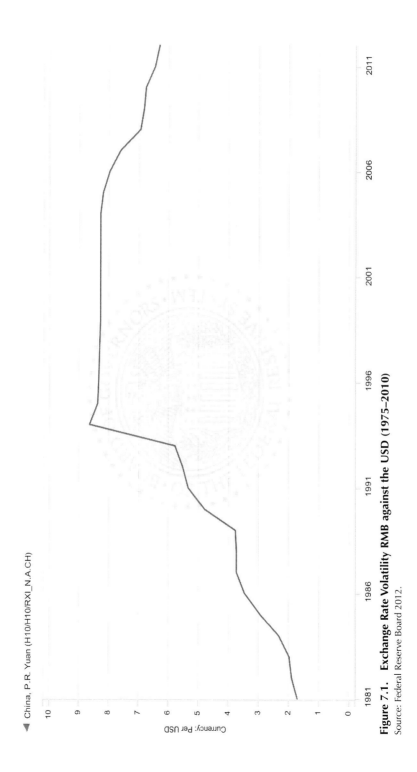

▼ China, P.R. Yuan (H10/H10/RXI_N.A.CH)

Figure 7.1. **Exchange Rate Volatility RMB against the USD (1975–2010)**
Source: Federal Reserve Board 2012.

reflected in its limited ability to exert influence abroad for the past two decades, China's economy has been enjoying a 7–12 percent GDP growth rate per year owing to a large-scale domestic investment and massive influx of foreign direct investment. From outside the region, the United States currently faces trade imbalances with all three Northeast Asian states, the largest of which is with China.

Currently, the U.S.-China trade imbalance stems from the growing U.S. consumption of Chinese manufactured goods and Chinese acquisitions of U.S. assets, particularly in the form of U.S. treasury bonds. The figures indicate that Mainland China took over Japan as the top foreign holder of U.S. treasury securities since 2008. The more China seeks to engage in deeper economic relations with its regional neighbors of East Asia, the more intense the U.S.-China regional competition for leadership can get. With Japan holding the door open for continued U.S. engagement in the region to balance against China, the U.S.-China-Japan Triangle creates a difficult dynamic in building regional leadership regarding economic policy making and prolongs the preference for bilateralism over multilateralism or regionalism in the region.

Regional Financial Cooperation and Renminbi Internationalization

Before the Asian Financial Crisis (AFC) of 1997, an "organizational gap" prevailed in Northeast Asia due to the absence of a power balance and different state structures.[6] While it was widely understood that Northeast Asia featured the paradox of growing economic integration and stagnant political cooperation, the AFC was a turning point for regional institution building in the region. The Asian Financial Crisis inevitably gave awareness to East Asian countries of the need to promote regional financial cooperation to prevent further crises and to retain stable economic growth. Northeast Asia remains a region that demonstrates relatively slow formal and legal integration, due to income disparities and differences in business cycles amongst economies.

With regard to regional financial cooperation, the major economies of Japan, China, and Korea acknowledged the need for a regional framework in the aftermath of the 1997 financial crisis, and implemented a common regional bond market, the Asian Bond Market Initiative (ABMI), and the Chiang Mai Initiative (CMI), a network of currency swap agreements among ASEAN+3 countries to secure liquidity against future financial crises. In the course of the global financial crisis, the CMI has evolved into a regional fund under the Chiang Mai Initiative Multilateralization (CMIM), with the proportions of the contributions to the fund decided upon diplomatic negotiations (China: Japan: Korea = 2:2:1, the remaining 2– percent of the fund contributions from ASEAN). In the course of the negotiations, China has created a level-playing field with Japan in the regional financial cooperation framework. While this is a good start for regional financial cooperation, the use of the fund is still partially subject to IMF conditions and has never been put into practice under actual circumstances of financial emergency. So far, neither China nor Japan has demonstrated willingness to lead the charge to make substantial progress to develop this institution into a full-fledged cooperative mechanism in regional finance. Very recently, the CMIM pool of funds was doubled to $240 billion by unanimous agreement of CMIM member states. China and Japan have always vied for leadership in the regional financial cooperation mechanisms, as Japan had previously pursued an Asia Monetary Fund (AMF) proposal, only to be turned down by the United States in 1999 following the Asian Financial Crisis.

Another development in East Asian regional financial cooperation is the establishment of the Credit Guarantee Investment Facility (CGIF) capitalized at $700 million. The launch of the CGIF was decided at the 13th ASEAN Finance Ministers Meeting, in which the ministers of ASEAN+3 agreed to establish ASEAN+3 macroeconomic research office (AMRO) based in Singapore, which was incorporated in April 2011 as a company limited by guarantee under the Companies Act, Cap. 50, of the Republic of Singapore as ASEAN+3 Macroeconomic Research Office Limited (AMRO Limited). It is currently composed of four members—finance ministries of China, Japan, Korea, and Singapore—and led by a Chinese director, Mr. Wei Benhua, who is to be succeeded by a Japanese head in the coming years.[7] The CGIF has the objectives for corporations to issue bonds in their domestic markets as well as in neighboring markets and across the ASEAN+3 countries. Again equal shares for investment was provided for China and Japan. The CGIF will be governed by an eight-member board drawn from contributing countries, including one representative from the Asian Development Bank (ADB), of which the Japanese government is a main sponsor. Once the $700 million capital has been used up, the board will review the CGIF's role, organizational structure and operations to decide whether the capital or 1:1 leverage ratio should be increased.

Regional Leadership and Economic Rivalry with the United States—TPP

The U.S. balance against China's economic outstretch in the China-oriented trade agreement in the ASEAN+3 framework in the East Asian region is reflected in the Obama administration's change of gears and the drive for the Trans-Pacific Partnership (TPP) or the Trans Pacific Strategic Economic Partnership Agreement. The TPP aims to abolish tariffs completely, without exceptions. Originally a framework comprising Brunei, Chile, New Zealand, and Singapore, the TPP has expanded to include the United States, Australia, Peru, Vietnam, and Malaysia. So far, four formal rounds of TPP negotiations have been held since 2010, led by the United States and Australia. In the beginning phase, it was difficult to judge the U.S. level of intensity and interest in the TPP agenda, just after the inauguration of President Barack Obama in January 2009, as the anticipated March 2009 negotiations were postponed. However, President Obama's first trip to Asia in November 2009 reaffirmed the U.S. commitment to the TPP, and the United States is currently leading the negotiations with the objective of shaping a high-standard, broad-based regional pact. China has expressed its interest in joining the TPP, although it is unclear how serious China is about joining. Japan is still in the course of deciding whether it should join the talks or not, and Korea has been requested to join by the United States following the KOR-US FTA renegotiations.

CONCLUSIONS: THE TWO-DIMENSIONS OF CHINA'S TRADE BARGAINING

Will China's rise and intent for economic regionalization be a catalyst or a hindrance for East Asian institutionalization? At this stage, there is no definite answer to this question; nevertheless, there is truth to interpreting China's initiative and drive for economic regionalization in East Asia. What really matters from this point forward is the response from the neighbors: at a stage in which China's rise is perceived both as a threat and an opportunity, how much validity in China's economic outreach are they willing to take in? Whether China will transform into a responsible actor and leader in the global political economy and also in the East Asian regional economic cooperation remains to be seen, and China faces the tasks of having to meet expectations in the areas of international trade practices and implementations of international standards and regulations in the domestic economy as well as in its external trade relations. Strictly speaking, however FTAs and EPAs are signed and implemented outside the WTO framework, the significance of regular trade practices are what constitutes the basis and outcome of reciprocal expectations of bilateral parties in free trade and economic partnership negotiations. In this respect, the cases of WTO dispute settlement cases reflect the deficiencies of China's practices in trade and services (i.e., sanitary and phytosanitary measures, intellectual property, financial opening) that have yet to be met with international standards. It is also all the more difficult to impose a certain standard on an economy that is dual-positioning itself as (1) a developing economy that is rent-seeking and also aims at exclusive treatment from international standards practiced by trading partners, and (2) a growing economy holder of strong purchasing power in the global economy that also retains the ambitions of a regional leader. The transitional period in between these positions may take longer for the case of China than it did for Japan and Korea, as China has not yet been met with a critical juncture that shook its economic fundamentals entirely, whereas Japan had gone through a currency readjustment via the Plaza Accord in 1985, the burst of the bubble economy at the end of the 1980s, and a major financial reform during the Big Bang in 1996; Korea had a nationwide structural reform in finance and trade under the IMF guidelines in recovering from the Asian Financial Crisis.

Two decades past the economic reform launched in 1989, China is throwing itself into a power game in a region in which the history of bilateral trade relations and development of the financial markets in East Asia reveals the significance of the role of the United States Accordingly, as China progresses its regional outstretch, a confrontation with the United States in economic policy making at both global and regional levels is unavoidable. In the meantime, Northeast Asian states' increasing involvement in cross-regional or bilateral trade agreements and partnerships elsewhere (i.e., the European Union, India) demonstrates an ongoing struggle among East Asian states based on the principle of self-help. Inevitably, the East Asian regional economic integration process has been and will continue to be heavily skewed by strong bilateral relations, extra-regional pressures, and intra-regional self-help seeking behavior for national interests of states. China's pursuit of regional leverage will continue to serve as a diplomatic tool for economic regionalization in East Asia, in the midst of intra- and extra-regional competition in the years to come.

NOTES

1. Naughton, B., *The Chinese Economy* (MIT Press, 2007).

2. Gallagher, K., and Roberto Porzecanski, *The Dragon in the Room: China and the Future of Latin American Industrialization*. (Stanford, CA, Stanford University Press, 2010).

3. Press briefings by press secretary of the Ministry of Foreign Affairs (MOFA) of Japan, Hatsuhisa Takashima (December 11, 2003). For instance, Japan's FTA and EPA strategies have been highly selective, in order to maintain political burdens of having to open its agricultural markets very low in the event of a free trade or economic partnership agreement.

4. While China is regarded as both an opportunity and a threat to many Latin American export economies such as Mexico, Brazil, Chile, and Argentina, the most vulnerable economy under China's influence is Mexico. Contest with China's economy is all the more difficult for the Mexican economy, its manufacturing sectors having been already distraught under the NAFTA (North American Free Trade Agreement of 1994).

5. Calder, K. a. M. Y. (2004). "Regionalism and Critical Junctures: Explaining the 'Organization Gap' in Northeast Asia." *Journal of East Asian Studies* 4(2) 2004: 191–226.

6. AMRO Official Website (www.amro-asia.org).

III

CHINA AND GLOBAL
ENERGY AND ENVIRONMENT

8

China's Quest for Energy Security: A Geoeconomic Perspective

Jieli Li

INTRODUCTION

China is on the rise. Unlike its past, China at the first decade of the twenty-first century is rising more visibly as a formidable geoeconomic power venturing actively into the world market. China's fast-growing economy, having already surpassed Japan to become the second largest economy in the world and arguably set to overtake the United States in the next two decades, is in high demand for energy resources to sustain its growth momentum. The ever-increased momentum of China's overseas venture is unprecedented and probably the most active one since after Chinese Ming Dynasty when Admiral Zheng He who commanded the largest vessels ever built in the world at the time that sailed as far as the east coast of Africa on its seven naval expeditions (1405–1430). Nowadays, in the same sea route, much of China's imported oil is being shipped though the Malacca Strait to its homeland. If we see Admiral Zheng He's overseas ventures as motivated by the geopolitical rise of Ming Dynasty in attempt to seek geoeconomic space for a potential global tributary system to the Chinese empire, current Chinese state seems to follow the similar trajectory of power-prestige projection for a big power. Indeed, like most rising world powers in history, particularly since the world entered what Wallenstein calls "the modern world system of capitalism,"[1] there has been a clear pattern of geopolitically induced geoeconomic spatial expansion, that is, with growing geopolitical power-prestige always comes a global search for raw materials and markets. Yet unlike its predecessor, the imperial Ming, China in the twenty-first century does not reach out across the oceans merely for a showing of diplomatic appeal and power status, but rather more pragmatically in search of markets in the world for its outbound capital, particularly in the regions where energy resources are located.

Indeed, over the past decade, China's increased demand in particular for energy and mineral resources has prompted the country's imports growing almost as fast as its exports. Since 2003, for example, China's annual purchase of raw materials has shot up from $73 billion to $240 billion, and China's fast-growing dependence on the imports of oil, copper, and iron ore has also prompted Chinese companies to invest abroad, up from $3 billion in 2003 to $19 billion in 2007.[2] In search for overseas energy market, the most noticeable change is China's thriving overseas trade and investment in the wake of the United States decline in those traditionally western dominant regions such as Southeast Asia, Africa, and Latin America. Over the past ten decades or so, while the U.S. has seen its economic aid, investment, and trade decrease significantly in the above regions due to its attention fully diverted to wars in Iraq and Afghanistan, China quickly stepped into the void and set its footing in trade and investment through effective economic diplomacy. The 2008 financial crisis that swept the United States and Europe has further provided Beijing with more geoeconomic opportunities to expedite its market expansion across the world. By all accounts, as China is marching more assertively into the world, securing future energy supplies has become the core of China's foreign policy and a vital national interest.

"CHINA INC."—A RISING GEOECONOMIC POWER

Geoeconomics is broadly defined as a study of the spatial, temporal, and political aspects of economics and resources. An analytical framework presented here is about how geoeconomics follows and intersects with geopolitics that works well for China. World history reveals a pattern of such dynamics in the state change: the expansion or contraction of the state's geoeconomic configuration often correlates with the rise and fall of its geopolitics in which the power of geoeconomics is projected through the state's geopolitical position and resource advantage at either the regional or the global level. As proposed, the state's geoeconomic advancement is a function of its geopositional advantage in the interstate system. Geopolitical advantage would help to facilitate economic development and market expansion (induced by its power-prestige and political leverage). Conversely, geopolitical disadvantage would likely impede economic development and market expansion (largely because of resources constraints stemming from war-preparation, war, and international sanctions). In other words, if all variables are held equal and constant, geopolitics tends to interact with geoeconomics in four distinctive patterns: (1) a state is likely to gain a "marchland" geopositional advantage when its rival states suffer from geopolitical decline in the interstate competition, (2) a state in a "marchland" geoposition with fewer rivals on its path is likely to grow stronger and acquire more geoeconomic opportunities, (3) a state's geoeconomic fortunes are likely to be gained through its geopolitical influence at either regional or global level as the state's power-prestige tends to promote or facilitate its business deals, and (4) on the opposite direction of one continuum, geoeconomic space is likely to shrink in direct proportion to the decline of state's geopolitical influence.

The rise of "China Inc" (as coined by Ted Fishman) has obviously benefited from the shift of geopolitical conditions turning favorably to China at the beginning of the twenty-first century.[3] China's quick reach-out for global energy resources neatly illustrates the interactive and cumulative dynamics of how the state's geopolitical advantage helps gain its geoeconomic foothold in the desirable regions of the world. Two major factors have apparently contributed to China's geoeconomic trajectory: (1) China as a beneficiary of drastic shift in the balance of power in world politics as both the fall of the Soviet Union and the United States diverted attention to wars in the 9/11 terrorist attack in the United States created an unprecedented geopolitical vacuum for China to grow unchallenged, and (2) China as a beneficiary of economic globalization as there has emerged, as never before in history, a liberal global trade regime that turned China's labor and venture capital to its full advantage in world market, and brought about huge trade surplus in favor of China.[4]

By 2010 China has overtaken Japan to become the second largest economy in the world next only to the United States. China has also become the second largest consumer of oil in the world as it is the second-largest net importer of oil behind the United States since 2009. According to the U.S. Energy Information Administration (EIA), China's oil consumption is projected to reach 17.0 million barrels per day by 2035 with a growth rate of 2.9 percent and so is its natural gas consumption up to 11.5 trillion cubic feet by the same period with the growth rate of 5.5 percent—both growth rates are considered the highest in the world. [5] While the country's domestic energy production has reached its peak limit, China seems to find itself with little alternative but to move more aggressively beyond its borders in search for new energy sources. China's current global energy search reflects its urgent need to diversify its energy suppliers in the world in order to meet its growing demand. Such strategy is further justified by China's recent move to build strategic petroleum reserves (SPR) as a safeguard for the sudden disruption of oil and gas supplies in the future.

Accordingly, China's foreign policy in the new century reflects its growing national concern over energy demand as China's economic and commercial interests in global market clearly prioritized its policy strategy. Historically China's foreign policy was never economic-centric or swayed by pure commercial motivation as its diplomacy always followed political agenda in the area of international relations. A good case in point is that China's economic aid and investment in Africa (as well as in Albania) in late 1960s and early 1970s were hardly driven for profit but rather primarily guided by its political strategy to gain visibility and reentry into the world stage. The strategy proved to be very successful as China reaped a huge diplomatic gain by winning the majority votes, mostly from African countries, in its bid to replace Taiwan as a permanent member nation in the *United Nations Security Council* (UNSC). What is worth noting here is that China's aid to Africa took place at the time when China itself was in economic difficulty, but the reason why China was still willing to devote generous economic investment can be answered by its political consideration to counterbalance the western power influence in the Third World countries as China saw itself as a leader or an ally to those poor countries. Clearly China won its geopolitical game in the late twentieth-century and the turning point for geopolitical shift was distinctively marked by formalization of Sino-U.S. diplomatic relations in 1979. With geopolitical ascendance comes the shift of China's foreign policy on its track toward a big power status.

In the post–Cold War period, China is in much better geopolitical position than ever before (since after the founding of People's Republic of China) and this favorable geopolitical position brought China a peaceful environment in which it could engage itself fully with economic reconstruction. In this process, China's huge population and lucrative market happened to fit right into the rising demand of outsourced western capital induced by a shift of international division of labor in the post–Cold War period in which the manufacturing industries of many developed countries were migrated to China for cheaper labor and higher profit. At this juncture, China's sustained peaceful environment caused by improved geopolitical conditions facilitated the graduate and smooth transition from planned economy to market-oriented economy. As previously discussed, China's geoeconomic rise benefited directly from two dramatic events that fundamentally reshaped the geopolitical landscape in the world: one is the disintegration of the Soviet Union (1991), and the other is the 9/11 terrorist attack on U.S. soil (2001) that immediately threw the United States into wars against Iraq and Afghanistan. The fall of the Soviet Union made China's longstanding northern military pressure evaporate, and weak Russia in the post–Cold War era was in no capacity to maintain its traditional domain of influence as it used to be in the Soviet era, thus leaving the entire central Asia region open for a new "great game" to play out between newcomers. China seized the opportunity and step in.

On the other hand, the United States was carried away to great extent by the emergent 9/11 incident and engaged the wars that followed, and worse, the protracted war in Afghanistan further diverted U.S. attention and resources away from its traditional domain of influence, thus leaving Southeast Asia, Africa, and Latin America (seen as the U.S. backyard) feeling unattended and neglected. Such negligence worsened when the United States and other western powers were caught in a financial crisis in 2008 and slumped into economic recession. China, on the contrary, was little affected by this economic crisis that swept across the western world due to its closed and well-guarded banking system and came up as a top financier in the world market. After years of attracting foreign investment to develop and consolidate its industrial infrastructure, China is now investing overseas itself, spearheaded by its state-owned corporations, making its move into resource-rich regions where the United States and other western powers fall back.

All the changes in the world over the past two decades, directly or indirectly, helped promote an unprecedented geopolitical opportunity for China to rise quickly and the significance of China's role in the new era has come to be more recognized. While the United States was eager to get China as a strategic partner into its global anti-terrorist campaign, Russia joined China in forming a new inter-governmental security organization called the Shanghai Cooperation Organization (SCO) which comprises all major nations in or near central Asia including China, Russia, Kazakhstan, Kyrgyzstan, Tajikistan, and Uzbekistan. A clear sign of China's rising geopolitical power-prestige is that the United States not without hesitation yielded and finally granted China permanent most favored nation status (MFN). MFN status is important in terms of its trading privilege as it entitles China to economic preferences offered by the U.S. government only to its best trading partners. Winning the MFN is a big step forward for China to get further integrated into the world economy—a clear sign of geoeconomic ascendance.

China's geoeconomic status was further reinforced by its accession to the World Trade Organization (WTO), and gaining the WTO membership has put China in direct access to a lucrative global market through a multilateral trade system, and more importantly it puts China in a better geoeconomic position to compete with the West in doing business with other countries. "China Inc." has quickly grown into a global economic powerhouse and its thirst for raw materials and energy resources to feed its thriving economy is altering the global geoeconomic landscape.

China's global market expansion powered by its rising geopolitical influence can be seen in the flow of investment from inbound foreign direct investment (IFDI) to outbound foreign direct investment (OFDI). While IFDI dominated the Chinese market throughout the 1980s and 1990s, in recent years China started using its newfound wealth to invest overseas. Data indicate that China's OFDI has reached as high as $170 billion.[6] Indeed, China has sped up its acquisition of overseas assets to meet its energy needs.[7] China's oil refiner, Sinopec, made China's largest overseas acquisition by buying Addax Petroleum—a Swiss oil company for $7.24 billion, which gives China access to the oil fields in Nigeria and Iraq. Furthermore, China National Petroleum Corp (CNCP) won a joint bid with BP to buy oil assets in Iraq. For even bigger bids, CNCP once attempted to take over Argentina's YPF—largely owned by Spain's Respol—for $17 billion, and China Aluminum Corp also attempted to buy a share of Australia's Rio Tinto for $19.5 billion. Although both bids failed for undisclosed reasons, the attempt itself indicates how ambitious and eager China is to seize the world's resource market. The report also revealed that the Chinese government would be willing to take $2 trillion out of its huge foreign exchange reserves and use it to acquire much needed resources all around the world.[8] In exchange for access to oil and other raw materials to fuel its booming economy, Beijing has boosted its bilateral relations with resource-rich states, sometimes striking deals with what the U.S. defined as "rogue" states or treading on the regions that traditionally belonged to the western turfs as long as these deals fit into Chinese geoeconomic interest for its own energy security.

STEPPING INTO THE GEOECONOMIC NICHE IN SOUTHEAST ASIA AND AFRICA

In Southeast Asia, when the U.S share of trade with the region is in decline, China has steadily strengthened its trade links with the Association of Southeast Asian Nations (ASEAN) whose member nations include Brunei, Cambodia, Indonesia, Laos,

Malaysia, Myanmar, Philippines, Singapore, Thailand, and Vietnam. Sino-ASEAN trade has grown from $8 billion in 1981 to over $130 billion in 2005, and then increased to $179 billion in 2008.[9] China is now one of the two largest trading partners with the ASEAN. As early as 2004, China signed an accord with ASEAN to create the ASEAN-China Free Trade Area (ACFTA) which came into effect in 2010 and this ASEAN trade bloc is expected to serve as a common market rivaling Europe and North America.[10] The 2009 global financial crisis hardly slowed down China's market penetration into Southeast Asia, and late that year a Chinese construction company obtained from the Malaysian government a commercial contract involving $2.2 billion for building a railway from Gemas to Johor Baharu.[11]

For China, Southeast Asia is strategically important to its vital geopolitical and geoeconomic interests because in this region lie the Straits of Malacca linking the Pacific Ocean and the Indian Ocean through which about 80 percent of China's oil ships pass, and further in the South China Sea lie the Spratly Islands surrounded by China, Vietnam, Brunei, Malaysia, and the Philippines, which are said to be potentially rich in oil. In addition, the Mekong River is a strategically important trade route for China to get deep into the Southeast Asia market. In recent years, China has built several inter-regional highways that connect Southwestern China to Vietnam, Thailand, and Burma to meet the fast-growing trade demand. In fact, China's influence became irresistible when it flexed its geoeconomic muscle in the 1998 Asian financial crisis by assuring some hard-hit Southeast Asian nations of China's commitment to keeping its currency stable to prevent the region from financial meltdown.

To further strengthen its influence in the region, China quickly came to aid the crisis-stricken ASEAN in the 2008–2009 global financial "tsunami." More than any other countries, Beijing made a pledge of USD 10 billion investment cooperation fund in addition to an offer of $15 billion in credit to ASEAN, in which a special aid of 270 million yuan (USD 39.7 million) was allocated to what are considered pro-Beijing ASEAN nations such as Burma, Cambodia, and Laos.[12] The United States is aware of the change, but its recent effort to counterbalance the Chinese influence may not be as effective as it wishes to be.[13] The reason is simple: geopolitics still matters. The fact that China's influence has risen and America's has ebbed also has much to do with China's close proximity to the region which makes China sit in a better geographical position than the United States in contending for regional domination. Geoeconomics follows geopolitics as China's position has been clearly reinforced in recent years by its easy logistical access to the region through the means of its booming trade, economic aid and venture capital. Southeast Asian countries that are connected with China through the Mekong River—Myanmar (formerly Burma), Cambodia, Laos, Thailand, and Vietnam—offer lucrative markets for Chinese investment. For example, China's investment in Burma seems more favorable than other Southeast Asian countries as China sees Burma has both geopolitical and geoeconomic benefits as the two proposed gas and oil pipelines that are under discussion which would connect Kunming, China, with central Burma (gas) and Burmese port of Sittwe (oil), and the latter would provide an alternative route to China for the Middle Eastern crude oil transportation, thus making China rely less on the geopolitically vulnerable Malacca Strait.

On the other geoeconomic front, China is now thrusting deeply into the African continent. Historically China has fostered friendly diplomatic relations with African countries. China has long treated Africa as in brotherhood of the Third World against Western imperialism and colonialism. Yet, geoeconomically, Africa is still largely under the domain of western influence. However, this traditional western domination has been seriously challenged as Africa becomes a new target region where Chinese companies are now vigorously moving in to carve out their own geoeconomic niches suitable for investment and business opportunities. In 2009, China surpassed the United States as Africa's largest trading partner in a total trade of $79.8 billion as compared with that of $78.9 billion with the United States.[14] China is competing with the West in business sectors ranging from oil, lumber, refining, agriculture, mining, textiles, and banking to the construction of dams, railroads, highways, bridges, airports, and housing.[15] China has become Africa's No. 1 trading partner, and more than one-third of African oil is on its route to China. From 2000 to 2006, China's bilateral trade with African regions quintupled to $55 billion and surpassed $120 billion in 2010.[16]

Although China is not a newcomer to Africa, its economic presence in the region before the new century was very limited in terms of investment. In the early 1990s, China's investment in Africa came largely from government projects and state-owned enterprises, but since 2000, hundreds of Chinese private companies have thrown themselves into the investment frenzy in the continent. The recent data show that China's total investment in the African region has now amounted to $40 billion and the African production in China's total oil import has increased from 10 percent to 40 percent over the past decade.[17] According to the statistical data of the Chinese ministry of commerce, Sino-African trade was merely $10 billion in 2000, but by 2008 it skyrocketed to a "historic" level of $106.8 billion, with an average yearly growth rate of more than 30 percent.[18]

It is worth noting that the Chinese investment tends to flow into regions that are shunned by Western countries due to what is perceived as inadequate economic profit. As some analysts pointed out, by being willing to take short-term meager investment returns, China is aimed at its long-term geopolitical goal for forming strategic alliance and friendly relations with Africa and this strategy would serve its global geoeconomic interest in securing energy and mineral supplies to fuel its economic growth. The "no-strings" attached investments made "Chinese deals" more appealing to African governments than Western ones, which are often linked to conditions for improvements in human rights and democracy. For example, China has invested billions of dollars in contracts involving oil and gas drilling rights with Nigeria, Sudan, and Angola, and is now working on other exploration or extraction deals with Chad, Gabon, Mauritania, Kenya, the Republic of Congo, Equatorial Guinea, and Ethiopia. In Nigeria, Chinese companies invested almost $5.5 billion in acquiring a 45 percent stake of an offshore oil field and developing oil reserves.

Under Chinese finance, Angola is contracted to export 25 percent or more of its oil production to China. In Sudan, China's investment brought her a 7 percent supply of China's total oil imports. In Zambia, Chinese investment in copper and coal reserves makes up 7.7 percent of the country's GDP.[19]

Leading China's geoeconomic thrust is China's diplomacy in fostering a closer political relation with the African continent. As of 2000, China began sponsoring the Forum of China-Africa Cooperation (FOCAC), which has held every three years. The past Forums gathered together the leaders of forty-nine nations to talk over how and what China could do to help Africa. In so doing, China has acquired the geopolitical leverage in contending with western powers while at the same safeguarding its own economic interests. Furthermore, as a permanent member of the U.N. Security Council, China is equipped with the veto power and other means to block any move that it perceives would threaten its global geoeconomic interests, as demonstrated by its success in preventing the U.N. from taking action against Sudan for the alleged genocide in its Darfur region and against the Mugabe regime in Zimbabwe.[20] In addition, Chinese peacekeeping forces in the name of the U.N. sent into Africa helped boost China's power-prestige, being in the vanguard to translate geopolitical needs into geoeconomic benefits.[21] Around Darfur, Sudan—the war-torn but oil-rich region—China once dispatched a 4,000-strong peacekeeping force in a U.N. mission to safeguard its invested oil projects.

FILLING THE GEOECONOMIC VOID— CENTRAL ASIA AND LATIN AMERICA

China's economic expansion in central Asia is clearly under its grand geopolitical design—to boost its power-prestige and ensure its energy security in the region. Strategically, the Central Asian region came into a close watch of China since the disintegration of the Soviet empire and particularly since the United States waged the anti-terrorist war in Afghanistan. The U.S. military presence in the region aroused China's national security concerns as its northwestern border was exposed directly to mounting geopolitical pressure. Yet, a turning point for China to have its northwestern geopolitical pressure lessoned came up when the U.S. military was marred in the battlefield of Afghanistan as the war became protracted and costly, thus becoming increasingly unpopular on America's home front. On the other hand, the U.S. military was strained by its resource shortfall due to its financial crisis that started in 2008 and the nation shows no clear sign of quick recovery from its economic recession. China's geoeconomic advantage was further gained as its neighbor Russia—another big power player in Central Asia—also experienced a sluggish economy, which severely limited its investment capacity in the central Asian region. With the result that both the United States and Russia were weakened by their economic difficulties, their traditional allies lost financial assistance much needed for the ailing economies. For example, Kazakhstan suffered from decreased foreign investment by half as of 2008.

All this subsequently created geoeconomic opportunities for Chinese aid and venture capital to move in, with most of it flowing into energy resource sectors. In this process, China's state-owned energy enterprises were the vanguard in China's expeditions.

China's move was quick and decisive. China National Petroleum Corporation (CNPC) took the lead and in 2005 it purchased Petrokazakhstan, whose assets included eleven existing oil fields with licensed permits to explore seven other fields. In 2006, CNPC moved further to establish a joint venture with Kaz Trans Oil to build the Sino-Kazakh Pipeline, which was considered the major step for China to develop a non-Russian oil import route. In the following three years, with massive capital venturing actively into the region, China succeeded in breaking traditional Russian domination over gas and oil markets to be able to use its own economic leverage in making local governments turn to China-favored energy policies. However, this economic leverage wouldn't have been effective if China's position were not bolstered by the key role it played in the Shanghai Cooperation Organization (SCO), which is aimed at securing central Asian stability and has its member nations across the region. While geoeconomics interacts with geopolitics, China has its advantage in close proximity to the Caspian region, which might be another oil-rich spot like the Middle East as some analysts predicted. As a USCC report points out, by playing in China's favor the Caspian region governments' common concern with separatism and extremism, China effectively used SCO as a venue to allow its state-owned energy companies to gain easy entry into the region[22] and facilitate making business deals and developing energy ties with local governments.[23]

Indeed, behind the economic motive of China's thrust into Central Asia is its political consideration for long-term national security on its northwestern boarders. For China, Central Asia is strategically important in its geographical position to check or combat the influence of the Muslim Turkic-speaking Uighur separatist movement around and in Xinjiang. On the other hand, China and Russia share the similar geopolitical concern over the encroachment of the U.S. influence into Central Asia, and both see the U.S. military presence in the region as an American strategic scheme to control energy resources in the Caspian Sea in order to make it an additional source to Persian Gulf oil supplies. It is true that for the U.S. geoeconomic interest, its military presence in the region can ensure that Baku-Tiblisi-Ceyhan pipeline remains open to counterbalance the "petro-power" of Iran.

In confronting the U.S. energy policy in Central Asia, China takes two distinctive strategies in securing energy supplies: (1) gaining full or partial ownership of resources through financing acquisition, and (2) constructing oil and gas pipelines that connect to China. The strategy China takes to concentrate on financing acquisitions let Chinese oil companies gain full or partial ownership of some nation's energy assets. China also extends loans to some national oil companies in the region in return for them to allow the Chinese oil companies an access to direct involvement in exploration projects or provide guaranteed oil supplies. In 2009 alone, China provided Kazakhstan with US$10 billion in a line of credit and another US$10 billion in a "loan for oil."[24] With all the investments, China has now increased its share in control of Kazakhstan's oil production by over 15 percent. In this process, as previously discussed, China's state-owned companies played the leading role. For example, China National Petroleum Corp (CNCP) and Kazakhstan's state-owned oil producer KazMunaiGas formed a joint venture acquiring MangistauMunaiGas from Central Asia Petroleum Ltd. of Indonesia. As part of acquisition, CNPC can gain priority access to future projects in exchange for a $5 billion loan offered by CNPC to KazMunaiGas, and China's Export-Import Bank of China also loaned $5 billion to Kazakhstan Development Bank to help improve infrastructure.[25]

Currently with China's investment, two major oil and gas pipelines are being under construction: one links Kazakhstan to China with Chinese investment up to $3 billion. The other pipeline, at a cost of $7.3 billion, starts from Turkmenistan via Uzbekistan and Kazakhstan to China.[26] With China's high-speed economic growth, the International Energy Agency (IEA) recently estimated that Chinese natural-gas demand would rise to 142 million tons in 2015 and 181 million tons in 2020. China turns to Turkmenistan for its enormous gas supply as the country holds the world's fourth-largest gas reserve. China Development Bank offered Turkmenistan a credit line of $4 billion in 2009 to help increase gas production fourfold to 250 billion cubic meters a year by 2030.[27] In its gas supply to China, Turkmenistan already sent 2.59 million metric tons, or about 2.9 billion cubic meters in 2010, and 17 billion cubic meters of the fuel in 2011 and is expected to reach 20 billion in 2012. However, China has its priority agenda in selecting and investing in Central Asian countries. For example, China's investment seems to weigh more in bordering Kazakhstan where there lives a large Uighur population—a potential source of ally for Uighur separatists in China's western border province—Xingjiang. In addition to huge investments in oil and gas, China has recently tapped into uranium mining in Kazakhstan as a Chinese nuclear power company is working with its Kazakh counterpart in a joint venture project. It turned out that China's geoeconomic "card" served the need of its geopolitical game very well as we found the Kazakh government chose to remain silent and neutral in its attitude toward the 2009 Uighur separatist riots in Urumqi, Xingjiang, China.

By tapping into the global energy resources market, China also found its geo-economic niche in Latin America. China's move into Latin America is considered to be driving a wedge into the region which the United States has always regarded as its "back yard" under its sphere of influence held up by the Monroe Doctrine of 1823. When the United States fell back in Latin America in recent years, China quietly moved in to take up the slack in trading and investment with Latin American countries left behind by the United States and other western powers. Trade between China and Latin America climbed from $10 billion in 2000 to $140 billion in 2008.[28] Since 2003, China's trade with Latin America has grown at an annual average rate of 40 percent.[29] In 2009, China surpassed the United States as Brazil's biggest trading partner. China's growing presence in Latin America again reflects its geo-economic strategy in search of greater access to energy resources wherever available. Indeed, China has become a significant importer of goods from countries such as Venezuela, Brazil, Chile, and Peru as Chinese imports from these countries generally concentrate on raw materials such as oil from Venezuela, zinc from Peru, copper from Chile, and iron ore from Brazil. China has also turned out to be the biggest foreign investor in Ecuador's oil industry.

Nonetheless, what should be considered China's most daring move in Latin America is its big stride into Venezuela, the fifth largest oil exporter in the world, doing business with anti-American president Hugo Chavez. China started forging close ties with Venezuela at the time when Chavez ran into conflict with the United States through his open defiance. Evidently Chavez played the "China card" in retaliation to the U.S. hostility and economic sanctions to his administration. By increasing its oil exports to China while reducing its shipments to the United States, Venezuela was able to keep its economy booming without depending on the U.S. market for its national revenue. Since he took office in 1999, Chavez made several official visits to China in search for economic cooperation with China. In 2004, Chavez entered into eight business deals on energy operation with China and some analysts claimed that all these energy deals would boost imports of oil to China up to 500,000 barrels per day.[30] In addition, Chavez attempted to seek a strategic alliance with China as a counterbalance to the United States by allowing Chinese companies to be entitled to developing fifteen oil fields in eastern Venezuela.[31]

China's success in setting its footing in Venezuela indicates that China's growing geopolitical clout has bolstered its geoeconomic expansion, and this process has also been reinforced by its double-digit economic growth percentage and increased trade surplus with the United States In this geoeconomic game, Hugo Chavez was fully aware that the United States could hardly use any leverage to stop or deter China from doing business with Venezuela. The same is true of the case of Iran. As the U.S. companies were prohibited and other foreign companies shied away from making any business deals with Iran, under the threat of U.S. punishment by the Iran-Libya Sanctions Act (ILSA), Chinese companies defied the U.S. threat and moved in while the western companies moved out. Since 2000, Iran provided China with more than 13 percent of its oil production, and the two countries went further in 2004 to agree to work on a joint project for liquefied natural gas for a period of thirty years. The fact that China dared to bypass the ILSA to do business with Iran and also with Libya indicates that China's geoeconomic thrust was driven in no small measure by its geopolitical prowess as China has become more assertive in playing its role in the world affairs as one of five permanent members in the governing body of the United Nations Security Council.

With China stepping up its presence in Latin America, the United States is now facing a powerful competitor in its traditional domain of influence. The United States seems incapable of holding China from marching into its "backyard," especially at the time when the United States itself is mired in financial crisis. For Latin American nations, then, cash-rich China has brought more business opportunities so that they can depend less on the U.S. market. As some analysts commented, the United States is losing not just its traditional status as the top trading partner in more Latin American countries, but its political influence as well.[32]

In a geoeconomic strategy different from the United States, China has adopted a more pragmatic, non-ideological stringed approach in doing business with Latin America, and this strategy effectively challenged the U.S. loan policy to some Latin American countries that are often conditioned by human rights and transparency of politics. While the United States attached political and ideological strings to loans, China's more pragmatic and business-focused approach became more attractive to Latin America. In terms of aid programs, Chinese development banks have become actively involved and taken over much of the function that used to be offered by the Inter-American Development Bank—a Washington-based major lender in its aid to Latin America as the latter's loan capacity is very much limited by money shortfalls due to financial crisis starting in 2008. For example, in 2009, China gave Brazil an access to $10 billion (almost as much as all the financing provided by the Inter-American Bank in the entire year of 2008) while at the same time increasing its development fund in Venezuela from $6 billion up to $12 billion. China also provided Ecuador and Argentina with $1 billion and $10 billion respectively in loan.[33] All these aid projects are largely in loan-for-oil deals between China and those recipient countries. In return to Chinese financing, Venezuela has agreed to boost its oil shipments to China up to one million barrels a day. Brazil will use the loan for further offshore oil exploration and plan to ship 150,000 barrels of crude oil per day to China.[34]

Like China's foreign policy in other regions of the world, China's geoeconomic expansion into some South and Central American countries also carries with it its geopolitical agenda to drive Taiwan's influence out of the region through economic assistance as mainland Chinese government sees Taiwan as a breakaway province (as the result of the civil war in the late 1940s) and wants to take it back for unification. Chinese strategy is clear: first to isolate Taiwan and limit its diplomatic space by winning over those countries with which Taiwan has a formal diplomatic relations, and second to get those countries turned into China favored policy to sever their relations with Taiwan.[35] The battle drags on for years between these two Chinese states, but which side would win the battle may depend largely on how much more the geopolitics and geoeconomic leverages each side can hold on to in the region.

CONCLUSION

China's relentless global search for energy resources in the first decade of the twenty first century showcases what I see it as an unprecedented geoeconomic expansion in Chinese history. As we discussed in preceding sections, the rise of Chinese geoeconomic power is closely associated with its rising geopolitical position in the world system which manifests itself in China's ascendance into a "marchland" geo-position resulting from the declining influence of both the United States and Russia in their traditional spheres of domination. What is worth noting is that in search of stable and secured sources of energy, Chinese foreign policy has been prioritized by its new geoeconomic strategy designed to support and protect its vital energy interest in Asia as well as in other regions of the world. This shift of policy priority demonstrates China is no longer a nation that intends to keep a low profile in international politics and put political consideration over commercial interest as it was in the Cold War period. From this perspective, China in the twenty-first century sees itself not just as what is conventionally perceived as a geopolitical power but as a rising geoeconomic power that tends to use geopolitical leverage to serve its geoeconomic interest just like any real super power would do in world politics. The recent tension arising from sovereignty dispute over the oil-rich South China Sea between China and several Southeast Asian countries such as Vietnam and the Philippines illustrates such trend as China seems to be firm with its stand and may not hesitate to use force to defend what it defines as a "vital interest of national security." Furthermore, China has even showed its confidence and is unhesitating in challenging the mainstream opinion such as vetoing the U.N. sanction against Syria in the Middle East Region where China definitely has its geoeconomic interests.

As China's energy demands continue to impact the world markets, its foreign policy will be more inextricably linked with its energy strategy to ensure the desirable economic growth for the nation.[36] China seems less interested in making alliances with other countries merely based on political rather than economic benefit as in contrast with its "good, old days," particularly during the Mao era (under the strategy of "Friendship First and Competition Second"). Nowadays, China's alliance strategy seems to orient toward both geopolitical and geoeconomic gains and such a pattern becomes evident when we examine its trade and investment strategies in Southeast Asia (as in Myanmar), Africa (as in Sudan), Latin America (as in Venezuela), and Central Asia (as in Kazakhstan) as documented earlier. Indeed, China's geoeconomic expansion would be impossible if it were not backed up by China's sound financial capacity. According to the *Financial Times*, Chinese state-owned banks such as Chinese Development Bank and China Export-Import Bank took the lead in Chinese overseas investment. Chinese Development Bank alone has its lending business totaling $141.3 billion in over ninety countries. Chinese overall economic aid/lending in 2008–2010 exceeded the World Bank's by about $10 billion.[37] In particular, China has now supplied more loans to poor countries than the World Bank, mostly in Sub-Saharan Africa in the past two years.[38]

Recent data point to China's new direction for its venture capital, which flows quickly into the production of renewable energy resources. According to *Global Trends in Renewable Energy Investment 2011*, China is emerging as the world's clean energy powerhouse as it becomes the largest investor in renewable energy technologies such as wind and solar projects.[39] A recent survey has also pointed out that China's investment in clean energy over the past five years has increased from $2.5 billion to $34.6 billion, far more than any Western country, whereas during the same period of time, total U.S. investment in the similar area was about half that at $18.6 billion. Evidently, the United States is lagging behind China in global competition for a renewable energy market.[40]

China's energy-driven expansion has indeed brought about the drastic change in the world's geoeconomic landscape characterized by energy production and market acquisition. The momentum of such change has been reinforced by China's ambitious strategy to advance in tapping renewable energy technologies and resources. As we discussed earlier, the success of China's geoeconomic advancement has benefited from its increased share of global governance as the result of its rising geopolitical power and its growing financial capacity. In the years to come, the same factor would also determine whether and how long China is able to hold or expand its geoeconomic fortune in competing with the rival powers in the world.

NOTES

1. Immanuel Wallerstein, *World-Systems Analysis: An Introduction*, Duke University Press, 2004.

2. See *China Statistical Yearbook (2007) of National Bureau of Statistics of China.*

3. Ted C. Fishman coined the term of "China Inc." in his book *China, Inc.: How the Rise of the Next Superpower Challenges America and the World* (New York: Scribner, 2006) in which the author claims that China's emerging corporations is aggressively competitive and marching into almost all sectors of world economy.

4. Benn Steil and Manuel Hinds (2009) point out that the outcome of globalization is the rise of liberal global trade regime at an unprecedented scale that exerts impacts on capital, markets and state sovereignty (Benn Steil and Manuel Hinds *Money, Markets and Sovereignty*, Yale University Press, 2009).

5. For China oil consumption projection, see http://www.eia.gov/oiaf/aeo/tablebrowser/#release=IEO2011&subject=0–IEO2011&table=5–IEO2011&region=0–0&cases=Reference-0504a_1630. For China's gas consumption projection, see http://www.eia.gov/oiaf/tablebrowser/#release=IEO2011&subject=0–IEO2011&table=6–IEO2011&region=0–0&cases=Reference-0504a_1630.

6. See "Inside Asia: Why China Will Keep Investing Abroad," By Alan Wheatley, *New York Times*, accessed July 21, 2009, http://query.nytimes.com/search/sitesearch?query=Inside+Asia%3A+Why+China+Will+Keep+Investing+Abroad&srchst=cse.

7. See "China's Thirst for Oil" by International Crisis Group, *Asia Report,* No. 153 (June 9), 2008.

8. See "China National Petroleum Corp in $17 Billion Argentina Oil Bid" by Dexter Roberts, *Business Week*, accessed July 03, 2009, http://search.newsweek.com/search?q=China+National+Petroleum+Corp+in+%2417+Billion+Argentina+Oil+Bid.

9. See "U.S. Strengthens Southeast Asia Ties, Playing Catch-up to China" By Daniel Ten Kate, *Bloomberg*, accessed July 22, 2009, http://www.bloomberg.com/apps/news?pid=20601080&sid=aHD_OIOLNMPM).

10. See "China, Southeast Asia Sign Trade Accord," *China Daily*, accessed November, 29, 2004, http://www.chinadaily.com.cn/english/doc/2004–11/29/content_395755.htm.

11. See report on Chinese President Hu Visited Malaysia in *Chinese Economic Net*, accessed November 23, 2009, http://news.wenxuecity.com/messages/200911/news-gb2312–956789.html.

12. "Politics: China Pulling Southeast Asia into Its Orbit" by Antoaneta Bezlova, *Newsmekong* (Beijing), accessed May 01, 2009, http://www.globalissues.org/news/2009/05/01/1371.

13. "Obama in Southeast Asia: Mending Fences in a Key Region" By Hannah Beech, *TIME*, accessed November, 14, 2009, http://www.time.com/time/world/article/0,8599, 1938753,00.html.

14. "In Africa U.S. Watches China's Rise" by Peter Wonacott, *Wall Street Journal* http://online.wsj.com/article/SB10001424053111903392904576510271838147248 .html?mod=WSJAsia_hpp_LEFTTopStories#printMode, accessed September 2, 2011.

15. Serge Michel and Michel Beuret, *China Safari: On the Trail of Beijing's Expansion in Africa,* Nation Books, 2009.

16. "The Chinese in Africa" at http://www.economist.com/node/18586448, accessed April 20, 2011.

17. *Reference News* (Chinese), "China desires African energy, aid to Africa increasing 30% annually," http://news.creaders.net/headline/newsViewer.php?nid=502992&id=1126421, accessed January 29, 2012.

18. "Sino-African Trade Passes $100 bln Mark in 2008," *China View*, retrieved January 27, 2009, http://news.xinhuanet.com/english/2009–01/27/content_10726493.htm.

19. Sannou Mbaye, "China's Grand Africa Strategy" Project-Syndicate at http://www .project-syndicate.org/commentary/mbaye7/English, accessed October 26, 2006.

20. "In Africa, China Trade Brings Growth, Unease: Asian Giant's Appetite for Raw Materials, Markets Has Some Questioning Its Impact on Continent" by Craig Timberg, *Washington Post*, accessed June 13, 2006, http://www.washingtonpost.com/wpdyn/content/ article/2006/06/12/AR2006061201506.html.

21. Trevor Houser and Roy Levy, "Energy Security and China's UN Diplomacy," *China Security*, Vol. 4 No. 3 (Summer) 2008, pp. 63–73, World Security Institute, http://www .chinasecurity.us/pdfs/cs11_5.pdf.

22. *USCC 2009 Annual Report* (Chapter 3) at http://www. uscc.gov.

23. See Threassy N. Marketos. *China's Energy Geopolitics: the Shanghai Cooperation Organization and Central Asia*, Routledge, 2009.

24. "Loan for Oil," http://www.economist.com, accessed July, 16, 2009.

25. See "China Lends Abroad to Ease Oil Deals," *Wall Street Journal*, April 20, 2009.

26. See USCC annual report, 2009, chapter 3.

27. "China Turns to Turkmenistan for Gas Amid Gazprom Pipe Talks" *Businessweek*, http://www.businessweek.com/news/2011–03–04/china-turns-to-turkmenistan-for-gas -amid-gazprom-pipe-talks.html, accessed March 4, 2011.

28. http://www.Mcclatchydc.com, accessed April 21, 2009.

29. "China Stepping Up Trade Presence in Latin America," July 10, 2009, Trumpet. com, and "The Dragon in the Backyard," *The Economist*, accessed Aug 13th 2009, http:// www.economist.com/search/search.cfm?rv=2&qr=The+dragon+in+the+backyard&area=1&x =15&y=11.

30. See "China, Venezuela Sign Energy Deal," *China National News*, August 25, 2006.

31. Chris Buckley, "China Gains Access to Venezuelan Oil," *The International Herald Tribune*, 28, December 24, 2007.

32. See *China's Expansion into the Western Hemisphere*, edited by Riordan Roett and Guadalupe Paz, Brookings Institution, 2008.

33. "Deals Help China Expand Sway in Latin America," http://www.nytimes.com/2009/ 04/16, accessed April 16, 2009.

34. See http://www.mcclatchydc.com/2009/04/16, accessed April 16, 2009.

35. Daniel P. Erikson and Janice Chen, "China, Taiwan and the Battle for Latin America," *The Fletcher Forum of World Affairs*, vol 31:3, Summer, 2007, pp. 69–89.

36. Philip Andrews-Speed and Roland Dannreuther, *China, Oil and Global Politics,* Routledge, 2011.

37. Teresita Cruz-del Rosario and Phillie Wang Runfei, "Is China the New World Bank?" *Project-Syndicate* at http://www.project-syndicate.org/commentary/rosario1/English, accessed February 21, 2011.

38. "The Chinese in Africa" at http://www.economist.com/node/18586448, accessed April 20, 2011.

39. Global Trends in Renewable Energy Investment 2011, http://www.fs-unep-centre.org/publications/global-trends-renewable-energy-investment-2011.

40. Shaun Tandon, "China Overtakes U.S. in Green Investment," *Industry Week*, March 25, 2010, http://www.industryweek.com/articles/china_overtakes_u-s-_in_green_investment_21415.aspx?Page=1.

9

Breaking the Impasse in International Climate Negotiations: A New Direction for Currently Flawed Negotiations and a Roadmap for China till 2050

Zhong Xiang Zhang

Concerned about a range of environmental problems and health risks from burning fossil fuels to steeply rising oil imports,[1] China had incorporated for the first time in its five-year economic plan a requirement that energy use per unit of GDP be cut by 20 percent during the 11th five-year period running from 2006 to 2010. This five-year plan also incorporated the goal of reducing SO_2 emissions and chemical oxygen demand discharge by 10 percent by 2010, relative to their 2005 levels. This is widely considered an important step toward building a "harmonious society" through "scientific development." Given that China is already the world's largest carbon emitter,[2] and its emissions continue to rise with its rapid industrialization and urbanization, China is seen to have greater capacity, capability, and responsibility for taking on climate commitments. Combined with great internal and external pressure on China to be more ambitious in limiting its greenhouse gas emissions, just prior to the Copenhagen Climate Change Summit in December 2009, China pledged to cut its carbon intensity by 40–45 percent by 2020 relative to its 2005 levels in order to reach an international climate change agreement at Copenhagen or beyond.

While this is consistent with China's longstanding opposition to hard emission caps on the grounds that such limits will restrict its economic growth, this marks a point of departure from its longstanding position on its own climate actions. The unilateral commitments clearly indicate China's determination to further decouple its energy use and carbon emissions from economic growth. This is a welcome step toward helping to reach an international climate change agreement.

China's unilateral commitments raise the issue of whether such a pledge is ambitious or just represents business as usual. Moreover, as long as China's commitments differ in form from that of the United States and other major greenhouse gas emitters, China is constantly confronted with both criticism on its inadequate carbon intensity commitment and the threats of trade measures whenever the US Senate is shaping its climate bill, given that the inclusion of border measures is widely considered the "price" for passing any US legislation capping its greenhouse gas emissions. Moreover, the US Senate can always use China as an excuse for its own failure to pass a long-awaited bill to cap US greenhouse gas emissions.

This chapter will first examine these issues and concerns. On this basis, the paper will lay out a realistic roadmap for China till 2050. Its main distinguishing features include China taking on absolute emission caps around 2030 and the three transitional periods of increasing climate obligations before that. Current international climate negotiations are flawed with a focus on commitments on the targeted date of 2020 as this does not accommodate well the world's two largest greenhouse gas emitters, namely the United States and China. The chapter concludes with a suggestion that international climate change negotiations need to focus on 2030 as the targeted date to cap the greenhouse gas emissions of the world's two largest emitters in a legally binding global agreement.

CHINA'S CARBON INTENSITY PLEDGE FOR 2020: STRINGENCY AND IMPLICATIONS

Stringency Issues

Zhang envisions that China could make a voluntary commitment to total greenhouse gas emissions per unit of GDP at some point around 2020.[3] However, it is not until just prior to the Copenhagen Climate Chang Summit that China pledged to cut its carbon intensity by 40–45 percent by 2020 relative to its 2005 levels. Wen Jiabao, China's prime minister, made it clear at Copenhagen that China's pledges "are unconditional and they are not dependent on the reduction targets of other nations."[4]

While some question China's willingness to act, real discussion has since focused on whether such a pledge is ambitious or just represents business as usual.[5] While China considers it very ambitious, some Western scholars view it as just business as usual based largely on the long-term historical trend of China's energy intensity.[6]

There are several ways to evaluate how challenging this proposed carbon intensity target is. One way is to see whether the proposed carbon intensity goal for 2020 is as challenging as the energy-saving goals set in the 11th five-year economic blueprint. This involves two issues.

The first issue deals with the rationale for using energy intensity reduction as a reference. Given the fixed CO_2 emissions coefficients of fossil fuels, which convert consumption of fossil fuels into CO_2 emissions, and given that China's energy mix is coal-dominated, cutting China's carbon intensity is in fact cutting its energy intensity.

The second issue requires the justification for the high challenge posed by the 20 percent energy-saving goal for 2010. China had met its aforementioned pollution-cutting goals ahead of the schedule. However, as discussed by Zhang, China had faced great difficulty meeting its energy-saving goal.[7] In July 2010, China released its energy intensity number for 2009, and its final energy intensity numbers for the years 2005, 2006, 2007, and 2008, which are revised based on the second nation-wide economic census. Based on these revised numbers, China's energy intensity fell by 15.61 percent from 2006 to 2009.[8] The country would meet its energy-saving goal if it could cut its energy intensity by 4.39 percent in 2010. However, China's energy use rose faster than its economic growth in the first half of 2010, with seven provinces becoming even more energy intensive during this period. This suggests that the country as a whole needs to accomplish the goal set for the whole year only within a half year, with some provinces required to fill even big remaining gaps during this period. Given the annual energy-saving rate of 5.25 percent during the period 1980–2000 in which China achieved a quadrupling of its GDP while cutting its energy intensity by about three quarters,[9] achieving such high energy-saving rate within a half year poses a significant challenge for the country as well as for those provinces lagging behind schedule.

To achieve the goal, it was widely reported that several provinces issued a strict rotation of rolling blackouts for thousands of factories that required them to shut down five days for every nine they operate in the second half of 2010.[10] Clearly, the local blackouts were not what the central government intended. While they were neither rational nor consistent with the national policy, it seemed that local governments had little choice but to take such irrational measures in such a very short period of time. Despite taking such unprecedented measures, China in the end cut its energy consumption per unit of GDP by 19.1 percent, falling short of the 20 percent energy-saving goal.[11]

Moreover, these reductions in China's energy intensity have already factored in the revisions of China's official GDP data from the second nationwide economic census as part of the government's continuing efforts to improve the quality of its statistics, whose accuracy has been questioned by both the general public inside of China and many analysts both inside and outside of China. Such revisions show that China's economy grew faster and shifted more toward services than previously estimated, thus benefiting the energy intensity indicator. Even so, it was still not easy for China to achieve its own set energy-saving goal. If there were no upward revisions of GDP data, there would be an even bigger gap between the target and the actual performance.

All this clearly indicates that even by closing 60.06 gigawatts (GW) of small, inefficient coal-fired power plants in the past four years, ahead of the national schedule to decommission 50 GW of smaller and older units in the five years through 2010, China has managed to get to where it currently stands.[12] However, those easy opportunities can only be captured once. The new carbon intensity target set for 2020 requires an additional 20–25 percent on top of the existing target. Achieving this will clearly be even more challenging and costly for China.

Another way is to assess how substantially this carbon intensity target drives China's emissions below its projected baseline levels, and whether China does its part to fulfill a coordinated global commitment to stabilize the concentration of greenhouse gas emissions in the atmosphere at the desirable level. The World Energy Outlook (WEO) 2009 has incorporated many policies into the baseline projection that were not incorporated in the WEO 2007.[13] This projection puts China's baseline carbon emissions at 9.6 gigatons of carbon dioxide ($GtCO_2$) in 2020. Under the ambitious 450 parts per million (ppm) of CO_2 equivalent scenario, China's CO_2 emissions are projected to be 8.4 $GtCO_2$ by 2020, 1.2 $GtCO_2$ less than that in the baseline.[14]

Now let us put China's proposed carbon intensity target into perspective. The calculations of the paper show that cutting the carbon intensity by 40–45 percent over the period 2006–2020 would bring reductions of 0.46–1.2 $GtCO_2$ in 2020, which are equivalent to a deviation of 4.8–12.7 percent below the WEO 2009 baseline set for China in 2020.

Two key points need to be made. First, even the lower end of that range does not represent business as usual, because it represents a deviation of 4.8 percent below the WEO 2009 baseline levels. Second, if China would be able to meet its own proposed 45 percent carbon intensity cut, the country would cut emissions of 1.2 $GtCO_2$ in 2020 from its baseline levels as is required under the ambitious 450 ppm scenario. That is equivalent to 31.6 percent of what the world would need to do in 2020 under the 450 ppm scenario, a share higher than China's share of the world's total CO_2 emissions (28 percent in 2020). Clearly, the high end of China's target, if met, aligns with the specified obligation that China needs to fulfill under the 450 ppm scenario.

These two key points clearly show that the proposed carbon intensity target does not just represent business as usual as some Western scholars have argued.

Implications of China's Carbon Intensity Pledge

At Copenhagen, China eventually compromised to agree to open its emissions data to international consultation and analysis. The European Union has identified building a robust and transparent emissions and performance accounting framework as a key element of implementing the Copenhagen Accord.[15] How all this will be worked out remains to be seen. China has not agreed to releasing its GDP figures to international consultation and analysis. But as long as China's commitments are in the form of carbon intensity, establishing a robust and transparent emissions and performance accounting framework is helpful, but not enough to remove international concern about the reliability of China's commitments. As discussed by Zhang, the revisions of China's GDP figures and energy consumption in recent years show that GDP figures are even more crucial to the impact on energy or carbon intensity than data on energy consumption and emissions.[16] As shown in table 9.1, such revisions lead to a differential between preliminary and final values as large as 123 percent for the energy intensity in 2006. The aforementioned revisions of China's GDP figures reflect partly on the government's continuing efforts to improve the accuracy and reliability of China's statistics on economic activity. While they are certainly not being calculated to make the energy intensity indicator to make the government look good, such revisions have huge implications for meeting China's energy-saving goal in 2010 and its proposed carbon intensity target in 2020.

Table 9.1. A Reduction in China's Energy Intensity: Preliminary Value versus Final Value[a]

Year	Preliminary Value (%)	Revised Value (%)	Re-revised Value (%)	Final Value (%)	Differential between Preliminary and Final Values (%)
2006	1.23 (March 2007)	1.33 (12 July 2007)	1.79 (14 July 2008)	2.74 (15 July 2010)	122.8
2007	3.27 (March 2008)	3.66 (14 July 2008)	4.04 (30 June 2009)	5.04 (15 July 2010)	54.1
2008	4.59 (30 June 2009)	5.20[b] (25 Dec. 2009)		5.20 (15 July 2010)	13.3
2009	3.98[c] (March 2010)	3.61[d] (15 July 2010)			

Notes:

[a]The dates when the corresponding data were released are in parentheses.

[b]Based on China's revised 2008 GDP from the second nationwide economic census, released in December 2009, which raised the growth rate of GDP to 9.6 percent from the previously reported 9 percent for that year and the share of services in GDP.

[c]My own calculation is based on the National Development and Reform Commission's reporting that China's energy intensity was cut by 14.38 percent in the first four years of the 11th five-year plan relative to its 2005 levels (Xinhua Net, 2010).

[d] Based on China's energy intensity number for 2009, and its final energy intensity numbers for the years 2005 and 2008 (NBS et al., 2010), my own calculation for this value would be 3.23 percent, instead of the official reported cut of 3.61 percent.

Sources: Zhang, Z. X., "Assessing China's Carbon Intensity Pledge for 2020: Stringency and Credibility Issues and their Implications," *Environmental Economics and Policy Studies*, Vol. 13, No. 3, 2011, pp. 219–235; Zhang, Z. X., "Energy and Environmental Policy in China: Towards a Low-Carbon Economy," in *New Horizons in Environmental Economics Series* (Edward Elgar, Cheltenham, UK, and Northampton, USA, 2011).

In addition to the criticism on its inadequate carbon intensity commitment and the threats of trade measures, China is also expected to face increasing pressure from the European Union, which will find it increasingly hard to convince its citizens in general and companies in particular why the European Union has taken the lead but they do not see China following. This is because overall competitiveness concerns mean that no country is likely to step out too far in front.

A ROADMAP FOR CHINA TO 2050

Indeed, the format and timeframe under which China would take on climate commitments is significant because it faces great internal and external pressure in international climate negotiations to exhibit greater ambition and at the same time it is confronted with the threats of trade measures. It has significant global relevance as well because when China's emissions peak is crucial to determine when global emissions would peak and because China's intent and action have significant implications for the level of ambition and commitment from other countries.

There is no question that China eventually needs to take on binding greenhouse gas emissions caps. The key challenges are deciding when that would take place and determining the credible interim targets that would be needed during the transition period. These results will no doubt be a combination of China's own assessment of its responsibility, economic and political benefits, and climate change impacts, taking also into consideration, the mounting diplomatic and international pressure and the give-and-take of international negotiations.

In the run up to and at the Copenhagen Climate Change Summit in December 2009, China not only took the initiative to ally with India and other major developing countries, but also took full advantage of being the world's largest carbon emitter, and attempted to secure a deal to its advantage. It is widely reported that China walked away "happy." But that came with a high price tag. Whether to admit or not, China angered allies and abandoned principles that it stuck by during the two weeks of talks, stoking anti-China sentiment in Western nations. The early appearance of this sentiment does not do China any good because it still has to evolve from a large country to a country that is truly strong in fields of science, technology, innovation, economy, and others. Officially China was backed by allies like India and Brazil but they admitted in private that this was mainly China's battle.[17]

Given that US President Obama's pledge "yes, we can" had raised high expectations for that meeting, Copenhagen was disappointing to many. However, the situation could be worse because the negotiations could have completely collapsed. While falling far short of the legally binding global agreement, the Copenhagen Accord reflects a political consensus on the main elements of the future framework among the major emitters and representatives of the main negotiating groups.

For the first time, China was blamed for dragging its feet on international climate negotiations. Previously such accusations were always targeted at the United States. French President Nicolas Sarkozy publicly criticized China for impeding the progress in climate talks.[18] British Energy and Climate Change Secretary Ed Miliband wrote in *The Guardian*,

> We did not get an agreement on 50 per cent reductions in global emissions by 2050 or on 80 per cent reductions by developed countries. Both were vetoed by China, despite the support of a coalition of developed and the vast majority of developing countries.[19]

A furious Angela Merkel, German chancellor, demanded, "Why can't we even mention our own targets?" Kevin Rudd, Australian prime minister, was annoyed enough to bang his microphone. Brazil's representative also pointed out how illogical China's position was.[20] Being asked in the early hours of December 19, 2009, why a pledge that applied only to rich nations and to which all those nations seemed to agree could have vanished from the final document, the spokesperson for the Swedish government that was serving the EU presidency at that time gave the flat reply after the seconds of what-can-I-say silence: "China didn't like numbers."[21]

It is not so hard to understand why China rejected the aforementioned two numbers. The need to cut both global greenhouse gas emissions by 50 percent and that of industrialized countries by 80 percent by 2050 means that emissions in developing countries are only allowed to increase by 15 percent by 2050 relative to their 1990 levels. Given their very low levels in 1990, China considers this unacceptable.

There could be a misinterpretation here. Some may interpret that a 15 percent increase by 2050 would mean that the developing country's emissions are allowed to only increase by 15 percent in any specific year from now on to 2050. This is not correct. Emissions in developing countries can be much higher than the level allowed by a 15 percent increase prior to 2050 and then come down to that proposed allowable level by 2050. Indeed, under the 450 parts per million of CO_2 equivalent scenario, CO_2 emissions in China are projected to go from 2.2 $GtCO_2$ in 1990 and 6.1 $GtCO_2$ in 2007 to 8.4 $GtCO_2$ in 2020, while the corresponding figures for India are estimated to go from 0.6 $GtCO_2$ in 1990 and 1.3 $GtCO_2$ in 2007 to 1.9 $GtCO_2$ in 2020.[22] Relative to their levels in 1990 and 2007, CO_2 emissions in 2020 increased by 282 percent and 37 percent for China and by 117 percent and 46 percent for India, respectively. More importantly, rejecting a long-standing, widely reported proposal without putting forward alternatives, had cast China in a very bad light. It gave the impression that rich countries should not even announce their unilateral cut, which was reported by the Western media.[23]

In response to these concerns and to put China in a positive position, I propose that at current international climate negotiations, China should negotiate a requirement that greenhouse gas emissions in industrialized countries be cut by at least 80 percent by 2050 relative to their 1990 levels and that per capita emissions for all major countries by 2050 should not exceed the world's average at that time. Moreover, it would be in China's best interest if, at the right time (e.g., at a time when the US Senate is going to debate and ratify any global deal that would emerge from current international climate negotiations), China signals well ahead that it will take on binding absolute emission caps around the year 2030.[24] While this date is later than the time frame that the United States and other industrialized countries would like to see, it would probably still be too soon from China's perspective.

However, it is hard to imagine how China could apply the brakes so sharply to switch from rapid emissions growth to immediate emissions cuts, without passing through several intermediate phases. After all, China is still a developing country, no matter how rapidly it is expected to grow in the future. Taking the commitment period of five years that the Kyoto Protocol has adopted, I envision that China needs the following three transitional periods of increasing climate obligations, before taking on absolute emissions caps.

Further credible energy conservation commitments starting 2013. China has already committed itself to quantified targets on energy conservation and the use of clean energy. It needs to extend its level of ambition, further making credible quantified domestic commitments in these areas for the second commitment period and aiming for a 46–50 percent cut in its carbon intensity by 2020.[25]

Voluntary "no lose" emission targets starting 2018. During this transition period, China could commit to adopting voluntary emission reduction targets. Emissions reductions achieved beyond these "no lose" targets would then be eligible for sale through carbon trading at the same world market price as those of developed countries whose emissions are capped, relative to the lower prices that China currently receives for carbon credits generated from clean development mechanism projects. This means that China would suffer no net economic loss by adhering to the targets.

Binding carbon intensity targets starting 2023, leading to emissions caps around 2030. While China is expected to incorporate the carbon intensity target as a domestic commitment for the first time in its 12th five-year plan period starting 2011, adopting binding carbon intensity targets in 2023 as its international commitment would be a significant step toward committing to absolute emissions caps during the subsequent commitment period. At that juncture, having been granted three transition periods, China could then be expected to take on binding emissions caps, starting around 2030 and subsequently, aiming for the global convergence of per capita emissions by 2050.

Overall, this proposal is a balanced reflection of respecting China's rights to grow and recognizing China's growing responsibility for countering increasing greenhouse gas emissions as living standards rise over time. The commitments envisioned for China are basic principles. They leave ample flexibility for China to work out the details while international climate change negotiations proceed. The value of this proposal lies in the format and timeframe under which China would be included in a post-2012 climate change regime, not in the numerical details. It should not be taken for granted that China can take on such increasingly stringent commitments because that would entail significant efforts to cut China's projected emissions below its baselines.

Political reality may limit the ability of the United States to take on significant emissions cuts by 2020 that developing countries called for. But as a tradeoff, the United States should significantly scale up its technology transfer and deployment, financing, and capacity building to enable China to do that. This is the least the United States could and should do. By setting the example, the United States can encourage other developed counties to do the same. As Winston Churchill said, "[you] can always count on the Americans to do the right thing—after exhausting every other alternative." After what is viewed as eight years of lost time under US President Bush, the whole world bets that the United States will not disappoint us this time. Only history will tell us whether that will be the case.

In the meantime, commitments by China would send a signal well in advance that China is seriously committed to addressing climate change issues. They will also alleviate, if not completely remove, the United States and other industrialized country's concerns over when China will join them. This is an indication that the world has long awaited for China to help the United States take on long-expected emissions commitments, thus paving the way for reaching a post-2012 international climate change agreement.

A NEW DIRECTION OF FUTURE INTERNATIONAL CLIMATE NEGOTIATIONS

However, current international climate negotiations have been focused on commitments on the targeted date of 2020. With the commitment period only up to 2020, there is very little room left for the United States and China, although for reasons very different from each other.

The Intergovernmental Panel on Climate Change (IPCC) calls for cutting global greenhouse gas emissions at least in half by 2050. To achieve that goal, the IPCC fourth assessment report recommends that global greenhouse gas emissions should peak by 2020 at the latest and then turn downward in order to avoid dangerous climate change consequences. It also calls for developed countries to cut their greenhouse gas emissions by 25–40 percent by 2020 relative to their 1990 levels.[26] This recommendation was incorporated into the Bali Roadmap at the United Nations Climate Summit in 2007. This seems a logical choice. Once the long-term goal (namely the target for 2050) is set, one needs a mid-term goal to help facilitate the long-term one. From then, the negotiations on industrialized countries' commitments have focused on projected 2020 emissions reduction targets.

However, 2020 is just around the corner. More importantly, this date does not accommodate well the world's two largest greenhouse gas emitters, namely the United States and China. Because the United States withdrew from the Kyoto Protocol, it has not made any substantial preparations to cut emissions as other Kyoto-constrained industrialized countries have done over the past decade. Whether you like it or not, this is a political reality. It is very hard for an unprepared country like the United States to take on a substantial cut in emission in 2020 as demanded by developing countries, although it should still do so on moral grounds.

In the meantime, China overtook the United States to become the world's largest greenhouse gas emitter in 2007, at least twenty years earlier than what was estimated by the US IEA as late as 2004.[27] The IEA (International Energy Agency) estimates that about half of the growth of global energy-related CO_2 emissions until 2030 will come from China. Combined with huge trade deficit with China, the United States has pushed for China to take on emissions caps as early as 2020. Otherwise, the goods exported from China to the United States markets might be subject to carbon tariffs.[28] However, as argued by Zhang, 2020 is not a realistic date for China to take on the absolute emissions cap because its carbon emissions would be still on the climbing trajectories beyond 2030, even if some energy saving policies and measures have been factored into such projections.[29] Meanwhile, taking on commitments for 2050 seems too far away for politicians.

If the commitment period is extended to 2030, it would really open the possibility for the United States and China to make the commitments that each wants from the other in the same form, although their scale of reductions would differ. By 2030, the United States will be able to commit to much deeper emission cuts that China and developing countries have demanded, while, as argued by Zhang, China would have approached the threshold to take on the absolute emission cap that the United States and other industrialized countries have long asked for.[30]

Being aware of his proposed provisional target in 2020 is well below what is internationally expected from the United States, President Obama announced a provisional target of a 42 percent reduction below 2005 levels in 2030 to demonstrate the US leadership commitment to find a global solution to global warming. While the US-proposed level of emission reductions for 2030 is still not ambitious enough,

President Obama inadvertently points to the right direction of international climate negotiations, namely, international climate negotiations need to look at the targeted date of 2030. If international negotiations could lead to much deeper emission cuts for developed countries as well as the absolute emission caps for major developing countries in 2030, that would significantly reduce the legitimacy of the US-proposed carbon tariffs and, if implemented, enhance their prospects for withstanding a challenge at the World Trade Organization. That will also alleviate any concern about when China's greenhouse gas emissions will peak and what China is going to do. More importantly, it really opens up the possibility of capping the greenhouse gas emissions of the world's two largest emitters in a legally binding global agreement.

I repeatedly called for international climate negotiations moving the targeted date beyond 2020.[31] International climate negotiators have gradually recognized its importance and merit in getting the cooperation of all countries, at least all major emitting economies, and international climate negotiations very much move into this direction. This is clearly reflected by the Durban Climate Change Conference's decision in December 2011 on the Establishment of an *Ad Hoc* Working Group on the Durban Platform for Enhanced Action. This decision formally launches a process to develop a protocol, another legal instrument or an agreed outcome with legal force under the United Nations Framework Convention on Climate Change applicable to all parties.[32] While the road ahead is widely expected to be bumpy, this is a very positive development and a right direction of international climate negotiations.

NOTES

1. Ho, M., and C. Nielsen, "Clearing the Air: The Health and Economic Damages of Air Pollution in China" (Cambridge, Massachusetts: MIT Press, 2007); World Bank, "Cost of Pollution in China: Economic Estimates of Physical Damages," Washington DC, 2007 http://siteresources.worldbank.org/INTEAPREGTOPENVIRONMENT/Resources/China_Cost_of_Pollution.pdf; Zhang, Z. X., "Is It Fair to Treat China a Christmas Tree to Hang Everybody's Complaints? Putting its Own Energy-Saving into Perspective," *Energy Economics*, Vol. 32, 2010, pp. S47–S56; Zhang, Z. X., "China in the Transition to a Low-Carbon Economy," *Energy Policy*, Vol. 38, 2010, pp. 6638–6653.

2. IEA, *World Energy Outlook* 2007; IEA, *World Energy Outlook* 2009; Netherlands Environmental Assessment Agency, "China Now No. 1 in CO2 Emissions; USA in Second Position," 19 June 2007.

3. Zhang, Z. X., "Decoupling China's Carbon Emissions Increases from Economic Growth: An Economic Analysis and Policy Implications," *World Development*, Vol. 28, No. 4, 2000, pp. 739–752.

Zhang, Z. X., "Can China Afford to Commit Itself an Emissions Cap? An Economic and Political Analysis," *Energy Economics*, Vol. 22, No. 6, 2000, pp. 587–614.

4. Watts, J, "China 'Will Honour Commitments' Regardless of Copenhagen Outcome," *The Guardian*, 18 December 2009, http://www.guardian.co.uk/environment/2009/dec/18/china-wen-jiabao-copenhagen.

5. See Qiu, J., "China's Climate Target: Is It Achievable?" *Nature*, 2009, 462: 550–551; Carraro, C., and Tavoni, M., "Looking Ahead from Copenhagen: How Challenging Is the Chinese Carbon Intensity Target?" VOX, 2010, http://www.voxeu.org/index.php?q=node/4449.

6. See Levi, M., "Assessing China's Carbon Cutting Proposal," Council on Foreign Relations, New York, 30 November 2009.

7. Zhang, Z. X., "Is It Fair to Treat China a Christmas Tree to Hang Everybody's Complaints? Putting Its Own Energy-Saving into Perspective," *Energy Economics*, Vol. 32, 2010, pp. S47–S56; Zhang, Z. X., "Assessing China's Carbon Intensity Pledge for 2020: Stringency and Credibility Issues and Their Implications," *Environmental Economics and Policy Studies*, Vol. 13, No. 3, 2011, pp. 219–235; Zhang, Z. X., "In What Format and under What Timeframe Would China Take on Climate Commitments? A Roadmap to 2050," *International Environmental Agreements: Politics, Law and Economics*, Vol. 11, No. 3, 2011, pp. 245–259; Zhang, Z. X., "Energy and Environmental Policy in China: Towards a Low-Carbon Economy," in *New Horizons in Environmental Economics Series* (Edward Elgar, Cheltenham, UK, and Northampton, USA, 2011).

8. National Bureau of Statistic (NBS), National Development and Reform Commission and National Energy Administration, "Bulletin on Energy Use per Unit of GDP and Other Indicators by Region," Beijing, 3 August, 2010, http://www.stats.gov.cn/tjgb/qttjgb/qgqttjgb/t20100803_402662765.htm.

9. Zhang, Z. X., "Why Did the Energy Intensity Fall in China's Industrial Sector in the 1990s?, The Relative Importance of Structural Change and Intensity Change," *Energy Economics*, Vol. 25, No. 6, 2003, pp. 625–638.

10. Sina Net, http://finance.sina.com.cn/focus/jpxcxd/index.shtml.

11. People Net, "Energy Consumption per Unit of GDP Expected to Fall by 19.06% during the 11th Five-Year Period," 11 February, 2011, http://env.people.com.cn/GB/13892587.html.

12. China had closed smaller and older plants with a total capacity of 76.8 GW during the period 2006–2010, relative to a total capacity of 8.3 GW decommissioned during the previous five-year period. See *China News Net*, "China Decommissioned 76.825 GW of Smaller and Older Coal-Fired Unites during the 11th Five-Year Period," 28 September 2011; http://www.chinanews.com/ny/2011/09–28/3358876.shtml; Zhang, Z. X., "China in the Transition to a Low-Carbon Economy," *Energy Policy*, Vol. 38, 2010, pp. 6638–6653.

13. IEA, *World Energy Outlook* 2009; IEA, *World Energy Outlook* 2007.

14. IEA, *World Energy Outlook* 2009.

15. European Commission, "International Climate Policy Post-Copenhagen: Acting Now to Reinvigorate Global Action on Climate Change," COM (2010) 86 final, Brussels, 9 March 2010, http://ec.europa.eu/environment/climat/pdf/com_2010_86.pdf.

16. Zhang, Z. X., "Assessing China's Carbon Intensity Pledge for 2020: Stringency and Credibility Issues and their Implications," *Environmental Economics and Policy Studies*, Vol. 13, No. 3, 2011, pp. 219–235; Zhang, Z. X., "Energy and Environmental Policy in China: Towards a Low-Carbon Economy," in *New Horizons in Environmental Economics Series* (Edward Elgar, Cheltenham, UK, and Northampton, USA, 2011).

17. Graham-Harrison, E., "Snap Analysis: China Happy with Climate Deal, Image Dented," *Reuters*, 18 December 2009, http://www.reuters.com/article/idUSTRE5BI0DH20091219.

18. Watts, J., "China 'Will Honour Commitments' Regardless of Copenhagen Outcome," *The Guardian*, 18 December, 2009, http://www.guardian.co.uk/environment/2009/dec/18/china-wen-jiabao-copenhagen.

19. Miliband, E., "The Road from Copenhagen," *The Guardian*, 20 December 2009, http://www.guardian.co.uk/commentisfree/2009/dec/20/copenhagen-climate-change-accord.

20. Lynas, M., "How Do I Know China Wrecked the Copenhagen Deal? I Was in the Room," *The Guardian*, 23 December 2009, http://www.guardian.co.uk/environment/2009/dec/22/copenhagen-climate-change-mark-lynas.

21. *The Economist*, "Climate Change after Copenhagen: China's Thing about Number," 2 January 2010, pp. 43–44.

22. IEA, *World Energy Outlook* 2009.

23. Some of China's stance and reactions in Copenhagen are generally well-rooted because of realities at home. Some reactions could have been handled more effectively for a better image of China, provided that there were good preparations and deliberations. For further discussion on China's stance and reactions in Copenhagen, see Zhang, Z. X., "Copenhagen and Beyond: Reflections on China's Stance and Responses," in E. Cerdá and X. Labandeira (eds.), *Climate Change Policies: Global Challenges and Future Prospects* (Cheltenham, UK and Northampton, MA: Edward Elgar, 2010), pp. 239–253.

24. For detailed discussion on why around 2030 is considered the timing for China to take on absolute greenhouse gas emissions caps, see Zhang, Z. X., "The U.S. Proposed Carbon Tariffs, WTO Scrutiny and China's Responses," *International Economics and Economic Policy*, Vol. 7, Nos. 2–3, 2010, pp. 203–225.

25. Zhang, Z. X., "China in the Transition to a Low-Carbon Economy," *Energy Policy*, Vol. 38, 2010, pp. 6638–6653; Zhang, Z. X., "Assessing China's Carbon Intensity Pledge for 2020: Stringency and Credibility Issues and Their Implications," *Environmental Economics and Policy Studies*, Vol. 13, No. 3, 2011, pp. 219–235.

26. Intergovernmental Panel on Climate Change, *Climate Change 2007: Mitigation of Climate Change*, Working Group III Contribution to the Fourth Assessment Report, (Cambridge University Press, Cambridge, 2007).

27. EIA , *International Energy Outlook* 2004, Washington, DC.

28. Zhang, Z. X., "The U.S. Proposed Carbon Tariffs, WTO Scrutiny and China's Responses," *International Economics and Economic Policy*, Vol. 7, Nos. 2–3, 2010, pp. 203–225; Zhang, Z. X., "Energy and Environmental Policy in China: Towards a Low-Carbon Economy," in *New Horizons in Environmental Economics Series* (Edward Elgar, Cheltenham, UK, and Northampton, USA, 2011).

29. Zhang, Z. X., "In What Format and under What Timeframe Would China Take on Climate Commitments? A Roadmap to 2050," *International Environmental Agreements: Politics, Law and Economics*, Vol. 11, No. 3, 2011, pp. 245–259; Zhang, Z. X., "Energy and Environmental Policy in China: Towards a Low-Carbon Economy," in *New Horizons in Environmental Economics Series* (Edward Elgar, Cheltenham, UK, and Northampton, USA, 2011).

30. Ibid.

31. Zhang, Z. X., "Assessing China's Carbon Intensity Pledge for 2020: Stringency and Credibility Issues and their Implications," *Environmental Economics and Policy Studies*, Vol. 13, No. 3, 2011, pp. 219–235; Zhang, Z.X., "In What Format and under What Timeframe Would China Take on Climate Commitments? A Roadmap to 2050," *International Environmental Agreements: Politics, Law and Economics*, Vol. 11, No. 3, 2011, pp. 245–259; Zhang, Z. X., "Energy and Environmental Policy in China: Towards a Low-Carbon Economy," in *New Horizons in Environmental Economics Series* (Edward Elgar, Cheltenham, UK and Northampton, USA, 2011).

32. United Nations Framework Convention on Climate Change, *Establishment of an Ad Hoc Working Group on the Durban Platform for Enhanced Action: Proposal by the President*, FCCC/CP/2011/L.10, Seventeenth session of the Conference of the Parties, Durban, 28 November–9 December 2011.

IV

CHINA AND
GLOBAL SECURITY

10

China's Approach to Nuclear Disarmament and Nonproliferation

Tong Zhao[1]

Since its first nuclear explosion in 1964, China's participation in global nuclear disarmament talks has been relatively limited. Controversy over China's interaction with the international nuclear nonproliferation regime has always existed. In recent years, the interplay between China's growing power and the changing dynamics in global geopolitics has elevated China to a leading role in the development of global nuclear security framework. China's voice and role in these areas can no longer be overlooked. The unique and increasingly significant influence of China on global nuclear disarmament and nonproliferation institutions will inevitably have profound implications for great power interaction and cooperation on a wide range of regional and international security issues. The following sections of this chapter will analyze China's approach to global nuclear disarmament and nonproliferation and shed light on how China will affect the future evolution of institutions in these areas and why this will be the case.

Specifically, China rejects the traditional framework of addressing nuclear disarmament issues. China's small nuclear arsenal determines that its nuclear retaliation capability is limited to a range of military capabilities that are non-nuclear in nature. Constructive dialogues on conventional arms control, missile defense, and space weaponization are necessary to bring China into future multilateral nuclear arms control discussions. China appreciates the role of nuclear taboo and the importance of regulating nuclear operation policies as part of future global nuclear disarmament framework. Discussions on de-alerting nuclear weapons and restraining the use of nuclear weapons will serve as important confidence-building measures to address Chinese concerns over arms race and nuclear coercion.

China possesses a deep-rooted skepticism about the discriminative nature of certain rules in existing nonproliferation regime. From its own experience of undergoing serious economic sanctions, it remains unimpressed with the utility of coercive measures to promote compliance with nuclear nonproliferation rules. This is why

China favors a persuasive approach over existing coercive approaches to resolve differences over nuclear nonproliferation issues. To China, the solution of North Korean and Iranian nuclear crises lies in integrating the isolated countries into the international community through support and confidence building.

THE PATH FROM BILATERAL TO MULTILATERAL NUCLEAR DISARMAMENT

International efforts to promote nuclear disarmament began soon after nuclear weapons were first created in 1945. Official nuclear disarmament negotiations between the United States (US) and Russia achieved initial results after the Soviet Union disintegrated but suffered difficulties in the following decade. In recent years global nuclear disarmament movement regains momentum after the Four Horsemen took the lead by coauthoring a series of *Wall Street Journal* op-eds.[2] The overall nuclear arsenals in the US and Russia have so far dropped substantially in comparison to Cold War figures while the two governments reach new agreements. The recent conclusion and ratification of the follow-on agreement for Strategic Arms Reduction Treaty (START) will further limit each country's deployed strategic nuclear warheads to a maximum of 1550 within seven years after the treaty enters into force.[3] Almost all the previous nuclear disarmament negotiations were carried out within a bilateral framework. None of the second-tier nuclear weapons states was formally involved.

The problem is, however, after decades of bilateral nuclear disarmament, the US and Russia found making progress in further nuclear arms reductions beyond the New START Treaty level extremely difficult. This is because second-tier nuclear weapons states continue to hold out and make no commitment to reduce their own nuclear stockpiles. In particular, China's position becomes critical, because the US, and Russia to a lesser degree, are very concerned about Chinese nuclear capability and its trajectory of future development. China is also frequently mentioned by Western policy makers and practitioners as the only nuclear weapon state under the Non-Proliferation Treaty (NPT) that is modernizing its nuclear arsenal, although this is not necessarily accurate.[4] China's position toward nuclear disarmament will presumably have considerable influence among other second-tier nuclear weapons states. In this sense, China's commitment will be critical for transformation of the global nuclear disarmament framework from a traditionally bilateral one to a more inclusive multilateral process. China's perceptions of nuclear weapons and its strategic thinking of national and international security will affect the dynamics of global nuclear disarmament mechanism in several ways.

NUCLEAR DISARMAMENT AND COMPREHENSIVE ARMS CONTROL

China's small nuclear stockpile determines that its nuclear forces are susceptible to potential impact of a range of military technologies and capabilities and its nuclear policies cannot be made independently of other relevant factors. Since its first nuclear explosion in 1964, China's nuclear arsenal has been kept much smaller than those of major nuclear powers. Currently, after significant reductions in the American and Russian nuclear stockpiles, the US and Russia still possess thousands of actively deployed strategic nuclear warheads, with thousands of strategic warheads in reserve and a large number of tactical nuclear weapons unaccounted for.[5] In comparison, China's nuclear arsenal has always been a fraction of those.[6] Within its small nuclear arsenal, only dozens of China's nuclear weapons are capable of reaching continental United States, and they are not mounted upon long-range delivery vehicles.

Classical deterrence theory mandates that a country maintain a survivable nuclear force and possess the capability to launch an effective nuclear retaliation after absorbing a first strike. New development in modern military technology, however, has challenged traditional thinking on nuclear deterrence and strategic stability by introducing advanced conventional weapon systems into the equation. Both conventional defensive systems like ballistic missile interceptors and offensive systems like conventional intercontinental ballistic missiles will have implications for nuclear policies of all major nuclear weapons states. But their impact on these countries is very unbalanced due to the huge gaps in nuclear stockpiles among nuclear weapons states. In the near-to-medium term, ballistic missile defense and conventional Global Strike weapon systems will be under development; their capabilities will be limited and their deployment will be constrained. Such limited conventional strategic weapon systems cannot significantly undermine nuclear second strike capabilities of the US or Russia, but might compromise or be perceived as capable of compromising second strike capabilities of much smaller nuclear powers such as China. As a result, it is unlikely that China's involvement in global nuclear disarmament will take the same form of previous arrangements that dealt with nuclear issues in isolation from conventional strategic military capabilities.

Previous nuclear arms control negotiation frameworks, such as Strategic Arms Limitation Talks (SALT), START, and Strategic Offensive Reductions Treaty (SORT) focused almost exclusively on nuclear warheads and their delivery systems. In most cases, conventional weapon systems were not taken into consideration in negotiations. The deployment of national ballistic missile defense systems were once restricted by the Anti-Ballistic Missile Treaty (ABM), but the restriction was then lifted as the treaty broke apart in 2002. The recent New START Treaty was concluded with no limitations on missile defense development and deployment. Such negotiation framework might no longer be useful if China is going to be involved in a general discussion on nuclear disarmament. China has been concerned for years that the ground-based ballistic missile interceptors in Alaska and Florida will significantly neutralize China's nuclear second strike capability. Obama administration's plan to substantially upgrade and expand the fleet of both sea-based and land-based Standard Missile (SM) Interceptors might pose even more severe threats to China's nuclear retaliation forces. Studies point out that advanced SM interceptors deployed in Asia-Pacific region have the potential to shoot down China's intercontinental ballistic missiles when the missiles are still in the boost phase of flight.[7] In addition, SM-3 missile defense systems are highly mobile and therefore can seriously undermine China's nuclear deterrence if they were relocated during a crisis from other regions to waters close to China.

Similarly, advanced conventional offensive weapon systems might acutely affect China's nuclear deterrence, but not necessarily challenge much larger nuclear stockpiles in the US or Russia. Even if the United States only develops conventional Global Strike weapon systems into a "niche capability" and limits their deployment to a small scale,[8] they might still pose a concern or at least create new threat perception in the Chinese mind of their vulnerable nuclear deterrence. For similar reasons, China's nuclear deterrence is more vulnerable to space weaponization than the US or Russia. China's confidence in the survival of its nuclear forces can be seriously undermined by space-based striking or surveillance systems such as Synthetic Aperture Radars. Taking all these into consideration, China's participation in nuclear disarmament negotiations is unlikely to follow the previous models. China will require a more comprehensive arrangement that can effectively deal with the new challenges of advanced conventional systems against strategic stability and nuclear security.

NUCLEAR TABOO AND UTILITY OF NUCLEAR WEAPONS

Scholars have pointed out that China's nuclear philosophy is quite different from that of other major nuclear weapons states.[9] Hence, China develops a relatively unique nuclear strategy and keeps a very small nuclear arsenal even though it has the resources and capacity to build a much larger one. Its relatively unique nuclear philosophy is also going to affect existing nuclear security mechanisms in which China is playing an increasingly important role. What is special about China's nuclear philosophy is its perception of the usability of nuclear weapons. Previous studies reveal that China is more skeptical of the usability of nuclear weapons on the battle field than other major nuclear states. As a result, it attaches little importance to tactical war fighting capabilities of its nuclear weapons. In other words, China is more receptive to the norm of nuclear taboo than others.[10]

China's appreciation of nuclear taboo is historically consistent and this has significant implications for China's understanding of external nuclear threats as well as its own nuclear strategy. China is highly skeptical that any nuclear country would ever launch a nuclear first strike against itself. Therefore, China is much more concerned about the coercive behaviors of its nuclear adversaries who might be emboldened by a misperceived nuclear supremacy over China.[11] As for its own nuclear strategy, China's depreciation of the utility of nuclear war-fighting capabilities results from its appreciation of the nuclear taboo, which led to a decision to keep its nuclear forces at a minimal level—capable of delivering a nuclear retaliation after absorbing a first strike. China's appreciation of nuclear taboo well explains its unconditional No First Use (NFU) policy, which categorically takes off from the table the option of nuclear first strike that is prohibited by the norm of nuclear taboo.

From the cultural perspective, China's security culture is believed to comprise two distinctive paradigms: the Confucian-Mencian paradigm and the *parabellum* (*realpolitik*) paradigm.[12] China's appreciation of nuclear taboo is a prominent reflection of the Confucian-Mencian tradition of its strategic culture. This, however, does not necessarily contradict rational *realpolitik* calculations. China's offering of its NFU commitment in the 1960s, for example, was consistent with its confidence that China had the conventional military capability to absorb and then defeat any conventional attack.[13] Such confidence was reasonable in the 1960s and 1970s when Chinese leadership was willing to sacrifice huge losses in terms of resources and wealth to fight a protracted conventional war of attrition. Nowadays, however, as China's economy becomes increasingly interconnected and interdependent with other parts of the world and as China's overall wealth accumulates, China seems more war-averse because it has much more to lose today than in previous decades if it is involved in a large-scale conventional military conflict. Nonetheless, China still holds firmly to its unconditional NFU policy and continues to reject any shift of policy that suggests using nuclear weapons as deterrence against conventional attacks.[14] Such persistency of policy is better explained by China's appreciation of nuclear taboo than by *realpolitik* calculations. This pressures other nuclear weapons states to take seriously China's position on nuclear taboo and no first use of nuclear weapons.

As China becomes a critical player in future global nuclear disarmament negotiations, the importance of nuclear taboo can no longer be dismissed by world powers. China's appreciation of nuclear taboo has been fundamental to its nuclear thinking, and it is predictable that China will adhere to the norm of non-use of nuclear weapons. As a result, the normative approach of nuclear disarmament will gain momentum and pose an unprecedented challenge to the traditional *realpolitik* approach to disarmament.

NUCLEAR OPERATION POLICY AND NUCLEAR POSTURE

China's participation in future global nuclear disarmament negotiations will probably drive a shift of focus from restricting nuclear development to regulating nuclear operation. Both nuclear development and nuclear operation are key elements of a country's nuclear strategy and policy. Nuclear development refers to qualitative and quantitative status of a country's nuclear forces, and it is represented by the size and destructive power of the arsenal; nuclear operation involves nuclear force training: nuclear signaling, targeting, covering, mobilizing, and launching. Traditional nuclear arms control agreements focus strongly on limiting nuclear development and deployment, but attach little importance to regulating nuclear operation policies. In SALT, START, and SORT negotiations, much attention has been paid to setting numerical limits for nuclear weapons and their delivery systems. In contrast, in striking agreements, too little attention has been paid to the regulation of nuclear weapon operations and alert status of nuclear forces.

Take the New START Treaty as an example. The treaty imposes constraints on the number of deployed strategic warheads that the US and Russia can possess and sets up verification mechanisms to enforce the rules. According to the New START Treaty counting rule, only strategic warheads that are deployed on delivery vehicles are counted. As some scholars pointed out, under this counting rule, China literally possesses zero nuclear weapons, because all Chinese nuclear warheads are kept unmated with their delivery vehicles and stored in separate facilities.[15] This shows that China's nuclear operation policy is very different from the US and Russia. As a result, the counting rule and other mechanisms in existing nuclear arms control treaties will have to be significantly revised before they can be applied to the Chinese case.

China attaches great significance to nuclear operation regulations. China agrees that numerical reduction has positive implications for international security. It also regards the agreements on maintenance and operation of nuclear weapons as more fundamental and critical for attaining mutual understanding and confidence-building. Hence, we see China's focus on regulations on nuclear operation as the foundation for trust building. We also see China's pursuit of the prerequisites for nuclear elimination in its persistent advocacy for unconditional NFU policy, comprehensive negative security assurances, and de-alerting of nuclear weapons.

For decades, China has sought for universal adoption of NFU policy by all nuclear countries. Although dismissed by the US in the early 1990s, China's efforts have put increasing pressure on other nuclear weapons states to consider the significance of regulating nuclear operation policies. Russia agreed to conclude with China the Sino-Russian NFU and De-targeting Agreement in September 1994, and the US also signed a non-targeting agreement with China in 1998. Throughout the process of conducting the 2010 US Nuclear Posture Review, NFU policy and negative security assurance received unprecedented attention and triggered the most heated debate. It is not difficult to imagine that as China's influence on future direction of nuclear disarmament grows, negotiations on nuclear operation policies would receive more attention. These nuclear operation policies include the NFU, negative security assurance, and de-alerting of nuclear weapons. The traditional approach of numerical reduction would face the challenge of a more balanced disarmament mechanism that takes nuclear operation regulations into consideration.

TRANSPARENCY AND CONFIDENCE BUILDING

Traditional nuclear arms control institutions call for greater transparency in nuclear development. Under such framework, revealing specific numbers of nuclear weapons and their physical capabilities is critical for mutual understanding and confidence building. China, on the other hand, emphasizes the importance of nuclear doctrinal and operational transparency. China's official documents contain detailed operational procedures of the Second Artillery and explanation for the training and operating conditions of China's nuclear forces.[16] Extensive information on the development and operation of China's nuclear forces is offered by state-run media. One recent research by Mark Stokes on China's nuclear storage system and facilities, for example, was conducted by collecting and studying such official releases.[17]

Two reasons explain China's distinctive approach on issues related to transparency. First and foremost, small nuclear countries disfavor promoting transparency on nuclear development. China's small nuclear arsenal dictates that its nuclear deterrence relies more on numerical and geographical ambiguity than bigger nuclear powers. From Chinese perspective, current verification mechanisms are too intrusive for China they challenge the key principle of China's nuclear operation—"hide and then retaliate." For the same reason, China has been reluctant to reveal the size of its current weapon-grade uranium and plutonium stockpiles, fearing that such information will uncover key features of China's existing nuclear weapons and undercut China's ability to deal with future uncertainties.[18]

Secondly, China believes that confidence building relies more on doctrinal transparency than numerical transparency. Chinese strategists see doctrinal transparency, such as an unconditional NFU commitment as important indications of a country's strategic objectives and political intentions, having direct and positive implications for promoting mutual understanding and trust and, therefore, laying the foundation for further nuclear disarmament. China's emphasis on doctrinal transparency might pressure current nuclear disarmament mechanism to shift from a lopsided focus on numerical transparency to a more balanced focus that includes both numerical and doctrinal transparency.

CHINESE APPROACH TO COUNTER-PROLIFERATION

Nonproliferation of nuclear weapons is a key pillar of the NPT regime. As many scholars have pointed out, China's relationship with global nuclear nonproliferation regime has changed dramatically since the very beginning and has gone through three main phases:

Phase 1: From 1964 to 1983, China was defiant toward global nonproliferation regime. It did not feel itself sharing a common identity with other nuclear weapons states; instead, it saw the Nuclear Nonproliferation Treaty as discriminatory and supported the pursuit of nuclear weapons by other developing countries as a means to break down the nuclear monopoly possessed by "imperialist countries."

Phase 2: From 1983 to 1992, as China took steps to transform its centralized economy to a market-oriented one, China changed its position and began to participate in international nonproliferation institutions under certain conditions.

Phase 3: Since 1992, China has fully accepted the norm of nonproliferation and has taken steps to bring its domestic legislation in line with international regulations.[19] Since China has joined most of existing nonproliferation institutions during the last couple of decades, its nonproliferation records have improved significantly.[20]

Nonetheless, China's compliance and cooperation with nonproliferation institutions does not mean its approach toward nonproliferation is completely consistent with the existing framework. China does have different views and priorities on issues related to nonproliferation, and such differences will continue to distinguish China from other countries and will inevitably affect the future evolution of global nuclear nonproliferation regime.

The Principle of Non-Discrimination

China's nonproliferation policy has been characterized by a combination of *realpolitik* pragmatism and Confucian-Mencian tradition.[21] Its signing of NPT treaty is a reflection of the pragmatist thinking, whereas its persistent criticism of the double-standard embodied in the regime is indicative of the Confucian-Mencian tradition. China has long been critical toward some of the discriminatory arrangements in the NPT framework and called for "a fairer and more just international nonproliferation regime, on the basis of universal participation."[22]

Within the broad framework of WMD nonproliferation, China is a member of NPT treaty, Chemical Weapons Convention, Biological and Toxin Weapons Convention, Nuclear Suppliers Group (NSG), and Zangger Committee. It signed Comprehensive Nuclear Test Ban Treaty (CTBT), and has applied for membership in the Missile Technology Control Regime (MTCR).[23] However, China is still outside of the Wassenaar Arrangement and Australia Group. China's primary concern is that these two institutions have specific target countries in mind and employ double-standard in their arrangements. The Australia Group, for example, is perceived as having an explicit objective to target Iran; and the Wassenaar Arrangement is believed to have Iran, Iraq, Libya, and North Korea as its main targets at the time of its establishment.[24] A most recent example of China's opposition against institutions that are targeted at specific countries is China's decision to stay out of the Proliferation Security Initiative (PSI) announced by President Bush in 2003. PSI is viewed as specifically designed to contain Iran and North Korea. As a result, China is not expected to join PSI in the near future.

Having chosen to hold out, China has considerably affected the overall efficacy of these regimes. PSI, for example, cannot fully deal with all suspected flights and ships that go in or out of North Korea or Iran without China's assistance and cooperation. As China is becoming an increasingly important player in international trade and transshipment, its role in multilateral counter-proliferation efforts and impact on nonproliferation regimes will grow correspondingly. Without China onboard, these regimes may face a persistent problem and need to make structural adjustment in order to deal with the pressure from China to address its concerns.

From Coercive to Persuasive Nonproliferation Framework

Another key difference that distinguishes China's nonproliferation approach from the traditional one lies in the mechanisms of compliance enforcement. One potential drawback of the NPT treaty is that there is no formal mechanism within the treaty to ensure that obligations will be met and noncompliance will be punished. The nonproliferation regime largely relies on its member states to take voluntary actions against noncompliance. The traditional way for Western countries to deal with NPT violators is to employ coercive measures. There were several cases that preventive military strikes were threatened or used to destroy nuclear facilities built by enemy states. When the chances of successful military actions were slim, other coercive measures such as trade embargo and economic sanctions were used to press the proliferator to give up its nuclear weapon programs. In dealing with the two present nuclear crises that involve Iran and North Korea, economic sanctions are the primary means that are employed.

China, however, takes a different view toward economic sanctions. China has been very reluctant to join the West in imposing comprehensive economic sanctions on Iran or North Korea. China's resistance toward employing economic sanctions has been widely interpreted as an effort to protect its energy and geostrategic interests in Middle East and Northeast Asia.[25] While it is certainly true that China wants to maintain its interests and influence in these regions, it is also important not to misunderstand China's perceptions of the efficacy of using economic sanctions against proliferators.

Chinese claim that they believe sanctions are neither effective nor helpful in resolving nuclear crises and therefore should not be recurrently employed.[26] Western policy makers and practitioners always dismiss such Chinese claim as convenient excuses. A careful study of China's perceptions of the efficacy of economic sanctions, however, reveals that China does view the value of economic sanctions differently from traditional Western perspective.

Since the foundation of the People's Republic of China more than sixty years ago, the country has only initiated a very limited number of unilateral economic sanctions.

Even among the only four historical cases, China's sanctions against Albania mainly took the form of aid cut-off, aiming primarily at reducing China's external economic burden and facilitating China's domestic economic reform.[27] Furthermore, China did not follow through on its threat to impose sanctions on American arms

Table 10.1.   Summary of China's Unilateral Economic Sanctions.

Target	Time	Objective	Sanction Details
Vietnam	1978–88	Dole out economic punishment in the context of political and military confrontation	Cutting-off aid
Albania	1978–83	Reduce China's economic burden	Cutting-off aid
France	2008–09	Elicit political compromise	Delaying trade negotiations in certain areas
U.S.	2010	Protest against US arms sales to Taiwan	Threatening to impose sanctions on U.S. arms companies

companies after the US made an arms sale to Taiwan in 2010. It is also debatable whether China actually carried out any substantive economic sanction against French companies in 2009 even though it was said to have made such threats. In short, China rarely used unilateral economic sanctions as a means to advance its foreign policy objectives.

In the very few cases when China did threaten to do so, it did not actually implement sanctions in the end. This is not only true during the Mao era when China lacked the capacity to impose economic sanctions, but also true during post-Mao era up till now when China does have the capacity to impose sanctions but still refrains from doing so.

In the foreseeable future, as China's economic interests become increasingly dependent on an open and stable global market, there is little reason to predict that China will change its behavior on economic sanctions. On the front of multilateral economic sanctions, the situation is similar. China is rarely an active participant in imposing multilateral sanctions. Even though China does not usually take steps to block multilateral sanction initiatives, it is always reluctant to join them. In most cases, pressure from foreign governments is necessary to lay the conditions for fostering China's ultimate compromise and cooperation.[28]

China's skepticism over using coercive measures such as comprehensive economic sanctions for the purpose of compliance enforcement has historical roots in its own experience of undergoing sanctions. Since the very beginning of the Cold War, China faced a series of severe trade embargos and economic sanctions. The most significant ones were imposed by the US and its Western allies during the 1950s and 1960s and by the Soviet Union during the 1960s and 1970s. None of these sanctions achieved their original objectives, and China managed to limit the negative impact of these sanctions on its economy and successfully developed its own nuclear arsenal. Such experience leaves the Chinese less impressive about the efficacy of coercive sanctions than most Western countries who themselves have rarely been targets of comprehensive sanctions.

China's reluctance to use comprehensive sanctions to serve counter-proliferation purposes is well manifested by its policies toward Iranian and North Korean nuclear crises. Even under tremendous pressure, China refused to impose comprehensive economic sanctions against Iran or North Korea. In the Korean case, when China was outraged by North Korea's provocative nuclear tests which seriously undermined the China-DPRK relationship, China still refused to employ comprehensive sanctions. China's unwillingness to get onboard with international sanction agreements significantly delayed the implementation of these sanctions. Even though China ultimately chose not to block United Nations resolutions to sanction Iran or North Korea, China's policies limited the scale and scope of the sanctions and made the sanctions less painful. In the case of North Korea, China not only refused to impose comprehensive sanctions, instead it offered resources to help North Koreans develop an open and market-oriented economy. In early 2010, for instance, instead of imposing sanctions, China revealed a plan to make a US$10 billion investment in North Korea.[29] On more than one occasion, China invited North Korean leader Kim Jong-il to visit China and showed him the Chinese model of economic development. In May 2011, China gave Kim another economic "study tour" in China.[30]

Therefore, China' approach for compliance enforcement within the nonproliferation framework is fundamentally different from the traditional Western approach. China dismisses the efficacy of coercive measures because of its own experience of resisting sanctions. As an alternative, China tends to offer resources and economic assistance as a means to elicit compliance. It favors a persuasive approach in dealing with proliferators or potential proliferators, and calls for confidence building measures that can address the root causes of disputes and reduce sources of threat perception.[31] While most Western countries have no trade or financial relationship with North Korea and Iran, China maintains a growing economic and political influence in these countries. Without China's participation, it is difficult for any multilateral economic sanction against these countries to bear substantive results. China's strong opposition against coercive measures and support for persuasive approaches will affect the relative importance of the two opposite approaches for compliance enforcement in the future.

CONCLUSION

As a recognized Nuclear Weapons State under NPT, China shares the goal of nuclear disarmament and the concern about further nuclear proliferation with other countries in the international community. However, due to a variety of reasons, China's approach to nuclear disarmament and nonproliferation differs from the traditional approaches adopted by many countries.

As China grows, so will its influence on the future evolution of these institutions increase. A world free of nuclear threat is impossible to achieve without China's substantive participation and cooperation. China's position will be critical for the direction and success of any future global nuclear disarmament process. China is also imposing increasing pressure on the current nonproliferation regime to transform its compliance enforcement measures from a coercive one to a more persuasive one. Therefore, the international community should not be overly concerned with China's potential influence in these areas. Rather, it should seek a clear understanding of China's approach and continue to engage with China on vital security issues such as nuclear disarmament and nonproliferation. China has the potential to play a constructive role in reducing global nuclear arsenals and preventing further proliferation of nuclear weapons as long as all countries are committed to continuous engagement and comprehensive communication.

NOTES

1. This chapter includes part of a work that was first published in its original form in St. Antony's International Review: Tong Zhao, "China's Role in Reshaping the Global Nuclear Non-Proliferation Regime," *St. Antony's International Review* 6, no. 2 (2011): 67–82.

2. Four prominent former American lawmakers and senior government officials—George Schultz, William Perry, Henry Kissinger, and Sam Nunn coauthored a series of *Wall Street Journal* op-eds and called for a world free of nuclear weapons. See, for example, George Schultz,

William Perry, Henry Kissinger, and Sam Nunn, "A World Free of Nuclear Weapons," *Wall Street Journal*, January 4, 2007; George Schultz, William Perry, Henry Kissinger, and Sam Nunn, "Toward a Nuclear Weapon Free World." *Wall Street Journal*, January 14, 2008.

3. "New Strategic Arms Reduction Treaty (New START)," The Department of State, http://www.state.gov/t/avc/newstart/c39903.htm.

4. Jeffrey G Lewis, "Chinese Nuclear Posture and Force Modernization," *The Nonproliferation Review* 16, no. 2 (2009): 197–209.

5. William J. Perry, Brent Scowcroft, and Charles D. Ferguson, "U.S. Nuclear Weapons Policy," in *Independent Task Force Report* (New York: Council on Foreign Relations, 2009).

6. For discussions on the size of China's nuclear arsenal, please see Robert S. Norris and Hans M. Kristensen, "Chinese Nuclear Forces, 2008," *The Bulletin of the Atomic Scientists* 64, no. 3 (2008): 42–45.

7. Riqiang Wu, "US and Japan Construct Three-Layer Defense to Undermine China's Nuclear Deterrent Capability," *Elite Reference* no. October (2009).

8. Senate Foreign Relations Committee *Statement of Eric S. Edelman before the Senate Foreign Relations Committee Hearing: The New Start Treaty (Treaty Doc 111–5): Benefits and Risks*, June 24, 2010.

9. Bin Li, "Understanding China's Nuclear Strategy," *World Economics and Politics* no. 9 (2006): 16–22.

10. Nuclear taboo generally refers to the norm that is derived from the discriminatively destructive nature of nuclear weapons and that prohibits the use of nuclear weapons on battle fields. For in-depth discussion on nuclear taboo, see, for example, Nina Tannenwald, *The Nuclear Taboo: The United States and the Non-Use of Nuclear Weapons since 1945* (Cambridge: Cambridge University Press, 2007); or T. V Paul, *The Traditions of Non-Use of Nuclear Weapons* (Stanford: Stanford University Press, 2009). For discussion on the relationship between nuclear taboo and China's nuclear strategy, see, for example, Riqiang Wu, "Just War, Nuclear Taboo and Nuclear-Weapon-Free World," *World Economics and Politics* no. 10 (2009): 51–58.

11. Li, "Understanding," 19.

12. Jing-Dong Yuan. "Culture Matters: Chinese Approaches to Arms Control and Disarmament," In *Culture and Security: Multilateralism, Arms Control and Security Building*, edited by Keith R. Krause, 85–128. (Portland: Frank Cass Publishers, 1999). According to Yuan, the Confucian-Mencian perspective views the world as harmonious rather than conflictual and assumes a world order with China the 'Middle Kingdom' at the center; in contrast, the *realpolitik* perspective emphasizes diversity over uniformity, conflicts over harmony, and economic/ military power over moral persuasion.

13. Li, "Understanding," 20.

14. "China's National Defense White Paper, 2008," Beijing: Ministry of Defense, 2009.

15. Gregory Kulacki, *China's Nuclear Arsenal: Status and Evolution* (Boston, MA: Union of Concerned Scientists, 2011).

16. The most recent National Defense White Paper was published in 2009, and is available at http://www.gov.cn/english/official/2009–01/20/content_1210227.htm.

17. "Expert: China Is the Only Country That Has a No First Use Policy," Xinhua News, http://news.xinhuanet.com/mil/2010–04/15/content_13358573.htm.

18. Bin Li, "Country Perspectives on the Challenges to a Fissile Material (Cutoff) Treaty: China" (Princeton: The International Panel on Fissile Materials [IPFM], 2008).

19. Baogen Zhou, "China and Global Nuclear Nonproliferation Regime: A Constructivist Analysis," *World Economics and Politics* no. 2 (2003): 23–27.

20. Gary K. Bertsch, "Challenge and Change in Chinese Export Controls and Industry Compliance," *China Currents* 7, no. 2 (2008): 2–6.

21. Yuan, "Culture," 87.

22. "China's National Defense White Paper," Beijing: Ministry of Defense, 1998.

23. China has applied for but so far declined membership of MTCR.

24. Jun Wang, "An Analysis on the Change of China's Nonproliferation Policy after the End of the Cold War," *Pacific Journal* no. 4 (2002): 61–71.

25. See, for example, David Shambaugh, "China and the Korean Peninsula: Playing for the Long Term," *The Washington Quarterly* 26, no. 2 (2003): 43–56.

26. "Ministry of Foreign Affairs Spokesperson: Pressure and Sanctions Won't Help Achieve Non-Nuclearization of Korean Peninsula," Ministry of Foreign Affairs, China, http://china .cnr.cn/jryw/200904/t20090409_505298400.html; and "Ministry of Foreign Affairs Spokesperson's Statement on Press Conference." Ministry of Foreign Affairs of China, accessed August 15, 2010, http://202.123.110.5/xwfb/2009–09/08/content_1412139.htm.

27. Yuhua Guo, "Sino-Albanian Relations: Close Allies That Ultimately Broke Up," *Across Fine and Space* 12, (2001): 17–23; and Hongqi Wang, "The Special Years of China-Albanian Relations That I Witnessed," *Chinese People* 8, (2007): 91–95.

28. Mark Landler, "Despite Pressure, China Still Resists Iran Sanctions," *The New York Times*, February 25 2010.

29. Jung Sung-ki, "China Plans $10 Billion Investment in North Korea," *The Korea Times*, February 15 2010.

30. Royston Chan, "Kim Jong-il Tours East China," Reuters, accessed May 29 2011, http://news.yahoo.com/s/nm/20110523/wl_nm/us_china_korea_north.

31. *Ministry of Foreign Affairs Spokesperson: Pressure and Sanctions Won't Help Achieve Non-Nuclearization of Korean Peninsula*, Ministry of Foreign Affairs, China 2009, http://china.cnr .cn/jryw/200904/t20090409_505298400.html.

Select Bibliography

Accominotti, Olivier. "The Sterling Trap: Foreign Reserves Management at the Bank of France, 1928–1936," *European Review of Economic History*, 13 (2009): 349–376.

Andrews, David M. ed. *International Monetary Power*. Ithaca, NY: Cornell University Press, 2005.

Barry, Eichengreen and Jeffrey A. Frieden. *The Political Economy of European Monetary Unification*, Second Edition. Boulder, Colorado: Westview Press, 2001.

Bearce, David, and Stacy Bondanella. "Intergovernmental Organizations, Socialization, and Member-State Interest Convergence," *International Organization* 61 (2007): 703–733.

Beeson, Mark, and Stephen Bell. "The G-20 and International Economic Governance: Hegemony, Collectivism, or Both?" *Global Governance*, Vol. 15, No. 1 (January-March 2009), pp. 67–86.

Bergsten, C. Fred, Charles Freeman, Nicholas R. Lardy, and Derek J. Mitchell. *China's Rise: Challenges and Opportunities*. Washington, DC: Peterson Institute for International Economics, 2008.

Bernstein, Richard, and Ross H. Munro. *The Coming Conflict with China*. New York: A.A. Knopf, 1997.

Bertsch, Gary K. "Challenge and Change in Chinese Export Controls and Industry Compliance," *China Currents* 7, no. 2 (2008): 2–6.

Blasko, Dennis J. "China's Views on NATO Expansion: A Secondary National Interest," *China Brief* 9, no. 5 (March 2009), 3.

Blustein, Paul. *Misadventures of the Most Favored Nations: Clashing Egos, Inflated Ambitions, and the Great Shambles of the World Trade System*. PublicAffairs, 2009.

Bottelier, Pieter. "China and the World Bank: How a Partnership Was Built," *Journal of Contemporary China* (2007), 16(51), May, 239–258.

Bowles, Paul. "Asia's Post-Crisis Regionalism: Bring the State Back in, Keeping the (United) States Out," *Review of International Political Economy*, 9 (2002), 245.

Bown, Chad. "Developing Countries as Plaintiffs and Defendants in GATT/WTO Trade Disputes." *The World Economy* 27 (2004): 59–80.

Bown, Chad. "On the Economic Success of GATT/WTO Dispute Settlement," *The Review of Economics and Statistics* 86 (2004): 811–823.

Bown, Chad. "Participation in WTO Dispute Settlement: Complainants, Interested Parties and Free Riders," *World Bank Economic Review* 19 (2005): 287–310.

Breslin, Shaun. "China's Emerging Global Role: Dissatisfied Responsible Great Power," *Politics*, 20 (S1) (2010): 52–62.

Brewster, Rachel. "Shadow Unilateralism: Enforcing International Trade Law at the WTO," *University of Pennsylvania Journal of International Economic Law* 30 (2009): 1133–1147.

Buckley, Chris. "China Gains Access to Venezuelan Oil," *The International Herald Tribune*, 28, December 24, 2007.

Bull, Hedley. *The Anarchical Society.* New York: Columbia University Press, 1977.

Bull, Hedley. *The Anarchical Society: A Study of Order in World Politics*, 3rd edition. Houndmills, Basingstoke: Palgrave Macmillan, 2002.

Busch, Marc and Eric Reinhardt. "Developing Countries and GATT/WTO Dispute Settlement," *Journal of World Trade* 37 (2003).

Busch, Marc, L., Eric Reinhardt, and Gregory Shaffer, *Does Legal Capacity Matter? Explaining Dispute Initiation and Antidumping Actions in the WTO*. Geneva: International Centre for Trade and Sustainable Development, 2007.

Calder, K. a. M. Y. (2004). "Regionalism and Critical Junctures: Explaining the "Organization Gap" in Northeast Asia." *Journal of East Asian Studies* 4 (2) 2004: 191–226.

Callahan, William A. "Chinese Visions of World Order: Post-Hegemonic or a New Hegemony?" *International Studies Review*, 10 (4), December 2008: 749–61.

Cao, Qing. "Confucian Vision of a New World Order?: Culturalist Discourse, Foreign Policy and the Press in Contemporary China," *International Communication Gazette*, 2007, Vol. 69(5), 435.

Carlson, Allen. "Moving beyond Sovereignty? A Brief Consideration of Recent Changes in China's Approach to International Order and the Emergence of the Tianxia Concept," *Journal of Contemporary China*, 20 (68), January 2011: 89–102.

Cattaneo, Olivier, and Carols A. *Primo Braga, Everything You Always Wanted to Know about WTO Accession*. World Bank, Policy Research Working Paper Series 5116, 2009.

Chan, Gerald. *China's Compliance in Global Affairs: Trade, Arms Control, Environmental Protection, Human Rights.* Singapore: World Scientific, 2006.

Chan, Gerald, Pak K. Lee, and Lai-Ha Chan. *China Engages Global Governance: A New World Order in the Making?* Abingdon: Routledge, 2012.

Chan, Lai-Ha, Pak K. Lee, and Gerald Chan, "Rethinking Global Governance: A China Model in the Making?" *Contemporary Politics*, Vol. 14, No. 1, March 2008, 3–19.

Chan, Lai-Ha. *China Engages Global Heath Governance: Responsible Stakeholder or System-Transformer*. New York: Palgrave Macmillan, 2011.

Checkel, Jeffrey. "International Institutions and Socialization in Europe," *International Organization* 59, 804, 804–5, 805, (2005).

Chen, Da. "First Hand Experience with the WTO Negotiation: Who Can Serve the WTO?" *Beijing Youth Daily*, September 23, 2001.

Chen, Fengying. "G20 yu guoji zhixu da bianju" ["G20 and the dramatic transformation of the international order"]. *Xiandai guoji guanxi* [Contemporary international relations] 11 (2009).

Chen, Jian. *China's Road to the Korean War: The Making of the Sino-American Confrontation.* New York: Columbia University Press, 1994, 85–90, 111–12.

Chen, Kaihe. "lun wo guo zai duobian waijiao huodong zhong de guoji gonggong guanxi celue" [China's international public relations strategies in multilateral diplomacy], *waijiao pinglun* [foreign affairs review], no. 100, December 2007, pp. 68–74.

Chen, Suquan."ba guo jituan, ershi guo jituan yu zhongguo" [G8, G20 and China], *dong-nanya Zongheng* [Around Southeast Asia], 2009, pp. 77–80.

Chey, Hyoung-kyu. "The Changing Political Dynamics of East Asian Financial Cooperation: The Chiang Mai Initiative," *Asian Survey*, 49 (2009), 450.

Chin, Gregory, and Eric Helleiner. "China as a Creditor: A Rising Financial Power?" *Journal of International Affairs*, 62(2008): 87–102.

Chin, Gregory, and Ramesh Thakur, "Will China Change the Rules of Global Order?" *Washington Quarterly*, 33:4, 2010, pp. 119–138.

Chinn, Menzie D. and Jacob A. Frankel. "The Euro May Over the Next 15 Years Surpass the Dollar as Leading International Currency," *NBER Working Paper*, No. 13909, April 2008.

Chow, Jack C. "China's Billion-Dollar Aid Appetite," *Foreign Policy*, 21 July 2010.

Christensen, Thomas J. "Fostering Stability or Creating a Monster? The Rise of China and U.S. Policy toward East Asia," *International Security*, 31 (2006), 81–126.

Chung, Jae Ho. "China and Northeast Asia: A Complex Equation for 'Peaceful Rise,'" *Politics*, 27 (3), October 2007, 159–61.

Chung, Jae Ho. "China's 'soft' clash with South Korea: The History War and Beyond," *Asian Survey*, 49 (3), May/June 2009: 468–83.

Cohen, Benjamin J. "The Seigniorage Gain of an International Currency: An Empirical Test,' *Quarterly Journal of Economics,* 85(1971): 494–607.

Cookson, Robert. "ADB Issues Landmark Renminbi Bond," *Financial Times*, October 19 2010.

Cookson, Robert, and Geoff Dyer, "Currencies: Yuan direction," *Financial Times*, December 13, 2010.

Cooper, Robert. *The Breaking of Nations: Order and Chaos in the Twenty-First Century.* New York: Atlantic Monthly Press, 2003.

Croome, John. *Reshaping the World Trading System: A History of the Uruguay Round.* Kluwer, 1998.

Cui, Liru. "G20 kaiqi le tansuo 'quanqiu zhili' xin lujin de jihui zhi chuang" ["G20 opens a window of opportunity for exploring a new approach to 'global governance'"], *Xiandai guoji guanxi* [Contemporary international relations], 11 (2009).

Davis, Christina, and Sarah Bermeo. "Who Files? Developing Country Participation in WTO Adjudication," *Journal of Politics* 71 (2009): 1033–1049.

Deng, Yong. *China's Struggle for Status: The Realignment of International Relations.* Cambridge: Cambridge University Press, 2008.

Diamant, Neil. "Conflict and Conflict Resolution in China beyond Mediation-Centered Approaches," *Journal of Conflict Resolution* 44 (2000): 523–546.

Dieter, Heribert, and Richard Higgott. "Exploring Alternative Theories of Economic Regionalism: From Trade to Finance in Asian Co-operation?" *Review of International Political Economy*, 10 (2003), 430–454.

Drezner, Daniel W. "Bad Debt: Assessing China's Financial Influence in Great Power Politics," *International Security*, 34 (2009): 7–45.

Dumbaugh, Kerry. "China's Foreign Policy: What Does It Mean for U.S. Global Interests?" CRS (Congressional Research Service) Report for U.S. Congress, July 18 2008.

Eichengreen, Barry. *Globalizing Capital: A History of the International Monetary System.* Princeton: Princeton University Press, 1996, p. 136.

Erikson, Daniel P., and Janice Chen. "China, Taiwan and the Battle for Latin America," *The Fletcher Forum of World Affairs*, vol 31:3, Summer, 2007, pp. 69–89.

Fairbank, John King (ed.). *The Chinese World Order: Traditional China's Foreign Relations.* Cambridge, MA: Harvard University Press, 1968.

Feng, Hui. *The Politics of China's Accession to the World Trade Organization: The Dragon Goes Global.* London: Routledge, 2006.

Finnemore, Martha. *National Interest and International Society.* Ithaca, NY: Cornell University Press, 1996.

Ferguson, Niall, and Moritz Schularick, "The Great Wallop," *New York Times*, November 16, 2009, accessed in November 17, 2009,

Ferguson, Niall. *The Ascent of Money: A Financial History of the World.* New York: Penguin, 2008.

Ferguson, Niall, and Moritz Schularick. "Chimerical? Think Again," *Wall Street Journal*, February 5, 2007.

Fishman, Ted C. *China, Inc.: How the Rise of the Next Superpower Challenges America and the World.* New York: Scribner, 2006.

Fonte, John. *Sovereignty or Submission: Will Americans Rule Themselves or be Ruled by Others?* New York: Encounter Books Inc., 2011.

Foot, Rosemary. "Chinese Strategies in a US-Hegemonic Global Order: Accommodating and Hedging," *International Affairs*, 82, 1 (2006) 77–94.

Gallagher, K., and Roberto Porzecanski. *The Dragon in the Room: China and the Future of Latin American Industrialization.* Stanford, CA: Stanford University Press, 2010.

Gao, Henry. "Aggressive Legalism: The East Asian Experience and Lessons for China," in *China's Participation in the WTO*, edited by Henry Gao and Don Lewis. London: Cameron May, 2005.

Gao, Henry. "Taming the Dragon: China's Experience in the WTO Dispute Settlement System," *Legal Issues of Economic Integration* 34 (2007): 369–392.

Garret, Laurie, and El'Haum Alavian. "Global Health Governance in a G-20 World," *Global Health Governance*, 4 (1), Fall 2010.

Garrett, Geoffrey. "G2 in G20: China, the United States and the World after the Global Financial Crisis," *Global Policy*, Issue 1, Vol. 1 (January 2010): 29–39.

Goldstein, Goldstein, and Morris Nicholas R. Lardy, eds. *Debating China's Exchange Rate Policy.* Washington, DC: Peterson Institute for International Economics, 2008.

Grimes, William W. "Internationalization of the Yen and the New Politics of Monetary Insulation," in *Monetary Orders: Ambiguous Economics, Ubiquitous Politics*, edited by Jonathan Kirshner. Ithaca: Cornell University Press, 2003, 172–194.

Grimes, William W. *Currency and Contest in East Asia: The Great Power Politics of Financial Regionalism.* Cornell University Press, 2009.

Gu, Jing, John Humphrey, and Dirk Messner, "Global Governance and Developing Countries: The Implications of the Rise of China," *World Development* Vol. 36, No. 2, 2008, pp. 274–292.

Guo, Xiangang. "zhongguo waijiao xin liangdian: yu xinxing guojia hezuo de tansuo yu shijian" [new spotlight in China's diplomacy: exploring and practicing cooperation with emerging powers], *guoji wenti yanjiu* [international studies], issue 1, 2010, pp. 5–9, 31.

Guo, Yuhua. "Sino-Albanian Relations: Close Allies That Ultimately Broke Up," *Across Fine and Space* 12, (2001): 17–23.

Guzman, Andrew, and Beth Simmons. "Power Plays and Capacity Constraints: The Selection of Defendants in WTO Disputes." *Journal of Legal Studies* 34 (2005): 557–598.

Helleiner, Eric. *States and the Reemergence of Global Finance*. Ithaca and London: Cornell University Press, 1994, 81–100.

Horn, Henrik, and Håkan Nordström, and Petros C. Mavroidis. "Is the Use of the WTO Dispute Settlement System Biased?" CEPR Discussion Paper 2340 (1999), Centre for Economic Policy Research.

Huang, Renwei."Xinxing daguo canyu quanqiu zhili de libi" ["Benefits and drawbacks of new emerging powers' participation in global governance"]. *Xiandai guoji guanxi* [Contemporary international relations] 11 (2009), 21–2.

Hudec, Robert E. *Essays on the Nature of International Trade Law*. London: Cameron May, 1999.

Hund, Markus. "ASEAN Plus Three: Towards a New Age of Pan-East Asian Regionalism? A Skeptic's Appraisal," *Pacific Review*, 16 (2003), 383–417.

Ikenberry, G. John. "The Rise of China and the Future of the West: Can the Liberal System Survive?" *Foreign Affairs*, January/February 2008.

Jacobson, Harold K., and Michel Oksenberg. *China's Participation in the IMF, the World Bank, and GATT*. Ann Arbor: University of Michigan Press, 1990.

Jacques, Martin. *When China Rules the World: the End of the Western World and the Birth of a New Global Order*. New York: the Penguin Press, 2009.

Jansen, Marius B. *The Making of Modern Japan*. Cambridge, MA: Belknap Press, 2000.

Johnston, Alastair Iain. "Is China a Status Quo Power?" *International Security*, 27(4), Spring 2003: 5–56.

Johnston, Alastair Iain. "Beijing's Security Behavior in the Asia-Pacific: Is China a Dissatisfied Power?" in *Rethinking Security in East Asia: Identity, Power and Efficiency*, edited by J. J. Suh, Peter J Katzenstein, and Allen Carlson. Stanford, CA: Stanford University Press, 2004, 34–96.

Johnston, Alastair Iain. *Social States: China in International Institutions 1980–2000*. Princeton, NJ: Princeton University Press, 2008.

Joseph, Jonathan. *Hegemony: A Realist Analysis*. London: Routledge, 2002.

Jung, Sung-ki. "China Plans $10 Billion Investment in North Korea," *The Korea Times*, February 15, 2010.

Kang, David C. *East Asia before the West: Five Centuries of Trade and Tribute*. New York: Columbia University Press, 2010.

Kent, Ann. "China, International Organizations and Regimes: The ILO as a Case Study in Organizational Learning," *Pacific Affairs*. Vol. 70, No. 4, Winter, 1997–1998: 517–532.

Kent, Ann. *Beyond Compliance: China, International Organizations, and Global Security*. Palo Alto: Stanford University Press, 2007, pp. 222–223.

Keohane, Robert O., and Joseph S. Nye, *Power and Interdependence: World Politics in Transition*. Boston: Little, Brown and Company, 1977.

Khoo, Nicholas. "Breaking the Ring of Encirclement: The Sino-Soviet Rift and Chinese Policy toward Vietnam, 1964–1968," *Journal of Cold War Studies*, 12 (1), Winter 2010: 3–42.

Kim, Moonhawk. "Costly Procedures: Divergent Effects of Legalization in the GATT/WTO Dispute Settlement Procedures," *International Studies Quarterly* 52 (2008): 657–686.

Kim, Samuel S. "International Organizations in Chinese Foreign Policy," *Annals of the American Academy of Political and Social Science*, Vol. 519 (1992).

Kim, Samuel S. *China, the United Nations, and World Order.* Princeton, NJ: Princeton University Press, 1979.

Kirshner, Jonathan. *Currency and Coercion: The Political Economy of International Monetary Power.* Princeton: Princeton University Press, 1995.

Krugman, Paul. "China's Dollar Trap," *New York Times,* April 2, 2009.

Kulacki, Gregory. *China's Nuclear Arsenal: Status and Evolution.* Boston, MA: Union of Concerned Scientists, 2011.

Kuntz, Diane B. *The Economic Diplomacy of the Suez Canal.* Chapel Hill: The University of North Carolina Press, 1991.

Kuruvila, Pretty Elizabeth. "Developing Countries and the GATT/WTO Dispute Settlement Mechanism," *Journal of World Trade* 31 (1997): 171–208.

Lardy, Nicholas R. *Integrating China into the Global Economy.* Washington, DC: Brookings Institution Press, 2002.

Legro, Jeffrey W. "What China Will Want: The Future Intentions Of A Rising Power," *Perspectives on Politics,* 5 (3), September 2007: 515–34.

Lewis, Jeffrey G. "Chinese Nuclear Posture and Force Modernization," *The Nonproliferation Review* 16, no. 2 (2009): 197–209.

Li, Bin. "Understanding China's Nuclear Strategy," *World Economics and Politics* no. 9 (2006): 16–22.

Li, Mingjiang. "Rising from Within: China's Search for a Multilateral World and Its Implications for Sino-US Relations," *RSIS Working Paper,* No. 225, March 25, 2011.

Li, Xiaojun. "Social Rewards and Socialization Effects: an Alternative Explanation to the Motivation behind China's Participation in International Institutions," *Chinese Journal of International Politics* 3 (2009): 347–377.

Li, Zuojun. "guoji jingji weiji de zhenzheng genyuan shi quanqiu zhili queshi" [the real source of global economic crisis is the lack of global governance], *zhongguo jingji shibao* [China economics daily], August 11, 2009.

Linklater, Andrew. *Theories of International Relations,* 3rd edition. Basingstoke: Palgrave Macmillan, 2005.

Linklater, Andrew, and Hidemi Suganami. *The English School of International Relations.* Cambridge: Cambridge University Press, 2006.

Marketos, Threassy N.. *China's Energy Geopolitics: The Shanghai Cooperation Organization and Central Asia.* Routledge, 2009.

McKinnon, Ronald I. *Exchange Rates under the East Asian Dollar Standard.* Cambridge: MIT Press, 2005.

Mearsheimer, John J. *The Tragedy of Great Power Politics.* New York and London: W.W. Norton & Company, 2001.

Mearsheimer, John. "The Gathering Storm: China's Challenge to US Power in Asia," *Chinese Journal of International Politics,* 3(2010): 381–396.

Michalopoulos, Constantine. *Developing Countries in the WTO.* New York: Palgrave, 2001.

Norris, Robert S., and Hans M. Kristensen, "Chinese Nuclear Forces, 2008," *The Bulletin of the Atomic Scientists* 64, no. 3 (2008): 42–45.

Olson, Mancur. *The Logic of Collective Action.* Cambridge: MA: Harvard University Press, 1965.

Perry, William J., and Brent Scowcroft, and Charles D. Ferguson. "U.S. Nuclear Weapons Policy," in *Independent Task Force Report.* New York: Council on Foreign Relations, 2009.

Roderick, Abott. "Are Developing Countries Deterred from Using the WTO Dispute Settlement System?" *ECIPE Working Paper* No. 01. 2007.

Roett, Riordan, and Guadalupe Paz. *China's Expansion into the Western Hemisphere*. Brookings Institution, 2008.

Schwartz, Herman. *Subprime Nation: American Power, Global Capital, and the Housing Bubble*. Ithaca, NY: Cornell University Press, 2009.

Setser, Brad W. *Sovereign Wealth and Sovereign Power: The Strategic Consequences of American Indebtedness*. New York: Council on Foreign Relations Press, 2008.

Sevilla, Christina R. "Explaining Patterns of GATT/WTO Trade Complaints," *Working Paper* 98–1 (1998), Weatherhead Center for International Affairs, Harvard University.

Shang, Huipeng. "'Lun ren' yu 'tianxia' – jiedu yi chaogong tixi wei hexin de gudai Dong Ya guoji zhixu" ('Human relations' and 'all under Heaven': an interpretation of the tribute-centred ancient East Asian international order), *Guoji zhengzhi yanjiu* (International Politics Studies), No. 2 (2009): 38.

Shorr, David, and Thomas Wright, "Forum: The G20 and Global Governance: An Exchange," *Survival*, 52: 2, 181–198, 2010.

Shu, Xiao, and Gong Yuping. "san ci fenghui hou kan ershi guo jituan de fazhan qianjing" [an analysis on the G20's prospect after three summits], *dangdai shijie* [contemporary world], issue 11, 2010, pp. 51–53.

Siddiqi, Javed. *World Health and World Politics: The World Health Organization and the UN System*. London: Hurst & Co., 1995.

Smith, James. "Inequality in International Trade? Developing Countries and Institutional Change in WTO Dispute Settlement." *Review of International Political Economy* 11 (2004): 542–573.

Spence, Jonathan D. *The Search for Modern China*, 2nd edition. New York: W.W. Norton, 1999.

Steil, Benn, and Robert E. Litan. *Financial Statecraft: The Role of Financial Markets in American Foreign Policy*. New Haven: Yale University Press, 2008.

Steil, Benn, and Manuel Hinds. *Money, Markets and Sovereignty*. Yale University Press, 2009.

Steinfeld, Edward S. *Playing Our Game: Why China's Rise Doesn't Threaten the West*. New York: Oxford University Press, 2010.

Strange, Susan. "The Persistent Myth of Lost Hegemony," *International Organization*, Vol. 41, No.4, 1987, p. 569.

Stubbs, Richard. "ASEAN Plus Three: Emerging East Asian Regionalism?" *Asian Survey*, 42(2002), 440–455.

Stueck, William. *Rethinking the Korean War: A New Diplomatic and Strategic History*. Princeton, NJ: Princeton University Press, 2002: 69–74.

Tannenwald, Nina. *The Nuclear Taboo: The United States and the Non-Use of Nuclear Weapons since 1945*. Cambridge: Cambridge University Press, 2007.

Thompson, Helen. "Debt and Power: The United States' Debt in Historical Perspective," *International Relations*, 21(2007): 305–323.

Volcker, Paul, and Toyoo Gyohten. *Changing Fortunes: The World's Money and the Threat to American Leadership*. New York: Times Books, 1992, 42–43.

Wallerstein, Immanuel. *World-Systems Analysis: An Introduction*. Duke University Press, 2004.

Walt, Stephen M. *The Origins of Alliances*. Ithaca, NY: Cornell University Press, 1987.

Wang, Hongying, and James N. Rosenau, "China and Global Governance," *Asian Perspective*, Vol. 33, No. 3, 2009, pp. 5–39.

Wang, Jun. "An Analysis on the Change of China's Nonproliferation Policy after the End of the Cold War," *Pacific Journal,* no. 4 (2002): 61–71.

Wang, Yusheng. "jinzhuan si guo de meili he fazhan qushi" [the charm of the BRICS and the trend of its development], *ya fei zongheng* [Asia-Africa studies], issue 5, 2009, pp. 27–29.

Wei, Liang. "China's WTO Commitment Compliance: A Case Study of the US-China Semiconductor Trade Dispute," in *China's Foreign Trade Policy: The New Constituencies*, edited by Ka Zeng and Andrew Mertha. London: Routledge, 2007.

Welch, Deborah Larson, and Alexei Shevchenko. "Status Concern and Multilateral Cooperation," in *International Cooperation: The Extents and Limits of Multilateralism*, edited by I. William Zartman and Saadia Touval (eds). Cambridge: Cambridge University Press, 2010: 182–207.

Welch, Deborah Larson, and Alexei Shevchenko. "Status Seekers: Chinese and Russian Responses to U.S. Primacy," *International Security*, 34 (4), Spring 2010: 63–95.

Wendt, Alexander. "Collective Identity Formation and the International State," *American Political Science Review* 88 (1994): 384–397.

Womack, Brantly. *China and Vietnam: The Politics of Asymmetry*. Cambridge: Cambridge University Press, 2006.

Wu, Guoguang, and Helen Lansdowne, "International Multilateralism with Chinese Characteristics: Attitude Changes, Policy Imperatives, and Regional Impacts," in *China Turns to Multilateralism: Foreign Policy and Regional Security*, edited by Guoguang Wu and Helen Lansdowne. Oxon: Routledge, 2008.

Yan, Xuetong, "Xun Zi's Thoughts on International Politics and Their Implications," *The Chinese Journal of International Politics*, 2 (1), Summer 2008: 159.

Yan, Xuetong, "The Instability of China-U.S. Relations," *Chinese Journal of International Politics*, 3(2010): pp. 263–292.

Yuan, Jing-Dong. "Culture Matters: Chinese Approaches to Arms Control and Disarmament," in *Culture and Security: Multilateralism, Arms Control and Security Building*, edited by Keith R. Krause, 85–128. Portland: Frank Cass Publishers, 1999.

Zhang, Feng. "Rethinking the 'Tribute System': Broadening the Conceptual Horizon of Historical East Asian Politics," *Chinese Journal of International Politics*, 2 (4), Winter 2009: 545–74.

Zhang, Xiaoming. "Deng Xiaoping and China's Decision to Go to War with Vietnam," *Journal of Cold War Studies*, 12 (3), Summer 2010: 3–29.

Zhao, Tingyang. *Tianxia tixi: Shijie zhidu zhexue daolun* (The Tianxia System: A Philosophy for the World Institution). Nanjing: Jiangsu jiaoyu chubanshe, 2005.

Zhao, Tong. "China's Role in Reshaping the Global Nuclear Non-Proliferation Regime," *St. Antony's International Review* 6, no. 2 (2011): 67–82.

Zhao, Xiaochun. "G20 fenghui yu shijie xin zhixu de yanjin" ["G20 summit and the evolution of the new world order"]. *Xiandai guoji guanxi* [Contemporary international relations] 11 (2009).

Zhao, Zongbo. "Guanyu ershi guo jituan huodong chengguo de ruogan sikao" [Thoughts on the achievements of the G20], *Dangdai jingji* [Contemporary Economy], February 2010, pp. 60–63.

Zheng, Yongnian, and Sow Keat TOK, "Harmonious Society and Harmonious World: China's Policy Discourse under Hu Jintao," Briefing Series, Issue 26, The University of Nottingham, China Policy Institute, p. 10.

Zhou, Baogen. "China and Global Nuclear Nonproliferation Regime: A Constructivist Analysis," *World Economics and Politics*, no. 2 (2003): 23–27.

Zou, Keyuan. *China's Legal Reform: Towards the Rule of Law*. Leiden, the Netherlands: Martinus Nijhoff Publishers, 2006, 245.

Index

List of Contributors

Gerald Chan is professor and head of the Department of Political Studies at the University of Auckland, New Zealand. His area of interest is Chinese international relations. His latest co-edited book (with Chan Lai-Ha and Kwan Fung) is titled *China at 60: Global-Local Interactions* . And his latest article is entitled "China's Response to the Global Financial Crisis and Its Regional Leadership in East Asia," *Asia Europe Journal*, 2012.

Lai-Ha Chan is Chancellor's Postdoctoral Research Fellow of the China Research Centre at the University of Technology, Sydney, Australia. Her major research interests include Chinese international relations, China's participation in global governance as well as non-traditional security issues, particularly contagious diseases. She is the author of *China Engages Global Health Governance: Responsible Stakeholder or System-Transformer?* Her joint publications have appeared in *Review of International Studies* (2012 forthcoming), *PLoS Medicine* (2010), *Global Public Health* (2009), *China Security* (2009), *Third World Quarterly* (2008), and *Contemporary Politics* (2008). The last one was awarded by *Contemporary Politics* the Best Article in the journal in 2008.

Yale H. Ferguson, Ph.D. (Columbia U.), is a professorial fellow in the Rutgers University graduate Division of Global Affairs at Rutgers University-Newark and Emeritus Professor of Global and International Affairs. Previously he was Professor II (highest rank at Rutgers) of political science and from 2002–2008 was co-director of the Division of Global Affairs. He also is Honorary Professor at the University of Salzburg (Austria). Ferguson is the author/co-author of eleven books and over fifty book chapters and articles. Books with frequent co-author Richard W. Mansbach include *A World of Polities; Remapping Global Politics; The Elusive Quest Continues; Polities; The Elusive Quest; The State, Conceptual Chaos, and the Future of International Relations Theory;* and

The Web of World Politics. Others are *On the Cutting Edge of Globalization* (with James N. Rosenau, David C. Earnest, and Ole R. Holsti); *Political Space* (with R. J. Barry Jones); *Continuing Issues in Global Politics* (with Walter Weiker); and *Contemporary Inter-American Relations.* He and Mansbach are currently working on two major book projects, one on changing patterns of globalization and the other a sequel to *Polities.*

Ferguson is on the editorial advisory board of *Global Governance.* From 2002 to 2010 he served on the editorial advisory board for *International Studies Review;* from 1999 to 2003, on the editorial advisory board of *International Studies Quarterly*; and from 1995 to 2000, on the international advisory board of the *European Journal of International Relations.* In 1999 he was honored with the Rutgers University Board of Trustees Award for Excellence in Research. He is a member of the European Academy of Sciences and Arts and has been a Visiting Fellow at the University of Cambridge (three times), the Norwegian Nobel Institute, and the University of Padova (Italy), as well as Fulbright Professor at Salzburg.

Henry Gao is a tenured law professor at Singapore Management University, and an Associate of the Centre for International Law at National University of Singapore. With law degrees from three continents, he started his career as the first Chinese lawyer at the WTO Secretariat. Before moving to Singapore in late 2007, he taught law at Hong Kong University, where he was also the deputy director of the East Asian International Economic Law and Policy Program. A leading scholar on China and WTO, Henry is the editor of the book *China's Participation in the WTO* (2005) and has published many articles in prestigious international journals including *Journal of International Economic Law* and *Journal of World Trade.* A frequent advisor to Asian governments, Henry has also been a consultant to the WTO, World Bank, Asian Development Bank, and APEC. As the academic coordinator to the first Asia-Pacific Regional Trade Policy Course officially sponsored by the WTO, he helped the WTO to establish this flagship training program in the region and has also been instrumental in building similar training programs in China, Singapore, and Thailand.

In 2009, when the WTO established the WTO Chairs Program to promote research, teaching and training activities on WTO issues in leading universities around the world, Henry was invited to join the international Advisory Board. Among the twenty plus distinguished members of the Board, Henry is the only non-governmental representative from Asia. Henry is the first Asian faculty member on the Master in International Economic Law and Policy (IELPO) program in Barcelona, and the only Chinese faculty member at the Academy of International Trade and Investment Law in Macau. His current research focuses on the interaction between China's trade policy and WTO rules, as well as WTO dispute settlement, trade in services and free trade agreements.

Pak K. Lee is a lecturer in Chinese Politics and International Relations/International Political Economy in the School of Politics and International Relations at the University of Kent, United Kingdom. His current research focuses on China's participation in global governance. He is the lead author of "China in Darfur: Humanitarian Rule-Maker or Rule-Taker?" in *Review of International Studies* (first published online in March 2011 and forthcoming in print in 2012) and "China's 'Realpolitik' Engagement with Myanmar," *China Security* 5(1), Winter 2009: 105–126 (all co-authored with Gerald Chan and Lai-Ha Chan). His joint book project with them on China's engagement with global governance, titled *China Engages Global Governance: A New World Order in the Making?* was published in October 2011.

Jieli Li is professor of sociology in the Department of Sociology and Anthropology at Ohio University. His research and teaching areas revolve around social change and development, historical and comparative sociology, sociological theory, conflict and resolution, and China studies. His research articles have appeared in some leading scholarly journals such as *Sociological Theory, International Journal of the Sociology of Law, Sociological Perspectives, Sociological Focus, International Journal of Public Administration,* and *Michigan Sociological Review.*

Mingjiang Li is associate professor at S. Rajaratnam School of International Studies (RSIS), Nanyang Technological University, Singapore. He is also the coordinator of the China Program and the coordinator of the MSc. in Asian Studies Program at RSIS. He received his Ph.D. in political science from Boston University. His main research interests include China's diplomatic history, the rise of China in the context of East Asian regional relations and Sino-U.S. relations, and domestic sources of China's international strategies. He is the author (including editor and co-editor) of nine books. His recent books are *Mao's China and the Sino-Soviet Split* (2012) and *Soft Power: China's Emerging Strategy in International Politics* (2009). He has published papers in various peer-reviewed journals including *Global Governance, Cold War History, Journal of Contemporary China, The Chinese Journal of International Politics, China: An International Journal, China Security, Security Challenges, the International Spectator,* and *Panorama.* He frequently participates in various track-two forums in East Asia.

Wei Li is assistant professor of International Political Economy (IPE) at the School of International Studies, Renmin University of China, Beijing. Before that he served as a postdoctoral research fellow at the Institute of International Studies, Tsinghua University, China. He earned his Ph.D at Fudan University, Shanghai. His current research focuses on the politics of currency competition and the reform of international monetary system. He was a visiting scholar at the Asia-Pacific Center for Security Studies (APCSS) based in Hawaii. He is the author of the book *The Institutional Changes and the U.S. International Economic Policies* (2010) as well as a number of articles on international monetary politics in leading Chinese IR Journals.

Xiaojun Li is a doctoral candidate of political science at Stanford University. His research interests include international and comparative political economy, comparative politics and Chinese politics. He has published in the *Chinese Journal of International Politics, Foreign Policy Analysis,* as well as edited volumes. A native of Shanghai, China, he received his bachelor's degree in English and international studies from Beijing Foreign Affairs University and master's degrees in political science and statistics from the University of Georgia.

June Park is a Fulbright Fellow and Ph.D. Candidate (ABD) in international relations and international political economy at the Department of Political Science, Boston University. Her Ph.D. dissertation in progress is titled "Unraveling the U.S. Trade Deficit Challenge in China, Japan, and Korea: Bilateral Trade Imbalances, Protectionism, and Currency Wars." For her dissertation, she has conducted on-site field research as a visiting scholar at the Policy Research Institute, Ministry of Finance, Japan and as a visiting research fellow at the Institute of Social Science, the University of Tokyo (2010–2011). She is currently continuing her field research in China as a senior visiting research student at the School of International Studies, Peking University (2011–2012).

ZhongXiang Zhang is Senior Fellow at Honolulu-based East-West Center. He also is an adjunct professor at Chinese Academy of Sciences, Chinese Academy of Social Sciences, and Peking University. He is co-editor of both *Environmental Economics and Policy Studies* and *International Journal of Ecological Economics & Statistics*, and is serving on the editorial boards of nine other leading international journals. He has authored over 170 journal articles, book chapters, and other publications, and authors/edits sixteen books and special issues of international journals (*Energy Economics, Energy Policy, International Economics and Economic Policy, International Environmental Agreements,* and *Journal of Policy Modeling*). He is among the most cited authors by the *IPCC Climate Change 2001* and *2007*, and by *Trade and Climate Change: WTO-UNEP Report*. He is among Social Science Research Network Top 100 Economics Authors, and among IDEAS/RePEc list of both the leading energy economists and the leading environmental economists in the world. He is listed in "Circle of Climate Gurus" by the current executive secretary of the United Nations Climate Change Secretariat.

Tong Zhao is a Ph.D. candidate in the program of Science, Technology, and International Affairs in the Sam Nunn School of International Affairs at Georgia Tech. He received his B.S. in physics and M.A. in international affairs both from Tsinghua University in China. He had experience of working in the Office of Foreign Affairs in the People's Government of Beijing Municipality. His area of interest is international security in general and arms control and China's security policy in particular. His scientific background, as well as his experience as a student in international relations provides him with the opportunity to do research on issues of arms control and international security through lenses of both science and technology and international politics. He joined the Sam Nunn Fellowship group on Science, Technology and International Security, and was a fellow of the Nuclear Threats Summer Fellowship (PPNT) program. He was a Young Scholar of the Nuclear Scholars Initiative at CSIS, is a fellow of the program on Strategic Stability Evaluation (POSSE) at Georgia Tech, and has worked on issues and published papers relating to nuclear security, missile defense, missile proliferation, regional strategic stability, and China's security policy. His recent work is on nuclear disarmament and strategic stability between major nuclear powers.